27391 24/5 HF

Phil Collins

Also by Ray Coleman

LENNON
The Definitive Biography

McCARTNEY
Yesterday And Today

THE CARPENTERS
The Authorised Biography

CLAPTON
The Authorised Biography of Eric Clapton

FRANK SINATRA
A Celebration

STONE ALONE
The Definitive Story of the Rolling Stones
Co-written with Bill Wyman

BRIAN EPSTEIN
The Man Who Made The Beatles

ROD STEWART
The Biography

I'LL NEVER WALK ALONE
Co-written with Gerry Marsden

Phil Collins

the definitive biography

Ray Coleman

SIMON & SCHUSTER
A VIACOM COMPANY

First published in Great Britain by Simon & Schuster Ltd, 1997
A Viacom company

Simon & Schuster Ltd
West Garden Place
Kendal Street
London W2 2AQ

Simon & Schuster Australia
Sydney

A CIP catalogue record for this book is available
from the British Library

ISBN 0-684-81784-5

Typeset in Joanna by Palimpsest Book Production Limited,
Polmont, Stirlingshire
Printed and bound in Great Britain by
Butler & Tanner, Frome & London

This book is dedicated to my sons,
Miles and Mark, with much love.

Contents

Acknowledgements

The author wishes to thank Phil Collins and Hit & Run Music (Publishing) Limited for permission to quote from the following songs.

You Know What I Mean by Phil Collins
   ©1980 Philip Collins Ltd/Hit & Run Music (Publishing) Limited

I Missed Again by Phil Collins
   © 1980 Philip Collins Ltd/Hit & Run Music (Publishing) Limited

The Roof Is Leaking by Phil Collins
   © 1980 Philip Collins Ltd/Hit & Run Music (Publishing) Limited

Thunder And Lightning by Phil Collins
   © 1980 Philip Collins Ltd/Hit & Run Music (Publishing) Limited

Please Don't Ask by Phil Collins

© 1980 Philip Collins Ltd/Hit & Run Music (Publishing) Limited

All lyrics by arrangement with Hit & Run Music (Publishing) Limited

Author's Note

The writing of this biography was a labour of love for Ray Coleman. But, as Phil Collins knows only too well, in the words of the old truism, the path of love never runs smoothly.

When Ray died in September 1996, among the myriad notes he had written to himself about the book were the following words, mostly in immaculate shorthand, on a scrap of paper which would have formed the basis of his Author's Note:

The politics surrounding this biography would be worthy of a separate book. At first Phil was totally in favour of the book and then, having given me many interviews covering his life and work and paving the way for my conversations with his family, friends and colleagues, he went cool on the idea.

In fifteen years of writing biographies, mostly authorized by the artists and their families, I never experienced such shenanigans as those surrounding this one.

I learned that Phil Collins, who has the public image

of Mr Nice Guy, is also a man who polarizes. Some of those interviewed wanted to be reassured that it was a book that would praise Phil to the skies, with no criticism, and others said they would talk to me as long as I put the verbal boot in. So, I decided to make this as much as possible an oral biography. Much of the text is for the reader to make up his or her own mind.

From Artful Dodger to Royal Groover . . . never was anyone so well cast.

What do I think of Phil Collins after all this research? I think exactly what I thought when I began: that he is an immaculate artist. And Phil Collins, the man? As he reinvents himself in Switzerland taking life a little easier with his new love, has he found peace at last? Ah . . .

Ray travelled the world gathering material for this biography. Little did he or any of us know that it would be his last book. A few weeks after returning from accompanying Phil on part of his *Far Side of the World* tour in Singapore and South Africa in 1995, Ray was diagnosed as suffering from cancer. After a serious operation we all thought he had made a complete recovery. Alas, the dreaded disease struck again in the spring of 1996 and, despite further surgery and bravely embracing enthusiastically every treatment the medical profession had to offer, and a steely determination to survive, Ray lost his heroic fight in September that year.

Throughout his illness he continued to work on this book. He took it with him into hospital and carried on writing at home even when he could summon up the energy to put in only less than an hour at a time at the typewriter. When it became obvious, even to him, that he might not complete the manuscript, he asked me to put the finishing touches to it. This has been my most heartrending and demanding assignment. I have done my best.

Those familiar with Ray's work will know the exceptionally high standards he set himself. I cannot hope to emulate the quality of his prose or his encyclopedic knowledge of popular music. He was always concerned, above all, that what he wrote was truthful and a fair and accurate record and I have meticulously checked the facts on his behalf.

Ray never hesitated to offer constructive criticism and he never 'stitched anyone up'; he kept his cool in a profession where tumult reigns. He loved music and he loved musicians; he often said that he could think of no better way of earning a living than writing about his hobby.

I have done all I can to ensure that this biography is worthy of the name of its author. If there are omissions or minor imperfections, please forgive me. So much knowledge was locked in Ray's head and even though he left copious notes and instructions, putting the finishing touches to so personal an enterprise has been a daunting task.

Ray's own list of the people he wanted to thank for their help follow at the end of this note but I should like to add one or two names, particularly that of Ravi Kulkarni, the surgeon at Ashford Hospital, Middlesex, who never gave up and gave Ray a few bonus months of life; the nursing staff at Ashford Hospital and the staff in the Radiology Department of Charing Cross Hospital and at the Princess Alice Hospice in Esher. Rabbi Fred Morgan gave spiritual comfort and much, much more. Ray Williams and Roger Greenaway, two of the kindest men in the music business, showed Ray and me what friendship really means. Even when Ray was desperately ill the house rang with their laughter as they gossiped unceasingly about 'the biz' and retold so many 'in' stories and remembered the good old days. With Roger, particularly, talk inevitably reverted to the Fab Four. Yes, he and Ray *Really Did Know The Beatles!*

Thanks are due, too, to David Grossman, Brian Quick and Barrington Daniels, to Ida and Sheila and Michael and Cate and Jane who helped us both in so many ways. Morry, Mary and Howard also gave moral support when it was most needed and my mother, Marjorie Rudd, and our sons, Mark and Miles, were always 'there'. Phil and Orianne and many, many music business friends sent faxes, letters and cards and phoned regularly and their messages were very much appreciated.

For help with the book Ray's thanks are due to: Phil Collins, his first wife, Andrea, and their children, Joely and Simon; June Collins and Barbara Speake, Jack Wild, Ronnie Caryl and Peter Newton. Thanks, too, to Tony Smith, Carol Willis Impey, Brian Southall, Pete Ikin, Deborah Sandvik, Terri Anderson, Chris Welch and Mark Lewisohn.

In Los Angeles, Brian Carroll painstakingly compiled the discography at the back of this book, and in London, James Oldham spent many hours researching material.

Megan Taylor and Martin Lewis helped considerably with valuable recollections, as did Pattie Clapton, Steve Hackett, Bill Bruford, Peter Gabriel, Daryl Stuermer, Nathan East, Greg Phillinganes, Stephen Bishop, Taylor Hackford, Chester Thompson, Brad Marsh, David Green, John Gee, Jack Barrie, Ronnie Scott, Virginia Lohle and Hugh Padgham. And thanks to Helen Gummer at Simon & Schuster for being so patient and to Annie Lee for her painstaking editing of the final manuscript.

Postscript:

I asked Ray how he thought Phil Collins would be remembered. Songwriter? Drummer? Singer? 'As a nice chap,' he replied . . . the ultimate accolade from my husband, who, when we met thirty-five years ago, was described to me as 'The nicest man in the music business'.

Pamela Coleman
Cornwall
January 1997

*'I want you to listen tight. I'm talking about all people everywhere
. . . that's what's important: to feel useful in this old world, to hit
a lick against what's wrong or to say a word for what's right even
though you get walloped for saying that word. Now, I may sound
like a Bible-beater yelling up a revival . . . but that don't change
the truth none. There's right and there's wrong, and you gotta
do one or the other. You do the one and you're living. You do
the other and you may be walking around . . . but you're dead
as a beaver hat.'*

(From the keynote speech by John Wayne in the 1960 film
The Alamo. Playing the role of Davy Crockett, 'king of the
wild frontier', Wayne mesmerized millions with his élan.
His co-stars included the charismatic Richard Widmark and
Laurence Harvey. Phil Collins was nine years old when the
film was released. He has seen it dozens of times and it
remains his all-time favourite movie. 'I think,' says Collins's
lifelong friend from childhood, Ronnie Caryl, 'that Phil has
always seen himself as a cross between John Wayne, Laurence
Harvey and Davy Crockett.')

Introduction

'I've never really known the guy'

In common with Julian Lennon, Frank Sinatra Junior, Natalie Cole and the progeny of so many internationally acclaimed artists, Phil Collins's children know only too well the seeming impossibility of following successfully in father's footsteps. Multi-talented Phil (singer, musician, actor, composer) is a hard act to follow, yet two of his children are determined to do just that.

Joely, whom Phil adopted when she was small, is a rising young actress who has appeared in a major Canadian TV series, won a coveted Gemini award, and followed this with a move to Hollywood in 1995. Born on 8 August 1972 in Vancouver, the vivacious and intelligent Joely is determined to succeed without the asset of her identity as the daughter of one of the world's best-known rock stars.

Simon, born in London on 14 September 1976, is, like his father, a drummer. 'It was always a dream of mine to be a musician,' he says. 'One day at the house in Shalford Dad took me up to the studio and there was this little drum-kit sitting there. And he said: "That's for you. You're going to play drums." He sat me down and spent the whole afternoon teaching me a basic rhythm 4–4. Then he left the room and left me to go at it.' Phil had been the same age, five, when he began with a toy drum, but he started his son off with more sophisticated equipment. Today, based in Vancouver, Simon plans his career as a drummer with the knowledge that, when he was thirteen, his dad told him he was far better than he himself had been at that age – a remarkable compliment.

Lily, Phil's daughter born on 18 March 1989 in Guildford, lives in Beverly Hills with her mother.

Fiercely loyal to each other and defensive of each other's sensibilities, Joely and Simon both speak candidly about the difficulties, and the pleasures, of being the children of Phil Collins. Joely recalls a happy childhood in England before moving to Vancouver after her parents' divorce. 'There were times when my dad wasn't around. I was aware that we weren't a normal family. My dad wasn't a huge rock star back then but I certainly was aware that we did things differently. I remember being taken on tour, as a kid, before my brother was born, and saying to my dad before every show: "I promise I'll stay awake for this one." And I never would. I'd fall asleep during the show.

'I wasn't a child who went to school in a limousine. We never had a nanny. Mum always took care of us. I knew all the other Genesis kids, Peter Gabriel's and Mike Rutherford's and Tony Banks's. We hung out together. I was the oldest but they were going through the same thing as I was: children of musicians on the road. There were two different realities I could relate to: I've shared a part of my dad's life, but I've also been very grounded throughout, being brought up by my mother. I'm very appreciative of that because I have a great balance.'

She recalls a sadness combined with excitement at the time of her parents' divorce, when she was eight. She believes that leaving England was probably good for all the parties concerned. 'But knowing I was going to be that far from my dad was really hard. I didn't seem to have been long in Shalford at all; the only thing I do remember is that that's where I learned to tell the time! It was an odd period. Being away from Dad was tough, but I had cousins in Vancouver I was excited about seeing and once I got there, in my new home, it was good. Getting there was hard.'

Separations from parents after holidays visiting Phil in England were particularly painful: 'For the first three weeks Simon would call Dad "Mum", and then we'd get back and for the next few weeks he would call Mum "Dad". And there would be a lot of tears, bawling at the airport saying goodbye to Mum and happy to see Dad; bawling our eyes out saying goodbye to Dad and happy to see Mum. It was really hard going back and forth like that. I'd say when we left: "I don't know when I'm going to see you again . . . it might be a whole year."' She felt a different, more distant relationship with her father than with her mother. 'Definitely. And I feel personally that I did a lot just to keep him happy.'

The period of Phil and Andrea's divorce and the arrival of a new woman in her father's life is set firm in Joely's memory. 'I don't even think I longed for my parents to get back together. I automatically accepted that the marriage was over. I remember living with my grandmother in Vancouver for three months while Mum was back in England dealing with everything. I hated my school in Vancouver as much as I hated the one in England. It was really a weird time for me, and it wasn't long into the divorce that I met Jill. I believe Jill probably tried her best but there were times when I didn't like her because she wasn't

my mum. And maybe I resented her being in that position.

'I was twelve when Dad and Jill married. I, and my brother,
really had my dad's interests at heart and we could have created
a lot of trouble for that relationship. We could have made it a
living hell, and maybe, had we been teenagers, it might have
been a lot different. But I think since we were so young we
just accepted it. Obviously I can see that Jill was in an awkward
position because she suddenly had two kids she didn't know
on her hands. And in the discipline area it was like: "How
far can I go?"'

Joely had known Jill since she was eight. 'A long time, but
not super super well.' Their friendship developed when in 1996
Joely located to Los Angeles. Of her childhood memories of her
stepmother, she says: 'There were times when my brother and
I went shopping with Jill. But as soon as she was around my
dad I felt the whole relationship changed. I don't know if it
was because they were trying to be parents. I didn't really
know who to connect with; I really wanted to connect with
Jill and we did at times. I can't say it was all bad but there
was definitely a lot of compromising. Because she wasn't my
mother and we both knew that.'

Joely remembered shows of strength sometimes: 'I was one
of those kids who had a huge appetite and my brother didn't.
She'd tell my brother to eat his dinner and she'd be persistent
about it. I would say: "You aren't his mum! You can't tell
him to eat his dinner!" I'll stand up for my brother no
matter what, and he'll always stand up for me. He and I
are very tight. So basically it was adjusting and a lot of
transition. At a young age it's sometimes hard to understand.
But I knew in my heart that my parents were not going to
get back together. And if my dad was happy with Jill, then
Simon and I accepted that. As I've grown older I've learned

a lot more about what happened and I can see things a lot clearer now.'

Joely and Simon's insights into their father's psyche reflect those of so many observers of Phil Collins. 'There are a lot of things about my dad I'll never know,' Joely told me. Simon declared: 'I've never really known the guy. I've had some good times with him but still don't know who the fuck he is. It's weird.'

Joely continues: 'The person he presented to me was a person who was always in control and who knew exactly what he wanted and got what he wanted. A smart businessman. There's a lot of aspects of his personal life that I may not be aware of.' Her sense of his elusiveness contrasts with admiration of his work ethic. 'He's earned what he's done. It wasn't handed to him, and he'll remind you of that any time he sees you. And he really admires people who go through the same process. He is married to his career, which comes first, more so than anything in this world. And he works hard. I've never known him in my life to take time off, except for summers when he would see us. Even then he would sometimes be in the studio at home, fiddling about. I've never known him to just kick back for a year. And he works solid.' Her own musical tastes are more aligned with artists of her own generation, such as Seal, but Joely has great respect for her father's achievements.

Phil's gift to Joely for her thirteenth birthday was a horse named Sussudio. Her mother bought her riding equipment, and Joely competed successfully in horse-riding competitions for six years, intending to compete internationally, until fracturing her spine in an accident in 1988.

She was also intrigued by theatre and drama in Vancouver, where her mother was working at a local theatre. Joely and Simon were taking classes nearby and Joely took part in plays.

After going to college and backpacking through Europe, she decided in 1991 to study film for three years. 'I knew inside me that I had to do it.' She secured an agent and started going for auditions. 'I was working within six months; my first paying gig was in 1993.'

Attending auditions, she found her surname both an asset and a pressure. 'It can be an asset when people think it's very cool. I've done auditions and gone from the room, and the casting director has come running after me saying: "I didn't know! My God, I'm the biggest fan of your father!" Some people are bowing down; others think it's very cool that I'm Phil Collins's daughter. It can be a disadvantage in the sense that sometimes it puts an expectation on me. It's not something I like to discuss before an audition because what if I bomb the audition? Then it's "Phil Collins's daughter sucks!" I like to do my work and if they find out afterwards, great. But if they don't know, that's fine. It works to my advantage because I can be who I am.'

In 1994 she auditioned successfully for a Canadian TV dramatic series called *Madison*, in a lead role. 'They had no idea of my identity.' She got the part and after twenty-six episodes she won the Gemini award in Toronto as best newcomer. Her father sent her a letter of congratulations via Jill. Another series is planned.

Andrea Collins confirms that her ex-husband's surname has been a mixed blessing professionally for her children. 'The name will open doors but you've got to have the talent too or the doors will close very quickly. Joely doesn't get every audition she goes for. When she was cast in *Madison* they didn't know she was Phil Collins's daughter until she was on the third episode. They're not cocky kids. Simon is having a hard time because he's such a spiritual musician, so mellow, meek and mild. He doesn't like the business aspect but he's learning now that you have to play the game, you can't just sit and write songs.'

Joely describes herself as 'not a big, Hollywood-flashy person, although there's a side to me that's very comfortable within that realm. Because it's something I've grown up around. It's weird to have friends who are Led Zeppelin fans and have Robert Plant altars and worship the man, and freak out when he's on stage. And I know him through my Dad!

'Going through school was really weird. Some of the kids had seen my picture, and Simon's, in the *Face Value* album. It wasn't something I talked about, not because I wasn't proud of it, but because it was not something I needed to bring to everyone's attention. They found out. Word got round. My Dad would come to Vancouver and say hello to us on the radio. We got instant friends . . . and I definitely learned how to feel out!

'Who likes me for what I am? One of the wonderful feelings about my career is that I've actually done it on my own.' As for paternal advice from the master: the firmest, sanest and most important words he said to her proved correct and were valuable, she says. 'He said, "It's not going to be easy." He also said, "If you ever need a hand . . ." Definitely he can get a foot in the door for me but I'm the one who ultimately has to do the job. I've done things my way because that's the way I am. Like Dad, I'm a person who likes to earn; I don't like being given things.'

The search for a fuller understanding of her father continues, she told me. 'There are a lot of unresolved issues in my past, and there's probably been a lot that I have never said to my dad in terms of Joely's needs being met and Simon's needs being met. The one thing about my dad is that he's very controlling and will only allow you to see of him what he wants you to see. And I know there's more behind that. And I've pried.'

For Simon, Phil Collins is not only a very hard act to follow, but sometimes a difficult father to fathom, and their relationship has sometimes been taut. Drawn to music from his boyhood, Simon played piano and then drums in a succession of high school bands before leaving school in Vancouver at seventeen. He has written about fifty songs, some with an autobiographical tinge of loneliness, and is determined to make his mark as a musician. He enjoys experimenting with different influences, from mellow love ballads to gritty rock. His influences include Genesis, Nirvana, Tears for Fears and Lenny Kravitz. Just like his father, Simon was always playing around with drumsticks for fun as a kid, showing an instinctive love of rhythm. 'Dad bought the drum-kit before he really knew if I was going to like it or not. When I was on tour with him before that, I was always fooling around with the drumsticks, though.' Simon recalls going on the road with Genesis, whose music he has always admired.

Building a career in the shadow of a father so triumphant in the same sphere does not come easily to him. 'I'm totally aware of it. There's a pressure that's always kind of looming over me. It's always in my subconscious. It's almost like I feel there is this expectation, or standard, that I have to rise up to.'

This feeling reached a peak when Simon travelled to England in 1994 to record an album at Peter Gabriel's Real World Studios near Bath. 'As soon as I got into the studio, I totally froze up. I couldn't do anything. Because I was constantly thinking about what other people were going to think, how they were going to compare me to my dad. You can't be creative with that on your mind.'

While the father and son relationship is naturally loving, Simon has found the musical association lacking until recently. He has been to his father's concerts many times. 'They're great. He's very busy though, and it's hard to get a word in, from the manager of the tour to the band. It's not like he's ignoring me, but he has so many people who need his attention. His solo stuff is not really my kind of music, but Genesis is amazing; all their older stuff is where I really connect. There are a couple of songs on my album with primal drumming, like they did on *Los Endos*. I have a lot of influence from that.'

He has found his father 'aloof' when he has attempted to discuss drumming with him. 'I try, but he's very aloof when it comes to talking about music, for some reason; it's annoying. Maybe he takes the view that I've got to make it on my own, but he bought me this equipment, so I know he's very supportive. But when it comes to after the shows, I'll say: "Man, I love what you did in that drum solo; can you teach me how to do it?" He'll go: "Maybe tomorrow," or "I don't know right now." He might teach me but he'll spend two minutes doing it and I still haven't figured it out. It's really hard to talk to him about that. Maybe he doesn't want to share his secrets; maybe he thinks I'll rip him off or something. I don't know.'

Phil's encouragement for Simon came through when he said he wanted to produce his début album. 'Which I found pretty shocking,' says Simon. 'He asked me that after I was already in a studio with a producer.' But even if that had not been so, he says he would not have accepted. 'Because he is a very hard man to work with. He's very impatient. I remember doing a drum track for one of my songs in his studio, because he was producing a little demo of mine at his house in Loxwood. Three takes later, I still hadn't gotten the track and he started getting really irritated, losing his temper and shouting. It was like: "Jeez, I can't work with you." So it's a good thing he didn't produce the album, because there probably would be total stress by now.'

Although Phil has heard his son's music of the early 1990s,

at the time of writing Simon said: 'He hasn't heard my recent stuff. So to me that's not really being very supportive. It's not like he says, "Hey man, can I help you out – can I play it to somebody?" It's kind of weird to say but I think maybe he feels kind of threatened or something. I don't know. He used to be very supportive. He actually taught me how to play drums, for one weekend. After that I just taught myself. But now there's nothing. My mum is brutally honest and frank about my music and has always encouraged me. I respect her opinions. Dad will come up and jam saying, "If I can find the time." But he was always a busy guy. So having father and son moments with him were rare.'

The events leading up to Simon's recording sessions provoked a family feud. In 1995, Phil funded $50,000 worth of studio time for Simon's sessions in England. 'He lent me that money hoping that from the record sales I would recoup that and pay him back. I was totally intending to do that, but because the album didn't even get finished, the money just went down the drain.' Phil took the view that the operation had been mishandled. A stand-off ensued in which no conversation between Simon and Joely and their father took place for more than a year from 1995. 'It's kind of pathetic,' Simon said in 1996, 'but I know that eventually we will talk again.* These things happen. It's all politics. I'm not too worried about it. I'll pay the money back if he wants me to. I've never had any intention of ripping him off.'

Phil has always appeared to his son as a strict parent. 'Only up until recently, I was not allowed to swear around him.

---

* Since this conversation took place father and son have been reconciled, says Andrea Collins. She, Simon and Joely are now in touch with Phil again.

It was always like that. And my mum's the exact opposite.' Like his sister, Simon says he finds it difficult to get through to his father, particularly in the short periods they have been together since his childhood.

'I still haven't figured him out. There's definitely a really sweet, sensitive, soft part to him. It's just battling your way through all the bullshit first . . . and then you find it, you find his heart. But you have to really sit down with him and just get to know him, I guess. I don't think he's very open-minded to change. He's called me an idealistic hippie. Do I look like a hippie? He's just very set in his old ways. It's hard to have an interesting conversation with him. When he did call me up he'd usually be on tour and we'd spend the whole conversation talking about what he's doing, how his tour's going, what new song he'd written, and what new video he'd done. Maybe two minutes would be dedicated to what I did. It was always very one-sided; he's a weird man.'

Simon is in awe of his father's talents. 'As far as his musicianship is concerned, he's amazing. He's a fantastic drummer, one of my biggest influences. He's an amazing songwriter. I don't know how he does it. And he does great vocals. He's so talented and deserves everything he's gotten. It's as a person that I'm still trying to figure him out. Everyone has a good and bad side and with anybody you haven't seen for a long time, there will be barriers, if, say, you haven't seen a person in a year. You have to get through that barrier, and if you're only seeing him for a short time, by the time you're leaving and you've started to get to know the guy, you're off. So it's always been a cycle.'

Like Joely, he experienced the same identity difficulties in high school. 'Who was hanging out with me because my dad was Phil Collins? Who really liked me for what I was? You learn to find out who your real friends are.' His compositions reflected the mental solitude of his school years, to a degree: 'I felt like a different person compared to everyone else; they treated me differently because of who my dad was. A lot of my music and lyrics relate to that.' After several years of feeling shy about his voice, he had begun to let his vocals flow, too.

In 1995 Simon visited his father at his home in Geneva. Communication was good, but not a lot could be achieved in two days, he felt. 'He seemed very hardened to me. That's one of the reasons I don't know him as well as I should, or as I could. Because he seems very thick-skinned. This is just the way I see my dad. As soon as we start getting close we get taken apart again.' The softer side, which Simon liked, he didn't see often. 'You usually have to be with the guy for more than a month. Or alone. A couple of times, we've gone on a car journey and had some pretty good conversations. But if you ask him one question he can go off for two hours, talking. He's a kind of control freak that way. He's definitely a different person on tour from how he is at home. I've seen a lot of his barriers and not a lot of what's inside.

'There are also a lot of good things about my dad. He does always make sure that he tells me that he loves me. So that's cool.'

①

'Music was my mistress'

Phil Collins's wife was distraught. Her husband, who was making his name as the singer with the rising rock band Genesis, had always been fiercely ambitious. But with a three-month-old son and a four-year-old daughter, Andrea Collins felt that Phil Collins's unswerving devotion to his work was placing an impossible strain on their family unit.

It was New Year's Eve, 1976. In the kitchen of their home in Ealing, West London, Phil told his wife that his band faced a crucial year. In Britain, Genesis were the darlings of the self-styled intelligentsia of rock, and had a substantial following. But the lucrative American market had not been properly cracked. And so 1977 would find them out of Britain for most of the year: on three American tours, two concert tours of Europe, and one of Japan.

Andrea was at breaking point. She had known Phil since they were both thirteen, and his obsession for success in show business had been legendary, even then. But since their marriage in 1975 she had felt the pressure of raising two children while Phil was away so much, pouring himself into his work.

Phil remembers that when he told Andrea of the heavy touring schedule facing him in the next year, 'She said, "Listen. If you go on this tour, we're not going to be married this time next year." And I said, "Come on. This is the band! We've got to think of the band." We had to get over a hump. We had to tour everywhere in America. We were big in Chicago, Philadelphia, New York and Montreal, but to actually sell records and achieve what we wanted to achieve, we thought we had to play everywhere. That involved three tours, and then also two tours of Europe for pretty much the same reasons. And also a tour of Japan, which was the first time we went there.'

Andrea remembers her tearful response in that kitchen differently. It was more a *cri de cœur* than an ultimatum, she insists. 'I did *not* say: If you go on tour, don't expect me to be around when you get back, which is the way he portrays it. I never said that. I said: "Oh no, I can't *do* this." I said: "I don't think I can make it if you go away for another year." I told him I was not sure I would be able to go it alone for such a long period of time, with two small children. I said: "I can't make it emotionally. I'm not strong enough." He told me he had no choice. His response to my cry was: "I can't do anything about it. I have to go on tour. The band has got to make it." And I just put my head in my hands and cried. He was tearful too.'

Phil describes the recurring difficulty with Andrea as like saying to someone who doesn't like spiders, 'It's only a spider.' 'It was me saying, "It's only a year. I'll be back," to someone who actually couldn't be alone, didn't like loneliness and wanted companionship. You can't tell people to go "on hold" for a year. And that was unreasonable of me. At the same time, she had been so supportive of my music. And the music was my mistress.'

Andrea says she began to suffer from depressions. 'Problems developed in our relationship due to Phil's workaholicness. He was never at home.'

With his fervour for making music, and his individualistic talent as a singer and drummer, Phil Collins had helped lift Genesis to huge success. The band assumed an aura of innovative musicianship among the hierarchy of rock. Yet the punishing schedule that ensured the achievements of Genesis never seemed enough to nourish the addiction to his work that has always been Phil Collins's central characteristic. In 1975, in tandem with his work with Genesis, he worked with a jazz fusion band called Brand X. His reputation as a ubiquitous drummer, popping up on sessions all over London, made him the most industrious player in Britain and one of the most respected musicians. This hunger for work was never motivated by money. 'Ambition, to me, sounds like something greedy,' Phil reflects. 'I was never greedy. All I wanted was to make a living at what I was doing. And at that time [the mid 1970s] we were spending an awful lot of money as well as we were earning it. And people rang me up and asked me to do sessions with them . . . and I was flattered. So I'd say: "How can I turn this down?"' After studio session work all day, he would go home, he recalls, and say, 'I'm just off' – to a Brand X show. 'I never actually believed I did it. But I did. I was working an awful lot. So in retrospect I suppose she [Andrea] had to put up with an incredible amount.'

As Phil hit the road in 1977, promoting the ninth album by Genesis, *Wind and Wuthering*, a turbulent two years had begun that would end his brief marriage to his childhood sweetheart. Neither he nor Andrea nor the millions of rock fans who knew him as the singer-drummer in Genesis could have dreamed that from the very ashes of his marital break-up he would propel himself to the pinnacle of success, fame, fortune and multi-millionaire status.

Despite his jammed diary of engagements, Phil was always a keen home-maker, and with Genesis optimistic about turning the corner to financial success, he wanted to move his family to somewhere more spacious than the rented flat at 22 Queen Ann's Grove, Ealing. So in 1978, as they faced the tensions of his extensive touring, Phil and Andrea went house-hunting. They wanted a house near the Thames in Richmond or Twickenham, but the one they sought eluded them. His colleagues in Genesis, Mike Rutherford and Tony Banks, both married, were also on the move and suggested that Phil and Andrea might follow their lead by looking for a house in the Surrey countryside. Eventually Phil bought Old Croft, in the pretty village of Shalford, near Dorking and the Collins family moved in during the late spring of 1978.

The move should have presaged an idyllic new life for Phil and Andrea and their two children. As they moved in, they both did some decorating and enjoyed furnishing the house together. Phil would take Joely to the local school, Longacre, and collect her in the afternoons. But as the months passed and Phil's absences took their toll on her, Andrea decided that for her the move to Shalford had been a mistake. The rural environment in which to raise children, which she and Phil cherished, brought her even more loneliness and anxiety than the flat in Ealing. She could not drive and felt isolated. The proximity of Angie Rutherford and Margaret Banks brought her little company, since, being at that stage without children, they could freely accompany their husbands on tour when they wished.

'I was stuck by myself in the middle of nowhere, taking Joely to school when Phil was away and raising Simon. That put a big stress on me,' she says. Phil, however, did not think that Andrea's state of mind posed any real threat to their marriage.

The three years from 1975 to 1978, during which Phil and Andrea married, had a son, and moved to Surrey, coincided with the most convulsive period in Phil's life with Genesis.

On the departure of singer Peter Gabriel in 1975 for a solo career, Phil took over as lead vocalist. In 1977, a huge world tour took them from a British tour to America, where they starred at such major venues as Madison Square Garden, New York, and the Forum, Los Angeles. They played football stadiums in Rio de Janeiro and São Paulo, and appeared in five sell-out concerts at the Palais des Sports, Paris. There they recorded the shows for a live album, *Seconds Out*.

In 1978, guitarist Steve Hackett quit the band, provoking a new studio album called *And Then There Were Three*. This, like *Wind and Wuthering*, was recorded in Holland, taking Phil away from home yet again. That year, too, Genesis scored their first top ten hit with a catchy single, 'Follow You, Follow Me', and they were among the stars at the rock festival at Knebworth, Hertfordshire.

Phil had by now become a celebrated singer as well as a lauded drummer. He had made a triumphant leap to the front of the stage from behind the drums. This major turning point in his life capped twelve years of progress towards what would inevitably be a life in the spotlight of show business. But while his frenetic schedule increased, so did his domestic strife. Back home, Andrea felt that he changed when he became the singer in Genesis.

The explosive event which sealed their fate occurred while

Phil was on the road in 1978. 'By September I was feeling lonely, isolated and depressed,' Andrea says. 'I needed emotional support and turned to someone who was working on renovating the house. I got involved with someone but it was a reach-out, emotionally, for support. It wasn't a horrible sexual affair. That was such a small part. It was something that happened over a very short period of time, a few weeks. It wasn't a long, drawn-out affair and I certainly didn't go off and live with this guy.'

Realizing that she had made a 'dreadful mistake' in her liaison with the assistant to the decorator, she told Phil about it when he returned home for a week during a gap in his touring schedule. Reflecting on the fling, she adds: 'I guess it was something that emotionally I needed. I needed some support and this person was very supportive and would listen to the problems of stresses and strains I was going through at that time. He was more of a friend. And when it led to other things, I said, "Right, this has got to stop." And I cut it off at that point.' It was not merely a physical association, she declares, but a deep-seated emotional need that caused it to happen. 'I felt awful about it. I basically had a nervous breakdown. Our marriage had not been working for the last two years, anyway. I had a lot of anxiety, knots in my stomach, because I didn't feel that Phil was really emotionally supportive of me. And was this someone I wanted to spend the rest of my life with?'

According to Andrea, Phil's response to her admission of an affair was supportive at first. He was quiet and seemingly understanding. 'But we were constantly rowing at this point because of all the stresses on our relationship.'

According to Phil: 'It's funny how two people can go through exactly the same thing, and both see things so differently. She left me for somebody else. It's a fact. And yet my son and daughter really believe to this day that I left, and because I left she found someone else. Whereas all I did was go on tour.'

Phil says: 'I think Andy has reasons for why she did what she did, which I guess I don't understand. Or she claims I never understood. And therefore she has whitewashed that particular aspect.' He reflects that her explanation to him was in effect a denial; she was virtually saying: 'I didn't *go* with someone else. You *made* me go with someone else. You were on tour; you weren't there; so you doing that forced me to do this . . . I didn't do this out of choice.'

'Whereas,' Phil emphasizes, 'it *is* a choice. It's the same fact, whichever way you colour it.'

Phil Collins's life now became a rollercoaster of emotional, physical and professional turmoil. His marriage was threatened and it hit him badly. His international touring year of 1978 lifted Genesis to new heights. He was conscientious in phoning frequently to chat to his wife and children, a habit that marked his life. Andrea states that her anxiety and depressions worsened amid the constant battles between her and Phil. 'The children and I were scheduled to go on the Japan leg of the Genesis tour, but he cancelled our tickets after a row. He went to Japan alone, leaving me and the children behind.' Later, Phil would say of the Japan tour to writer Johnny Waller: 'Maybe I should have cancelled the tour, but no, I went to Japan, and spent ten days drunk. I hated every minute of it. I couldn't sing and everyone was concerned about my welfare although there was nothing anyone could do about it.'

He returned to Andrea, who describes herself as feeling 'desperately unhappy, struggling to keep our marriage together, but not having the stability that I needed'. Just before Christmas, 1978, her own problems were diverted by the illness of her beloved aunt and surrogate mother, who was diagnosed as having lung cancer. After the aunt's death, Andrea's mother flew in from Vancouver, where she lived, to attend the funeral, and stayed with Phil and Andrea for about a week. 'She became increasingly worried about my mental state and the constant arguing, and especially at Phil's worsening temper,' Andrea says. By this time, Andrea says, she was taking tranquillizers. In January 1979, Andrea left London for Vancouver, taking Joely and Simon with her. They stayed at the home of Andrea's elder sister, Francesca.

Before she went, it was Phil's turn to feel an emotional trauma. 'I wanted to hold the marriage together. I used to get up and take Joely to school and I obviously used to take care of Simon when I was there, as well. Never having been through this before, I just looked at Simon . . . I remember looking at him in his cot and thinking that this little thing lying there did not know that he was not going to have a dad in the same way that we all have dads. I felt really bad about that. Then I felt angry and upset that someone was making this happen at the time I was desperate to keep it all together. I wanted it to hold together, for my kids more than anything else.'

Ensconced in Vancouver with their children, Andrea received a barrage of telephone calls from Phil in which, she says, he demanded that she returned to Shalford with them. 'Over a three-month period there was yelling and screaming and fighting on the phone,' she says. Phil remembers making endless phone calls in the master bedroom in Shalford to Vancouver trying to get the relationship back together again. She would hang up on him, he says. Trying to retrieve his family unit and return it intact to Britain, Phil even flew to Vancouver several times, arriving unexpectedly at Andrea's sister's house. He was not welcome. On each visit, alleges Andrea, he was 'hostile. He was going nuts because I wouldn't go back to England. He didn't seem to understand that I was unwell, needed some space, needed to heal with the support of my mother, sister, brother and friends that I had made over there.'

After some four months of these battles in person and by transatlantic phone, spanning the months of January to April 1979, both sides called a truce. Phil was dedicated to repairing his marriage, even if it cost him his coveted place in Genesis. Returning alone to London from Vancouver, Phil went to dinner with Mike Rutherford, Tony Banks and Genesis manager Tony Smith in a Surrey restaurant. The news he gave his colleagues was stark and astonishing. 'I said: "Listen, tomorrow, I'm going to Vancouver to patch things up. And if I have to live there, I'll live there."' If the band could tolerate the geographical problem of its singer residing in Canada, well and good. 'This was a totally irrational and impractical thing to suggest,' he says now, 'that I could go to Canada and that the band could possibly survive, and that they should come over there to do anything [such as record and rehearse]. This was a kind of ultimatum on my part.'

Back in Canada, Phil's peace plan to Andrea was, she remembers, that he was willing to leave Genesis. 'To say I had chronic anxiety at that point is an understatement. I was able to calm down for a bit, because he is very volatile. It was then he said: "I'm willing to leave the band for you. And I can do session work in Los Angeles, only a three-hour plane ride away from Vancouver. No problem." I said "Yes." And we actually went house-hunting in Vancouver.'

But it wasn't long before they began arguing again. Andrea cites now 'his short fuse and controlling temper, the inability to say no to work and the abandonment that went with it, his lack of concern regarding my feelings, the constant humiliation I felt while he openly flirted with other women in the presence of myself and others. I did not feel any of these issues would resolve themselves overnight.'

Phil, acknowledging now that the marriage was breaking up inevitably, says: 'I now know I can't be ten minutes in conversation with her. We could have been friends but it was never destined to be a long marriage, for some reason. Because of the incendiary relationship we had, and still do have, we both talk *at* each other. We start talking and within a short time we're talking *over* each other, trying to get the other person to listen.' He states categorically: 'The reason it split was because Genesis were working so much, on tour for the bulk of the year.'

Andrea views the final collapse of their marriage differently. If it was rooted in Phil's work pattern, their interaction had now, with the renewed bickering in Vancouver, turned so sour that Phil's persistent attempts at rescuing the situation were doomed. 'I had been hurt too much, and over too long a period of time,' she says. 'Quite simply, my love had turned to hatred.' In April of 1979, facing the reality of a split, they returned to England separately. With Joely and Simon, Andrea moved into a rented house in Ealing. Phil went, alone, back to Shalford.

Out of the ruins of this relationship, Andrea's resolute decision became the catalyst to a defining period in Phil Collins's creativity. So far he had been the singer and drummer, and occasional songwriter, in a top rock band. The dying embers of his marriage were to provide him with the inspiration to cross the line from entertainer to artist.

Returning to Shalford alone, he found that Mike Rutherford and Tony Banks had immersed themselves in solo album projects. These operations posed no threat to Genesis, and were firmly in the tradition of rock musicians with successful bands feeling the need to forge an individual, as well as corporate, identity. Phil had no such plan. But with Genesis temporarily on hold, he says he 'started to doodle' upstairs in the master bedroom which he had converted into a studio. 'I had nothing else to do . . . I was enjoying wallowing in it a bit,' he remembers of his isolation at Old Croft. 'And I just started mucking about, recording at the same time as writing. And if the metre was moving, I was really pleased.'

The soul-baring lyrics that tumbled out of Phil's head were starkly autobiographical. He projected his words as an open-heart diary to Andrea. The songs became his catharsis, unlike anything he had done before, and a powerful evocation of his sadness. The titles and themes of the songs were direct. In 'You Know What I Mean', he sang:

Just as I thought I'd made it
You walk back into my life
Just like you never left.
Just as I'd learned to be lonely
You call up to tell me
You're not sure if you're ready
But ready or not, you'll take what you've got and leave.

Leave me alone with my heart,
I'm putting the pieces back together again,
Just leave, leave me alone with my dreams,
I can do without you, know what I mean.

I wish I could write a love song
To show you the way I feel,
Seems you don't like to listen
Oh but like it or not, take what you've got and leave,
Leave me alone with my heart,
It's broken in two and I'm not thinking too straight.

Even more forcefully direct was the song 'I Missed Again', in which he sang:

> So you finally came right out and said it, girl,
> What took you so long,
> It was in your eyes, that look's been there for far too
>   long,
> I'm waiting in line
> Would you say I was wasting my time
> Or did I miss again,
> I think I missed again.

His desperation to keep his marriage together 'really fuelled the songwriting', Phil says. What he describes as 'letters and messages' to Andrea did not come from a man who was a natural diarist. The only time he had kept a diary was to log his professional engagements. But he says he is better at writing about how he feels than he is at talking about it, because his thought processes tend to jump. 'Before I finish one sentence, it triggers another thing, and I'm off . . . so you end with a tape full of half finished sentences.' The lyrics were meant, he says, to address Andrea head on: 'If she hears this she will understand what I mean and she'll come back. I never got anywhere with heartfelt speech.' He adds: 'The girls and women you grew up with have a big part of your life; the first loves. You can't dismiss them. But because the phone kept going down on me all the time, I had no alternative but to get in touch in another way.'

Some of the songs carried words and messages that were abstruse: in 'The Roof Is Leaking', he wrote more indirectly about the howling wind and crying kids, and his 'Wonder if she ever made the coast/She and her young man, they both moved out there/But I sure hope they write, just to let us know.' The winter looked like it was going to be a bad one, he continued, but 'I'm getting stronger by the minute . . .'

In 'Thunder and Lightning', he wrote that he 'Never thought I'd ever get tired of playing games/But I've been holding back for too long/Now the time has come, gonna get it right/Now's the time to show them all that they're wrong.' The song concluded with his conviction of 'A feeling deep down in my shoe . . . 'cos things look like they're going my way'.

If some of the lyrics were oblique, two tracks were naked and withering, carrying a confrontational force to his wife that demonstrated how seriously fractured he was by her self-confessed liaison with the decorator and then by her departure.

In 'If Leaving Me Is Easy', he wrote that if going away from his side was easy, returning would be harder:

I read all the letters,
I read each word that you've sent to me,
And though it's past now, and the words start to fade
All the memories I have, still remain.

I've kept all the pictures, but I hide my feelings so no
    one knows,
Oh sure, my friends all come round, but I'm in a crowd
    and on my own.

It's 'cos you're gone now, but your heart still remains
And it'll be here if you come again.

You see, I'd heard the rumours, I knew before you
    let me know
But I didn't believe it, not you,
No you would not let me go,

Seems I was wrong but I love, I love you the same
And that's the one thing that you can't take away,
   but just remember . . .

If leaving me is easy
Coming back is harder.

The killer punch came with 'In the Air Tonight', a tortuous
piece of invective that could not have been designed to lure
Andrea back to his side. A response to Andrea's affair, it would
go on to establish Phil Collins as a lyrically incisive artist; and
it would become his signature song:

I can feel it coming in the air tonight, Oh Lord,
I've been waiting for this moment, all my life, Oh
   Lord,
Can you feel it coming in the air tonight, Oh Lord.

Well, if you told me you were drowning
I would not lend a hand,
I've seen your face before, my friend,
But I don't know if you know who I am.
Well, I was there and I saw what you did
I saw it with my own two eyes
So you can wipe off the grin, I know where you've been,
It's all been a pack of lies.

Well, I remember, I remember don't worry,
How could I ever forget, it's the first time, the last time
   we ever met,
But I know the reason why you keep your silence up,
   no you don't fool me,
The hurt doesn't show; but the pain still grows
It's no stranger to you or me.

Phil Collins hated the music of the 1970s with a passion, for its accent on sounds rather than songs and on massed armies of hard rock/metal image and posturing triumphing over music. The end of the decade, however, was to have a cataclysmic effect on his work and his life. In early 1980, by which time he and Andrea had been separated for nearly a year and she was still living in Ealing, Phil's regular weekend trips to collect the children for the weekend brought about a rapprochement. 'Something happened between us,' she recalls, 'a reconnection. And we spoke about putting our relationship back together again. Because we still loved each other.' Having recovered from the nervous breakdown, she says, she insisted that they should move slowly towards any such reunion, 'over at least a six-month period, possibly longer, because I didn't want the children to suffer in any way if it didn't work out again'. The agreed plan was to 'go for dinners, spend some time together, get to know each other again and see if it was still there'. But, says Andrea, 'Of course, he went away on tour about a week after that conversation.'

The song that bared Phil's emotions most painfully, with words of angst and personal heartache, was called 'Please Don't Ask'. This was a searing mixture of a love letter and a lament for the loss of his children. In the song, he said he could remember when it had been easy to say he loved Andrea. But then he addressed her directly: she had lost weight, looked good, and had nice hair, he continued. When could he see and touch her? Repeatedly, he wrote, he asked himself: was he wrong? He knew the kids were well, because Andrea was 'a mother to the world'. Phil said he missed his boy. He also confessed that he cried a little and didn't sleep too well. Please, he told Andrea, don't ask him how he felt.

Phil's work schedule was as full as ever in Andrea's absence.

In spring 1979, Phil recorded his fifth album as the drummer with Brand X, the band in which he worked simultaneously with Genesis. At this time, too, Tony Banks and Mike Rutherford, having completed their solo projects, were ready to work with Phil on another Genesis album. Visiting him at Shalford, they realized that the old order of things, whereby they did most of the band's songwriting, ought to change. Phil, who was gaining confidence in his writing, should be integrated more into the Genesis songwriting team. As the acclaimed singer, he often found it hard to empathize with lyrics in which he had had no input.

Phil played to Mike and Tony his stark, somewhat primitively recorded songs 'In the Air Tonight' and 'If Leaving Me Is Easy'. But they seemed too simplistic, perhaps even too direct, for Genesis to take on board. 'Please Don't Ask' was earmarked by Mike and Tony because, Phil recalls, 'they thought it had a Beach Boys feel to it', and they chose another song called 'Misunderstanding'.

And so 'Please Don't Ask', which Phil considers his most personal composition ever, went on to the next album by Genesis, Duke, which was released in March 1980. This was an anachronism, partly because directly emotional songs never sat comfortably within the sterile music of Genesis: 'Please Don't Ask', particularly, was far too personal to go on to a band album. The reason he allowed such a song out of his own net and into the realms of Genesis can only be that it exposed his own vulnerability just a bit too much. Inside a Genesis collection his wounds became buried.

Genesis, meanwhile, released the Duke album and, after a British tour, took off for a marathon trek around America to promote it. It was a heady time for Phil, since 'Misunderstanding', his solo composition for the band, had hit the number 14 position in the American chart in June 1980.

It was during this tour that Phil met the woman who would mark his next fourteen years. After a Genesis concert in Los Angeles, Phil adjourned for a drink with the band's manager, Tony Smith, to the Rainbow Bar and Grill on Sunset Boulevard, the famous rendezvous for the entertainment world. In a nearby cubicle with her friends sat Jill Tavelman. A staunch devotee of British rock bands visiting California, she attended virtually every rock concert in town. She had a particular penchant for the swagger of Rod Stewart and David Bowie and for the tougher sounds of Led Zeppelin.

Jill had more curiosity than enthusiasm for Genesis, of whom she had hardly heard. That night she had attended a special performance by the band at the Roxy, next door to the bar; but the band was not in the top league so it had not commanded her attention. Their music seemed too arty for a girl who loved no-holds-barred rock 'n' roll.

Her friendship with Phil was immediate, however. 'We spent some time together while I was in LA,' Phil says. Then, when Genesis left town to continue their tour, 'I asked her if she would fly out to be with me.' Jill duly flew to join him in Houston. From there, funding her own travels, she stayed with Phil until the end of the tour. Her mother, shown a photograph of the now bearded Collins as Jill's new amour, remarked: 'Love is blind,' a line which Phil would use in a future song lyric.

Cautious though she was about their plans to move forward towards a reconciliation, Andrea Collins had good reason, during Phil's absence, to suspect that something was amiss. 'He was phoning me every night while he was on tour, and then one night the phone didn't ring. And I knew. My intuition: he's met someone.'

And lo, when Phil Collins returned to his Surrey home from that triumphant American tour, Jill Tavelman was by his side.

Maybe, rues Andrea, she should have accompanied Phil on that tour: 'There was a lot at stake. But I stayed at home with the children.'

As his marriage now slid inexorably towards divorce, Phil had to face mixed emotions. In his studio at home, as Jill shipped in her possessions from California, he had to revisit the traumatic lyrics that told of his embattled relationship with Andrea. Tony Smith had asked Phil what he had been doing during the period when Rutherford and Banks had been making solo albums, and Phil had replied by playing him very rough demonstration tapes of the songs he had written. 'They were all therapeutic, autobiographical,' Phil says of them now. 'There wasn't even an album. I wasn't even recording them properly and they were not intended as demos. It was just me dabbling in a studio and recording it. Eventually things became songs and there was the fridge going on and off and the phone ringing on a couple of tracks. But it didn't matter. I played them to Tony, who said: "This sounds like an album. This sounds great."'

Phil responded that he could not face doing those songs all over again. Smith said those raw sounds could be used as the basis of the album. They decided to recruit Hugh Padgham into the project as assistant producer to Phil and as the engineer. He had first met Phil when he was house engineer at the Townhouse, a new West London studio owned by Virgin; Padgham had worked on Peter Gabriel's third solo album. Phil had played drums on that.

As a drummer, and now as a singer with Genesis, Phil had brought to his work an effervescence and musicality that contrasted sharply with the trends of the 1970s. The first half of the decade, characterized by 'pomp rock', found many bands losing sight of the strength of songwriting and pretentiously turning out symphonic 'concept' albums in the

name of rock. Towards the end of the 1970s, punk rock and
'new wave' set out to destablize the established giants such as
Genesis, Emerson, Lake and Palmer, Deep Purple, Yes and Led
Zeppelin. The new bands were the antithesis of everything that
Phil Collins stood for as an exemplary musician who had paid
all his dues. They came with an anarchic attitude but were
largely inept as artists.

Phil did not like what had happened in pop and rock in
the 1970s. He had grown up in the 1960s, loving the sounds
of the Beatles and soul music. The overstated efforts of many
rock bands in the 1970s left him cold.

Hugh Padgham, who had worked with some of the newer
bands as well as making his mark with Peter Gabriel, felt the
same. 'The decade had spawned records that sounded too
studio-inspired,' he says. 'Everything had to be overdubbed
and drum sounds, particularly, had become dead and dry.
We'd been through punk, where you didn't need to have to
play at all. Having worked with a few new wave and punk
bands where the more awful the sound was, the better they
liked it, I yearned for a drum sound that was more real, loud
and clattery on a record. Raw!'

Visiting Phil at Shalford one sunny afternoon, Padgham
played frisbee with him in the garden but had no inkling
of the scenario that had prompted the invitation. Taking
him into his studio, Phil asked him what he thought of the
songs, adding: 'I don't know how to recreate them in the
studio.'

'I was not familiar with his personal situation,' says
Padgham. 'I had only met Phil on the Gabriel sessions.
We were not mates. He did not ring me up and say he
had split from his wife and had written these songs. His
wife could have been out shopping, for all I knew.' Though
the themes became obvious as the songs unfolded, Padgham

was more attracted to the simplicity of the music, and to the equipment Phil had assembled in his studio.

'He had a Brennel one-inch analogue eight-track recorder, an Allen and Heath mixing console, he had a Prophet 5 synthesizer. Portable studios with four-track cassettes didn't exist then. Polyphonic synthesizers had only just come out. Phil's equipment was very much state-of-the-art semi-pro level of its time. Drum machines were in their infancy.'

Retaining the 'good vibe' that Padgham told Phil he heard in the sounds, the two men decided not to entirely recreate the songs in the studio, but to copy the best of Phil's tapes from his eight-track machine to a twenty-four track. 'Then we'll put proper drums and proper vocals on it,' Padgham added.

As they moved to the Townhouse, the production developed into a model of simplicity and showed Phil's flair for marking his work with some unexpected ingredients. His friend Eric Clapton went to the Shalford studio to add some attractive guitar work to the song 'If Leaving Me Is Easy'. Another recruit to the recording session of 'If Leaving Me Is Easy' was Ronnie Scott, whose London jazz club had been one of Phil's stamping grounds. Surprised to get the call from Phil inviting him to the session, Scott expressed his reservations when he went to the studios to add his tenor saxophone to the track.

'I told Phil Collins I didn't think I was the kind of saxophone player he wanted,' Scott recalls, 'but he said he wanted me to do it.' Though he did very few sessions of this nature, Scott was intrigued; as an open-minded musician, he had guested on the Beatles track 'Lady Madonna' and he knew Phil was a strong young musician. 'I did my best, playing with those earphones on,' he remembers, 'and we did three or four takes on "If Leaving Me Is Easy". But it didn't feel to me like I was suited to the track.'

When the record was released, Scott saw it displayed in a shop in Edinburgh. 'I went and bought it, wondering what I sounded like. I felt a lot worse, when I came out of the shop, than when I went in. They had added some sound-effect noise that made it sound unlike a saxophone; it had a funny noise attached to it.'

Phil loved the sounds of the American band Earth, Wind and Fire, so he and Padgham flew to California to add punch to some of the tracks by getting that band's horn section on board. At the Village Recorders studio in Santa Monica, birthplace of hit albums by such bands as Fleetwood Mac and Steely Dan, Phil and Hugh gave some songs extra fire. The veteran production maestro Arif Mardin, who had worked with such luminaries as Aretha Franklin and Ray Charles, arranged a sixteen-piece string section to add a lushness to the song 'You Know What I Mean'. On 'I Missed Again', Ronnie Scott blew a mean solo.

A range of high-pedigree musicians was scattered through the album, but the aim to keep it simple held firm. Two songs ran counter to Phil's mood of despair about his marriage. To celebrate the arrival in his life of Jill, there was an upbeat composition by him called 'This Must Be Love':

Happiness is something I never thought I'd feel again
   but now I know
It's you that I've been looking for
And day by day, more and more.

The last of the album's dozen songs was 'Tomorrow Never Knows', from the Beatles album *Revolver*. Written by John Lennon and inspired by his reading of *The Tibetan Book of the Dead*, this futuristic song has rarely been attempted by other artists. Phil's love of the Beatles from childhood thus surfaced on his solo début.*

The use of a saxophone on one track, a banjo on another, a thick drum sound on 'In the Air Tonight' and a sparse effect on others, brought a totally unexpected solo outing for the drummer from Genesis. 'There was a confidence in Phil,' says Hugh Padgham. He had a concept for each song, quite unlike the tentative approach of so many artists. 'He had been in Genesis for a long time, and been involved, but it was the typical drummer-syndrome: the drummer wasn't really regarded as a musician in the band. I think he had been silently sussing it out and drinking it all in, keeping it to himself. So when it all came flooding out he was well sussed in terms of arrangements. We were both into the "less is more" philosophy. Having less on a track is much harder than putting the kitchen sink on it.'

Phil was not particularly confident that the album would be a winner. His mother recalls him going to see her, 'thin as a rake' from under-nourishment while living alone, in her view. After he played the songs to her, she enthused. 'Yeah, you like it,' said Phil, 'but it depends whether the public does.' Another visitor to Shalford was the drummer in Yes, Bill Bruford, now a friend of Phil's. The two had played together in the band Brand X. He expected Phil's solo outing to sound more like the rock fusion of that band. 'I was gobsmacked, really,' Bruford recalls. 'That ballad, "If Leaving Me Is Easy", was gorgeous with those

---

* Phil's album was recorded in 1980. By the time it was released on 21 February 1981, John Lennon had been killed (on 8 December 1980). This prompted Phil to add, at the end of 'Tomorrow Never Knows', a snatch of the standard 'Over the Rainbow', his tribute. Written by Yip Harburg and Harold Arlen, the classic was originally sung by sixteen-year-old Judy Garland in the 1939 movie The Wizard of Oz. Lennon's murder sent 'Imagine' and then 'Woman' to number 1 in the charts. Phil's single, 'In the Air Tonight', released on 17 January 1981, was number 2.

strings, and with those horn players he had made a complete leap to the American Atlantic sound. Even I, who was not in the mainstream pop business, was surprised by the commercial appeal of the songs, and by the very high quality.'

More important than record sales, to Phil, was that it was his first solo statement. With the precision and application to detail that would stamp his life and career, he set to work on the cover design. A mono close-up of his eyes, nose and mouth stared almost menacingly from the record he called, sardonically, *Face Value*. Inside the gatefold sleeve, in those years before the advent of the Compact Disc largely eliminated cover art, Phil assembled an attractive family album. He hand-wrote all the credits for every performer on every track; he reproduced his scrawled lyrics for the songs; he included photographs of many of the supporting artists, adding a snap of his daughter and son. Among those thanked in his own hand were 'my lovely children, Simon and Joely'. On the rear cover, against a picture of the back of his head, he wrote the list of titles. Inside, his handwritten list of the tracks adorned the actual labels of each side of the record. He had carried the 'home-made' atmosphere of the production through to every corner of the finished product.

An obsession for recording perfection, and supervision of every facet of his career, was born at this time. He recalls the problems he had with *Face Value* and his second solo work, *Hello, I Must Be Going!* When he made mistakes in handwriting all the credits and details of the publishers for the record label: 'I'd get down to the bottom and make a mistake and have to start again. In France and Germany, there were different numbers on the label.'

He was decisive, too, in the selection of a record company. Genesis were on Charisma, an enterprising label which featured such bands as Van Der Graaf Generator, Lindisfarne, Stackridge and Audience. The image of the label was loosely defined as 'art-rock'. In America Genesis were signed to Atlantic, part of the Warner Brothers conglomerate. Phil was insistent on a British home for his solo record that would forge for him a different identity from the singer in Genesis. 'I would have taken the record anywhere, frankly,' says Tony Smith. He talked to WEA, the Warner-Elektra-Atlantic conglomerate, and to Virgin, a hungry independent label which interested Phil because it had a fresh, hip image.

'I didn't want to be part of a bunch,' says Phil, remembering his conviction that he needed a new label for his solo work. With the iconoclastic Richard Branson at the helm, Virgin had blazed an astonishing trail through the record industry in the 1970s. Its apogee had come in 1973, with the multi-million-selling instrumental album *Tubular Bells* by Mike Oldfield. But by the end of that decade, Virgin was in financial trouble. The hits were not flowing and its various investments had not yielded enough to prevent its bankers, Coutts, from exerting great pressure. Nevertheless, Richard Branson moved ahead bravely and adventurously and his managing director, Simon Draper, was convinced that the first solo album by the drummer in Genesis was a worthwhile gamble. Virgin stumped up £65,000 as an advance upon royalties, which was, in 1980, a substantial sum to pay over to an unknown solo artist by a company under a banker's gun.

In America, however, Phil felt that Atlantic, with its strong history of soul music, would be the natural home for his solo work. Audiences in the States, he reasoned, did not have the same 'fashion view' of record labels that existed in Britain. And the boss of Atlantic, Ahmet Ertegun, had a contagious enthusiasm for *Face Value*; he was spreading the word of a huge-selling record long before its scheduled release. 'So we did three different deals,' Smith says. 'Atlantic for the USA, Virgin for the UK only – because it was in a fairly shaky state at that time so I wasn't prepared to commit us for the rest of Europe. And then we did a deal with WEA for the rest of the world.'

Virgin projected itself as a cottage industry to contrast with the giant record labels. Even so, Phil Collins took his music there with extraordinary assertiveness. 'I said: "I want to see everything. I want to see the way you're going to advertise the album. I want to hand-write the cover and the label. I want to know what you will put on the adverts for the record, and what the posters are going to look like." ' His total involvement stemmed from his view that the public believed the artist controlled the way he was projected. 'You can actually be responsible for that, which takes up more time, or you can say: "I know, it's terrible, isn't it? But it wasn't my fault [if criticism was made]." I dealt with the videos, the editing of them, every aspect, which became very time-consuming.' His handwriting would adorn all his future album covers and much of the artwork of his entire career, although he ceased dealing with the minutiae of writing the record labels after his first two albums.

Released at the start of 1981, *Face Value* was all over the airwaves round the world. The intensity of Phil's lyrics, and his passionate delivery, surprised the rock world. At the dawn of a new decade, the offensive of the punk rock and new wave bands fizzled. The most successful new bands of that period, Dire Straits and the Police featuring Sting, were on course to enduring careers. And so, powered by what the music industry fraternity traditionally calls the Divorce Album, was Phil Collins.

Supported by an energetic promotion campaign by Virgin Records, with Phil enthusiastically participating at every turn, *Face Value* quickly sold a million copies. His personal songs of anguish were single hits. In Britain, *Face Value* gave Phil three chartbusters. 'In the Air Tonight' went to number 2 in January 1981, while 'I Missed Again' and 'If Leaving Me Is Easy' went to numbers 14 and 17 respectively in March and May. In America, the album yielded two best-selling singles, with 'I Missed Again' and 'In the Air Tonight' both hitting the number 19 position in Billboard's Hot Hundred in November 1981.

Face Value would go on to sell nearly 10 million copies worldwide. It was an album for divorcees everywhere, and Phil reflects that had he not gone through the pain of separation, his first solo album would probably not even have featured vocals. 'It would probably have been more of a rock-jazz fusion in the style of Brand X,' he believes.

The chain of events in Phil's life had been perfect for the arrival of Face Value. Had he still been just the drummer in Genesis, his solo work would have been more narrow in its appeal. Becoming the singer gave him the confidence to sing. 'And had the marriage break-up happened when he was the drummer, we might not have got the album, either,' says Tony Smith. In the view of Hugh Padgham, 'That bust-up with Andrea was big-time in his heart. Some people might become drunkards or commit suicide or whatever. This bottling up of his emotions came flooding out with his music.'

'Excuse me, you're playing in the wrong key'

Phil Collins had just turned thirty when *Face Value* catapulted him to stardom. The inspiration for the album, and the speed with which it established his name internationally, might have shocked those who knew his cheerful personality. Songs of sad introspection were not expected from such an upbeat character. But his arrival at the top in show business was completely predictable. It was his destiny.

The youngest of three children, Philip David Charles Collins was born at a nursing home in Chiswick, West London, on 30 January 1951. His parents had met on a boat trip. June Collins, born on 6 November 1913, was twenty at the time and working as the manageress of a wine store. Greville Charles Collins, eight years older than her, was born on 4 December 1905 and worked for London Assurance, later absorbed into the insurance giant Sun Alliance, where he would contentedly spend his entire working life.

June and Greville dated for a mere six months before their marriage on 19 August 1934 at the church at Osterley, Middlesex, near Greville's home. Their first home was at 60 Constance Road, Hounslow, and their first son, Clive, was born on 6 February 1942. Eighteen months later their daughter Carole was born, on 23 August 1944.

The trip down the River Thames that marked June and Greville's first meeting stirred the latter's interest in boats, and soon after their marriage he joined Richmond-upon-Thames Yacht Club. Shortly afterwards, with his enthusiasm for the hobby of boating coupled with an organizational flair and precise manner, he was made president of the club. June shared his keenness and she helped to shape the club's social calendar.

Phil was eighteen months old when his parents moved house. Greville loved old houses and they found one he liked at Sheen, not far from Richmond. June hated it, however, and after only eighteen months the family moved again. They returned to Hounslow, buying a three-bedroomed semi-detached corner house at 453 Hanworth Road. There, Phil shared a bedroom with his brother. Clive slept in the top bunk, with Phil in the bed below him.

In these pre-rock 'n' roll years, music was always being played in the Collins house. Phil's sister and brother enjoyed listening to the hit sounds on the commercial station Radio Luxembourg, which beamed from Europe such hits of the mid 1950s as 'Sixteen Tons' by Tennessee Ernie Ford, 'Mambo Italiano' by Rosemary Clooney, 'The Man from Laramie' by Jimmy Young, 'Stranger in Paradise' by Tony Bennett, and 'The Ballad of Davy Crockett' by Bill Hayes. In 1955, Blackboard Jungle, the film of teen rebellion, was a precursor for the rock 'n' roll explosion, and Bill Haley scored with his anthem 'Rock Around the Clock'. The new music was not enjoyed by Greville Collins, who, with his friends, enjoyed singing the songs of Gilbert and Sullivan at the yacht club. Clive and Carole would go along, too, and get on stage to do sketches.

Phil, a striking young five-year-old with blond hair and piercing blue eyes, was a hyperactive child, constantly drumming his fingers on the table as he waited for his meals. It's a habit that persists to this day, says his mother. Soon after he had begun junior school at nearby Nelson Road, his parents bought him a toy drum. Eventually his uncles, Reg and Len, made him a drum-kit with triangles and tambourines attached, small enough to fit into a suitcase. For the boy with so much energy and enjoyment of music, this was a big encouragement. Setting up his kit in the living-room, he would play along to the music being played on television variety shows like *Sunday Night at the London Palladium*.

Phil was ten years old when he had his hair shorn. A friend at Nelson Road Junior School, John Beadle, cut his hair to half an inch all over. June Collins was horrified that her son's cherubic appearance and golden fringe had been so mutilated. 'I always said that if I ever got hold of the person who did it, I would kill him.' In 1994, thirty-three years after John Beadle had cropped Phil Collins's hair, his mother had a surprise awaiting her when she visited her son backstage after a concert. 'Mum, this is Beadle. Do you recognize Beadle?' He had a glint in his eye, June Collins recalls, and knew what was coming. 'Beadle! I've been wanting to get hold of you for years! You cut my Phil's hair! He looked awful and you had no right to do it.' (Laughter.)

At eleven, Phil passed the scholarship examination and was accepted into Chiswick County Grammar School. There, he shone briefly as a footballer and was adequate academically. But drumming was his consuming passion. It was now 1962, and Phil remembers playing along to hits of the day including the Shadows' 'Dance On' and Joe Brown and the Bruvvers' 'It

Only Took a Minute'. In October of that year the Beatles would score their first small hit with 'Love Me Do', but as Phil's interest in music was taking shape, the music scene lacked any real direction. Elvis Presley had a hit with 'Return to Sender', Cliff Richard with 'The Young Ones', and Ray Charles sang 'I Can't Stop Loving You'.

Model railways were another interest in the Collins house. At the age of about eleven, Phil exchanged his train set for a drum-kit with a boy across the street; later, hearing Phil tell this story on television, his brother Clive would dispute ownership of the train set, claiming that it was his that Phil had 'swapped'. By the age of twelve, with a new set of drums bought for his birthday by his parents, Phil was unstoppable. His father's aunt, a piano teacher, taught Phil a little of how to read music, and the rudiments of piano. Clive, meanwhile, had been encouraged by his father to go into the insurance agency, but after six months he gave it up and started sending out drawings. Eventually he would become a successful cartoonist. Carole became an internationally successful ice skater. Their mother says: 'Phil always had show business rammed down his throat. All his life. I knew he would go into it because he was the one who had the most talent. If we went out anywhere, we'd say: "Do you want to sing a song for auntie?" And he'd go into a song straight away. You never had him hiding behind your skirt saying: "I don't want to do it." He was there, before you'd got the words out of your mouth.'

His route to the top as a drummer, and eventually a singer, was not orthodox. His precocious talent for perform-ing, coupled with his outgoing personality and handsome boyishness, equipped him perfectly for the theatrical stage. That was the view of his mother, whose twinkling, forceful character was to crucially shape his teenage years.

*   *   *

June Collins had been convinced that her younger son was heading for a life in show business when he was only seven. The family were on holiday at a Butlin's seaside holiday camp, where Phil entered a talent contest. Before the show, he had told the band he wanted to sing 'The Ballad of Davy Crockett'. With typical precision, he had indicated to the musicians how he would sing it. As he walked to the microphone and the band struck up, Phil turned to them, and the crowd clearly heard him say peremptorily: 'Excuse me, you're playing it in the wrong key.'

'That brought the house down and he won the competition,' June says, 'not because of his talent but because of his cheek.'

By 1961, his energetic mother had become the booking agent for the Barbara Speake Stage School in nearby Acton. Together with such other institutions as the Corona and Italia Conti stage schools, Barbara Speake not only trained children as actors but provided child models for photo sessions for knitting patterns, as well as children for the West End theatre.

Shortly after Phil had started at Chiswick Grammar School, the pop revolution really began. In 1963, the Beatles hit the top of the charts with three singles, 'I Want to Hold Your Hand,' 'From Me to You' and 'She Loves You'. This was also the year of the Profumo affair, which threatened to bring down Harold Macmillan's government, and of the Great Train Robbery on 8 August, when £2.5 million was stolen from the Glasgow to London mail train by a gang including Ronald 'Buster' Edwards, who many years later was to figure so prominently in Phil's life. Like millions of other twelve-year-olds, Phil was mesmerized by the vibrant new sounds that came not just from the Beatles but from a host of other bands from Liverpool. The entire pop scene erupted; he played the new records endlessly in his bedroom. Clive, in the bed above, tired of hearing the records all night, but his young brother was now virtually obsessed by music.

While Phil's tastes were eclectic, stretching from big bands and jazz through to soul and the freshly minted sounds of Tamla Motown, he reserved a special place for the Beatles. The first two albums he bought were *Please Please Me*, the group's début, and the Rolling Stones' first album.

So the kudos of actually getting close to the Beatles in 1964 was enormous, especially so for a thirteen-year-old. Along with several other stage school agents, June Collins received a call in the spring of 1964 for youngsters to be booked, at the union scale rate of seven guineas, as extras in the Beatles' first film, *A Hard Day's Night*. Phil needed no encouragement.

On 31 March 1964, along with 349 others of his age group, he went to the Scala Theatre in Charlotte Street, London, to be part of the audience for a mocked-up sequence of a television studio. Phil saw the Beatles mime to their songs 'Tell Me Why', 'And I Love Her', 'I Should Have Known Better', 'She Loves You' and (though it was not used in the movie) 'You Can't Do That'. Although he could not be picked out amid the crowd, Phil cherished the brief experience, little knowing that one day he would be in a recording studio and on stage alongside his heroes. 'I used to stand in front of a mirror with a tennis racquet pretending to be John Lennon,' he told *Playboy* magazine in 1986.

At the end of 1964, Phil's mother received a call asking if she wanted to send any of the Barbara Speake pupils to audition for the role of the Artful Dodger in the West End production of the Lionel Bart musical *Oliver!* At the New Theatre in St Martin's Lane, Lionel Bart's brilliant adaptation of the Charles Dickens classic *Oliver Twist* had enthralled audiences since its opening in June 1960, not least because of its infectious songs. The show began with workhouse kids queueing for their daily bowl of food, with a chorus of 'Food, Glorious Food'. In the next scene, the rebellious little Oliver, who had the nerve to ask for more, is captured and put in a cell.

Competing with several other boys, Phil was called back for auditions several times before being offered the part, at £15 a week. There was one snag. He was a grammar school boy, and within the next year, academic pressure on him would increase as he prepared for the General Certificate of Education. As she gladly accepted the part for him in *Oliver!* June Collins wrote to his headmaster, saying Phil would need to have one afternoon away from school each week for matinée performances, and would also be working in London every evening.

The Greater London Council decreed that a boy actor could accept only three contracts of three months each per year, and within those three months the actor had to have three weeks off. 'But it was still a lot of work,' Phil observes. 'So the headmaster called me to his study and said: 'I'm very proud of you and very pleased for you but I can only let you do this for three months of the possible nine months.' He obviously saw my academic side going down the pan. I'd never have any time to do homework. He said: "The choice is yours. But you would have to leave. I would not be able to entertain the idea here." So I left.'

Luckily for Phil, the quandary about his future education was solved at a stroke. The solution came from the Barbara Speake Stage School. Launched with entrepreneurial flair in February 1945 as a dance class with eight pupils when Barbara Speake was sixteen, the school had grown slowly but triumphantly. By 1957 Barbara Speake ran dance classes for nearly 200 pupils in the evenings and on Saturday mornings. June Collins met her in 1961, when Phil was ten, and agreed to work from her home in Hounslow as the booking agent.

Children were supplied to such West End stage shows as *Oliver!*, *The Prime of Miss Jean Brodie*, *Maggie May* and *The Sound of Music*.

June did so well with her agency, getting jobs for so many children, that their school head teachers became annoyed that they needed so much time off. 'And I found that my best pupils were leaving me and going to a full-time stage school,' Barbara Speake says. Investigating the method propounded by the Parents' National Educational Union, she discovered that she could teach five pupils in a private house without pressure from the authorities. The children would be offered a full curriculum. She expanded into academic tuition with boys and girls who were all on the West End stage in *The Sound of Music*.

With an eye for growth, Barbara Speake hired the church hall in East Acton Lane where she had been teaching dance in the evenings and on Saturdays, so she now had it for use during the day. In September 1963 she was granted a licence to open as a full-time academic school with thirty full-time pupils. June Collins moved into a small office at the front of the building to run the booking agency.

Phil was both popular as a pupil and in demand through calls to the agency office. 'With his mother working here it could have been difficult,' says Barbara Speake, 'but it wasn't. June would never push herself. If a call came through for Philip Collins I took it. She wouldn't say how marvellous he was. She could do it about anybody else's child but not for Philip.'

Most of the students were in awe of the authoritarian Miss Speake. 'The sound of her high heels put fear into us,' says Jack Wild, one of Phil's fellow-students. But Phil seems to have struck an easy rapport with the headmistress, and not because his mother helped in the running of the agency. 'He caused no problems and got on with his work,' Barbara Speake says. And he did, of course, play a major role in the school social calendar with his commandeering of the band The Real Thing.

'I never had to tell Philip off. He was an absolutely model pupil,' says Barbara Speake. He arrived wearing his red socks from grammar school, saying he felt an obligation to wear them. In the mornings, the schedule was theatrical training, which she supervised. He also learned tap and modern dance, in which he shone under the tuition of June Williams. Afternoons were devoted to the academic curriculum, and here the head teacher was Miss Gadd, whose sons Philip and Martin were in the same class as Phil.

But Barbara Speake noticed that his emphasis was on theatrical work. 'He was conscientious about his academic work, but he wanted to perform. He always wanted to do anything and everything but June insisted he got his O-levels. He passed three. He failed English the first time but took it again and passed and the other two were, I think, Scripture and Art.'

At this school, Phil had found his natural home. 'I think his headmaster [at grammar school] was misguided,' says Barbara Speake. 'It wouldn't have hurt him to say: "Do Oliver! Then come back and work harder." Phil would have done that. If these people in authority would be a little more understanding of youngsters, they wouldn't have the rebellions. If we had not had an academic curriculum, he would have lost the experience.'

And so, in tandem with his schooldays at the Barbara Speake Stage School, Phil commuted every day to the West End to appear in Oliver! His daily travels took him from his Hounslow home to Acton for morning assembly, then straight to central London to the theatre, returning home around midnight. 'We had all the eight or nine boys cast in Oliver!' Barbara Speake remembers. 'Jack Wild was the Artful Dodger's mate Charlie

Bates; his brother Arthur was Oliver. We sent them dozens of Olivers.' Morning assembly was at nine-thirty but she allowed pupils to arrive at ten o'clock if they'd been working at night.

The daily underground journey to Leicester Square, where he was met by a chaperone, gave Phil a rich beginning to 1965, just as he celebrated his fourteenth birthday. As the Artful Dodger he was cast propitiously in his own image, as an ebullient, snappy lad with sharp repartee. He sang the pick-pocketing song, 'You've Got to Pick a Pocket or Two' and loved every moment. Later, he would regard it as his most enjoyable acting experience. Greville Collins, glowing with paternal pride, sat in the audience every week, a striking figure with his handlebar moustache.

Living nearby in Hounslow was a boy two years younger than Phil, and when he became a pupil at the Barbara Speake school, June Collins would often give him a lift, along with Phil. His name was Jack Wild. 'All Phil ever talked about was the drums,' Jack says. 'In his mother's car we went to school with his drum-kit. I was squeezed on the floor where the front passenger sits; all the space was taken by Phil and his kit.'

In the class below him, Jack Wild looked up to Phil, envying his appeal among the girls. They united, however, for stage shows at school, particularly at end of term. By the time Phil made his début in Oliver!, Jack Wild and his brother Arthur were in the show, too. 'I saw Phil come into Oliver!, and he was a natural Dodger,' Jack Wild says. 'Phil was a perfect actor. But he was strong-willed about being a drummer first. Barbara Speake used to tell him that pop music was full of one-hit wonders. It's a good thing he was not a weak-minded guy or he would not have got where he did.'

Phil and Jack worked together for school stage shows,

planning a song and dance routine around such numbers as 'Same Size Boots' from the show *Maggie May*. The two competed successfully in 1966 in Stubby Kaye's *Silver Star Show*, a talent contest for kids. Singing a song called 'That's the Law', they reached the final.

In that pre-video age, Phil and Jack shared an admiration for the comedy of Peter Cook and Dudley Moore, and mimicked their appearances on television. Once, puzzled by why Phil always headed for the theatre much earlier than he needed to when he was appearing in *Oliver!*, Jack Wild asked him where he was going. He expected him to reply that he went to amusement arcades or coffee shops in the West End. 'Phil said no, but most days he liked to go to the music shops and look at the drum-kits.'

His run as Dodger over, his mother advised Phil to accept all the smaller television and work as an extra that he was offered. 'Make a name for yourself,' she told him. 'Then it doesn't matter what you do.' Phil replied: 'No. I am going to drum and be a good drummer. And *then* I can do what I like.' June Collins says now: 'I was wrong and admit it. He wasn't so dedicated to what I suggested. Drumming came out of his ears.'

An important adjunct to Phil's experience in *Oliver!* reinforced his decision to be a musician. The drummer in the pit orchestra for the show was also the bandleader. 'He happened to be on my train coming home most nights,' Phil says. 'We talked. There was also a cello player I used to go up and down with.' Their lives as professional musicians, as they described them, were very attractive to Phil, and he visualized himself following exactly that route.

'I thought: as a drummer, what is open to me? I can be in a band. I want to play with other musicians and I'll do that for as long as it lasts, until the bubble bursts. I had a big interest in big bands, like those of Eric Delaney and Ray

McVay, and I thought that after the *Oliver!* stint finished, that was the way I could go. I had a love of big band music, not middle-of-the-road music. And what else was a drummer to do but that? And probably after that I would end up in a pit orchestra. I was really quite happy. I saw my life going like that and I would have been quite happy as long as I could keep playing and earn money.' And about that he 'never had any doubt: I was extremely confident of the fact that I would make a living at it.' He took lessons at two London drum shops from experienced teachers, but it was not long before he and his teachers felt he had learned enough. He was on his way.

Running the booking agency, June Collins had found her son in continual demand for a wide range of assignments. With his blond hair and blue eyes, he was photogenic and in demand for modelling clothes and knitting patterns. He modelled at the Venture Studios in Floral Street, Covent Garden, London, for mail order catalogues for British Home Stores. 'They phoned asking for someone with a certain chest size and we went round with a tape measure,' Barbara Speake says. 'Phil did it once or twice.' He loathed this work. 'He didn't mind modelling pullovers, but when it got to pants and pyjamas, he didn't like it,' says his mother. Once, she got a call saying there was a message to be passed to Philip Collins's mother: would she see that he went to the studio with clean feet. June was aghast. 'It was strange. He went in the bath every night. However, I said to Phil: "I had a call about you. You go up to the Venture Studios with filthy feet."' He replied that *en route* to the job, he played football. 'What?' asked his mother. 'In the mud? So when you go to modelling, your feet are dirty?' He said: 'Well, I don't want to go anyway. Get me out of it.' Once he discovered that playing football in Hyde Park was a deterrent to them booking him, he did it even more. In the end they asked for someone the same size as Philip Collins but not him.*

After seven months as a success in *Oliver!* Phil's voice broke. He vividly remembers the night he realized that he could no longer sing the songs. With school in the day and the evenings now free, he went to auditions. 'Interestingly, I never got a commercial, out of all the things I went for. I got television plays, films, lots of work as an extra. But I never got a commercial, which meant I never looked like I could sell anything; I did not have the face of a Milky Bar kid.' In later years, he would reflect on that, pointing out that he put his face on the cover of his albums with commercial success.

What did take root during those years was a natural thespian quality added to his restless energy, guilelessness and an utter devotion to the drums. He was also endlessly polite and spoke lucidly. This earned him a stint doing the voice-overs on BBC Television's weekly *Junior Points of View*, reading out listeners' letters on current events for several weeks.

'You'd never recognize his voice,' remembers his mother of Phil's elocution. 'It was very much how-now-brown-cow type of speech.'

Then a television producer asked June if 'Philip Collins' was available to take the part in a play, of a boy who spoke with a Welsh accent. She doubted his ability to do that, but Phil said he would have a go. June said the television people could not be deterred, but she warned Phil that he might 'fall flat on his face'. 'I said: "They're hooked on your face! That's what they want."' She was astonished when he performed the Welsh accent immaculately.

*   *   *

* Another former pupil went on to achieve international fame as a model: Naomi Campbell.

Phil's eye for the girls came early. And since he stood out as the most striking boy among the 180 pupils at the Barbara Speake school, he could not miss. He took full advantage of his appeal to the opposite sex. He was fortunate that in his senior class the ratio was firmly in his favour. There were six girls and two boys. He and Philip Gadd sat alongside Geraldine Rhodes, Sheila Whitnall, Cissy Duncart, Carol Reid . . . and two girls who were to have a cataclysmic effect on his life. They were Andrea Bertorelli and Lavinia Lang.

With her thick, cascading black hair and pronounced eyebrows, Andrea was a diminutive beauty whose Italian lineage was abundantly clear. Academically one of the brightest in the class, she had a strong artistic streak. She lived only a few minutes' walk from the school. She wanted to be a dancer, as did her best friend, Lavinia Lang, a classic English brunette who oozed soft femininity. Peter Newton, who was among Phil's core of friends at the school, remembers Andrea and Lavinia 'doing that immature thing that kids do, cutting their wrists to be blood sisters. They actually did that.'

Then, as throughout his life, Phil was a boy of fast action and very quickly he was dating Lavinia and Andrea simultaneously. 'We both knew when he was going out with the other,' Andrea says. 'We were best friends; there were no secrets between us.' One week Phil would go with Andrea, the next with Lavinia. 'Lavinia and Andrea spent their entire time enticing the boys,' says Barbara Speake. 'They were rather like kittens with a ball of wool. They'd play, and then they'd go away. June and I used to watch it. We'd say: "Oh, it's Lavinia this week." And the pair of them would break it up. Phil was definitely keen on the girls, and Mrs Bertorelli was determined that her Andrea would marry Phil.' Sometimes when he visited her home, Andrea would cut Phil's hair, noticing that even at fifteen, it was beginning to thin.

'I was the go-between,' says Peter Newton of Phil's romantic arrangements. 'There was also a tremendously attractive girl called Linda Jolliff. Phil came to see me and said would I have a word with Linda and tell her how he felt. And I said I wouldn't do it. I thought: this is just not on. In a week, I saw them holding hands under the table. Before I knew it, whoever he was going out with at the time, Andrea or Lavinia (I can't remember), was in tears. And I remember going up to Phil and saying: "I love you as a friend but I think what you've done is despicable." He was very matter-of-fact and said: "You don't want to get emotional."

'It was "pick and mix" for Phil. The girls loved him. He was the tallest and best-looking boy in the school. He had his pick of the pretty girls. There was no jealousy among them and no possessiveness once he had dated them. They were just glad to have gone with him. While we were still fumbling about with the affectations of youth, he had a maturity and a confidence.' His tunnel vision as a fledgling musician, and his assurance that he was going to turn professional, added to his appeal to the girls. For all the girls at Barbara Speake, there was, affirms Peter Newton, no choice about whom they should aspire to for a date.

Phil, wiry, full of intense energy and above all determination, was also the driving force in the formation of a school pop group, as they were called in those years long before they became 'rock bands'. The Real Thing, as Phil called the unit, would rehearse most lunchtimes in the room over the school dining-room. There was Peter Newton as lead singer, Philip Gadd as lead guitarist, his brother Martin on bass guitar, and Phil at the drums. Andrea and Lavinia were the back-up singers. They sang fresh arrangements, by Phil, of the hits of the day, with Phil showing his particular interest in the sounds of Tamla Motown songs, such as the Four Tops' 'Reach Out, I'll Be There' and the soul classics from Sam and Dave, 'Soul Man' and 'Hold on, I'm A-Coming'. Phil would sometimes sing from behind his drums.

It was a band which ran mostly for fun, with occasional appearances at school functions. But it was the earliest example of Phil's unyielding dedication to getting his music right. Once, when Peter Newton let his attention drift during a rehearsal, staring down into the playground where the pupils were having their lunchtime break, Phil's fuse blew. 'My mind wasn't on it; I got the harmony wrong. Whack! Phil slapped my face! It wasn't a macho I'm-taking-you-on blow that demanded a reciprocal blow. It was a slap given out of frustration. He said: "We haven't got much time to rehearse. The least you can do is give me your attention." I thought it was outrageous at the time, but it was an example of how serious and one-dimensional Phil can be. When it came to music, you were under no illusion. If Phil was going to be in a school band, it was going to be the best.' What Phil admired about the records by the Beatles and Tamla Motown artists such as Martha and the Vandellas and the Marvellettes was that they had a powerful, recognizable sound as well as memorable songs. Even at fifteen he was registering an interest in recording techniques. Together with his formidable memory and determination, he was, says Peter Newton, 'obviously going to be a drummer. All the time you saw him at school, he was constantly drumming his fingers on the desks.'

The year 1966, in which fifteen-year-old Phil Collins was continuing his romances with Lavinia Lang and Andrea Bertorelli, was marked by some vintage popular music. The Beatles, in the year when they stopped touring after an American concert, poured out hit singles like 'Eleanor Rigby', 'Yellow Submarine', 'Paperback Writer', 'Day Tripper' and 'We Can Work It Out'. In the space race, Russia's Venus 3 landed on Venus and Luna 9 landed on the moon. The record charts in Britain and America were ablaze with sounds that would stand for ever: Simon and Garfunkel with the 'Sounds of Silence', the Supremes with 'You Can't Hurry Love', the Walker Brothers with 'The Sun Ain't Gonna Shine Anymore' and the Kinks with 'Sunny Afternoon'.

There was black news: 144 people, 116 of them children, perished in a coal-tip disaster in Aberfan, South Wales. American planes continued to bomb Vietnam. But England's football team won the World Cup, defeating West Germany 4–2 in the final.

For pop students, the sounds that beamed illegally from pirate radio ships stationed in the North Sea were quite stunning. There were the Four Tops with the urgent passion of 'Reach Out, I'll Be There', the Rolling Stones with 'Paint It Black', the mod heroes the Small Faces with 'All or Nothing', the Spencer Davis Group with 'Keep on Running' and power ballads from Frank Sinatra '(Strangers in the Night'), Tom Jones ('Green Green Grass of Home') and Dusty Springfield ('You Don't Have to Say You Love Me'). All were records that would be played continually by radio round the world thirty years later.

It was against this rich tapestry of sounds that Phil Collins began making an afternoon pilgrimage straight from school to Wardour Street, Soho, where at number 90 there was the Marquee.* Though the club did not open until 7 p.m., the assistant manager, Jack Barrie, became familiar with the sight of the boy who invariably arrived to head the queue, sometimes wearing his cap and school uniform and carrying a bag of school books. Phil would often get there as early as

* The site is now occupied by Mezzo, a restaurant owned by Sir Terence Conran.

4.30 and wait as the queue gathered from 5 p.m., eventually spilling over the pavement and stretching back fifty yards to St Anne's Court.

Sometimes, if it was cold or wet, Barrie would ask Phil if he would like to sit and wait in the foyer. John Gee, the manager, was assured by Barrie that the boy was a member, and a regular at the club. Gee questioned why he had been given priority treatment over others, but Barrie said: 'It does no harm. He's here every Tuesday. Let the lad in; maybe he can lend a hand in the cloakroom.'

After two or three weeks of this, Jack Barrie told Phil: 'Look, the manager's a bit cheesed off about me letting you sit here. This is what you can do to help: go in the club and put the chairs out.' So began Phil's weekly ritual of spreading out the seventy chairs into four rows in front of the bandstage. John Gee recalls that, thereafter, he let Phil in free of charge, to the boy's delight. 'This came as an incredible surprise because he had always faithfully paid his five bob at the cash desk.' Endearingly, Phil did not take his privilege for granted, but when he arrived, invariably before any queue had formed, would go straight to Gee or Barrie and say: 'Can I do anything?' Sometimes he would sweep the floor, or help in the cloakroom. 'He became my unofficial assistant,' says Gee.

This unique club, so central to the evolution of Phil Collins and thousands of musicians, originally opened in 1958 in Oxford Street. At first it was a jazz club under the aegis of the National Jazz Federation, whose founding fathers were bandleader Chris Barber and Harold Pendleton. It moved to Wardour Street in 1964, and although the generic term 'rock' had not yet arrived, the club began to be infiltrated by a new wave of 'beat groups' and 'rhythm-and-blues bands'. Jazz, especially the traditional and Dixieland bands, was becoming marginalized by the sound of youth, but Phil would go occasionally to Ronnie Scott's club in London, and on one occasion saw a mesmerizing appearance by American drum maestro Buddy Rich and his band. He was very impressed by Rich's showmanship and theatricality at the drums.

By the time Phil became a regular at the Marquee in 1966, the young musicians arriving on the rock scene were becoming ambitious to create sounds more permanent than hit singles. It was the year of Swinging London, Carnaby Street, Flower Power, and a Labour government with Harold Wilson as prime minister. The Marquee was a membership club, and Phil joined upon payment of five shillings (25 pence). Unlicensed, it was the biggest customer in the West End for Coca Cola at that time. Members received a newsletter every month and had the opportunity to book in advance to hear certain groups. 'People liked joining things in those days,' says Barrie.

The Marquee was the citadel of rock, the world's most important club, throughout the 1960s and 1970s. Tuesday was 'star night', when John Gee and Jack Barrie presented rising bands that had enjoyed a little success elsewhere. A typical calendar of Tuesday night shows in 1966, which Phil would have seen, featured appearances by John Mayall's Bluesbreakers with twenty-one-year-old Eric Clapton, the Spencer Davis Group with singer Stevie Winwood, the Yardbirds featuring Jimmy Page (later to lead Led Zeppelin to glory) and the Manfred Mann band with Paul Jones. Standing at the back, Phil and his friend Ronnie Caryl were also mesmerized by the Mahavishnu Orchestra with John McLaughlin.

One evening, as he spread the chairs, Jack Barrie noticed that Phil looked glum. Asked why he appeared so miserable, 'he said he was fed up at school, wanted to leave, but his mother wouldn't let him. She said he had to take his GCE exams.' Phil relayed what he had told his mother; that he wanted to be a drummer. Barrie responded that he thought

Phil's mother was right. 'By all means join a band and be a rock 'n' roll drummer. But keep it as a hobby. Go to university, get a degree. Then, if you reach your late twenties and nobody wants you as a rock 'n' roll drummer any more, you'll have something to fall back on.'

But Phil was adamant. Soon he was mingling with the musicians in the band room. John Gee introduced him to Carl Palmer, a creative drummer with The Nice who would star with Emerson, Lake and Palmer, a top band of the 1970s. The club was the perfect spot for Phil to absorb the work, and the conversation, of such drummers as Ginger Baker, who played with the Graham Bond Organization, Mick Fleetwood (with Fleetwood Mac), Mickey Waller (with Long John Baldry), Peter York (with Spencer Davis) and Aynsley Dunbar (with John Mayall). A special favourite of Phil's was Keith Moon of The Who.

If the Barbara Speake Stage School was the nursery for Phil's theatrical career, the Marquee was his academy of music. In the years that followed his earliest days as a club member and unofficial 'assistant', the names that dominated British rock made their first impact there (with the notable exception of Liverpool's Beatles). Marquee bands included the Rolling Stones, Pink Floyd, The Yardbirds, The Who, Ten Years After, Procol Harum, Joe Cocker, Free, Rory Gallagher, Jethro Tull and the Jimi Hendrix Experience, who established the attendance record at 1,318 in 1967. Paul Simon played there on special folk nights before he returned to America and teamed with Art Garfunkel.

Two particular bands had Phil transfixed. One was Yes, in which Phil admired the fluorescent vocals of lead singer Jon Anderson and the skills of drummer Bill Bruford. The other was The Action, an incisive, fiery band with a modish appeal. The front row seat which was Phil's reward for working in the Marquee enabled him to study such bands from a few yards away.

Wardour Street pubs like the Intrepid Fox and the Ship were the regular haunts of most Marquee regulars. With the Marquee still 'dry' in 1969, Jack Barrie opened La Chasse, a members-only drinking club, five doors away. This quickly became the 'green room', dispensing hospitality to the musicians and their entourages. As the years passed, Phil's entrée into such hallowed portals would provide a pivotal moment in his career.

At the Richmond Yacht Club at Eel Pie Island, Phil had begun a vital friendship with another boy that was to be lifelong. His name was Ronnie Caryl and he attended the Corona stage school. Pupils from the schools intermingled happily and many knew each other from working as extras on stage in the London theatres. On his way to school one morning, Caryl told a Barbara Speake boy that he was a guitar player. The boy said to Caryl: 'There's a fantastic drummer at our school. Why don't you come and meet him?'

At thirteen, two years younger than Phil Collins, Ronnie Caryl learned that Phil was about to perform with his school band at the yacht club. Since Caryl was in a school band at Corona, he thought he might go along to compare. It was a revelation. When Phil Collins, the Gadd brothers, Andrea and Lavinia and Peter Newton took the club stage, Caryl was 'blown away . . . it was quite something, tremendously slick compared with my band. Two girl singers! A black lead singer with slick white shoes! And even then, Philip was very forward in his whole manner.'

When he left the stage Phil began chatting to Caryl, who informed him that he played both rhythm and lead guitar. 'Hey, man, do you want to get up and play something?' Phil asked. Caryl joined The Real Thing for one number, the

Supremes song 'I'm So Glad'. That night Phil went home and pondered what he might do about the young lad who had guested with his band. His musicianship had impressed him. Next morning he arrived on Ronnie Caryl's doorstep.

'Philip was slightly harder than me,' Ronnie remembers, 'because he was from Hounslow. I lived in Hanworth, and though it's just down the road, it was a bit more genteel as an area. He had this tougher attitude. He dressed as a mod in mohair suit and green leather coat. He smoked cigar-lets [Hamlets] and went to the clubs to see acts like Stevie Winwood. It was all very adult to me; and two years is a huge difference at that age.'

Collins said to Caryl tersely: 'I'm forming a new band. Do you want to be in it?'

'Who else is in it?' came the reply.

'Well, if you join,' said Phil, 'there's you and me.'

A fast friendship developed. The two boys were going the same route as stage kids and coincidentally both had worked as extras in the London musical *Chitty Chitty Bang Bang*. They began bunking off school, setting their sights on lives as musicians. They would go to Denmark Street in London's West End, sit in the Gioconda coffee bar, and soak up the atmosphere and attitudes of the musicians who frequented it. 'I was thirteen and he was fifteen but Phil was already phenomenally focused on what he wanted to do,' Ronnie Caryl says. 'That was: to be in the music business. I remember very clearly him saying to me: 'I want to earn £40 a week or £200 a week." That was the professional wage scale for musicians.'

Phil undoubtedly inherited his drive, determination and application from his mother, who, as Ronnie Caryl observed: 'Powers away all day.' His pipe-smoking father, a sweet-natured man, was much more passive and not unlike John Cleese in his Britishness. Phil never had any serious confrontations with his parents and he recalls a very happy childhood. But from these speedy youthful years he remembers, and regrets, not conversing much with his father, whom he grew to adore. Years later he was to place a photograph of his dad, in his yachting cap and smoking his pipe, on the mantelpiece of every home he owned.

Phil's proclivity for girls extended beyond the confines of the Barbara Speake Stage School. 'He used to come and raid the girls at my school,' says Ronnie Caryl with a smile. 'He'd hang by the school gate to meet me and off we'd go to various parties. He was always Jack the Lad, a good-looking guy and funny, too. We had a few rows about girlfriends. As I found nice ones, he'd move in and nick 'em.'

Phil was still dating, alternately, Lavinia and Andrea. At this time, his friendship with Ronnie Caryl intensified and their prowess as musicians improved. They rehearsed in the front room of Phil's home. June Collins had met Lonnie Donegan, a pioneer of skiffle music whose number 1 record in 1956, 'Rock Island Line', had inspired thousands of young players. She invited him to the Collins household and proudly introduced her son the drummer.

'He came in to give his advice,' says Ronnie Caryl, 'and asked Phil if he could immediately do a paradiddle [a drum roll in which the principal beats are struck by the left and right sticks in succession]. Phil did this, and Donegan said: "You're not getting anywhere." And to me, he said: "The volume's the only thing you've got. Rubbish!" That was supposed to gee us up into being better musicians.'

Collins and Caryl practised as a two-piece, with the guitarist emulating the ambitious, innovative work of Eric Clapton in Cream and of Jimi Hendrix. They also performed songs from *West Side Story*.

This passion for making music with a kindred spirit was to mark Phil's life. Ronnie Caryl noticed how, in his earliest memories of his friend, he would differ from so many musicians, particularly American players. Phil firmly believed in using his theatrical experience on the stage to entertain the audience as well as make good music. It was to be one of the most significant decisions of his life, for many great players restricted themselves by believing that to deliver fine music was enough.

In 1968, when his parents went to work in Germany, Ronnie went to live with Phil. 'We were very, very close, literally like brothers; we lived in the same room. In fact his mother thought we were gay because we used to disappear for weekends. She said: "Why don't you bring some girls in?" We would argue a lot, but only in the way friends do.' There was an extraordinary symbiosis between the two boys. 'We could be walking down the road and both start singing the same part of the same song at the same time. Out of thin air.'

Days at Hanworth Road in the year that Caryl lived there consisted of getting up and putting on Phil's wonderful collection of records for the day (mostly American black music from the embryonic rhythm-and-blues labels Stax/Volt and Chess and Cream). With an eclectic taste, Phil swung between the pop hits of those years and the psychedelic work of Jimi Hendrix. He loved, also, the pyrotechnics of Keith Moon, the rumbustious drummer with The Who. With Phil's parents out at work, Ronnie Caryl became the cook for them both; their regular favourite meal was Spam, beans and cheese.

They rehearsed every afternoon and then played records again all night, seven days a week. Phil's father bought an album of *Waterside Down* and found there was hardly a gap in which he could get it on to the record player.

*   *   *

Around this time, Phil's mother was told of a major film, about to be made, for which the Barbara Speake Stage School was invited to offer boys and girls. The director was Franco Zeffirelli, and the film *Romeo and Juliet*, a big-budget screen version of the play by William Shakespeare. Phil asked to audition for the lead role, musing that the story-line of two star-crossed lovers of Verona bore an uncanny resemblance to his love for Lavinia. Unknown to Phil, Zeffirelli had first offered the role of Romeo to Paul McCartney, who turned it down because he feared it was too big a part for what would have been his screen début.

Phil was upset that he did not get the part, which went to an unknown seventeen-year-old British teenager, Leonard Whiting. Perhaps because of his experience in acting, Phil did not have the innocence the part required. His regret at losing it, and also the chance to play opposite Olivia Hussey, who attracted him, never left him. When the film was released in 1968 he went to see it several times, warming to the theme, which hit a perfect chord with the mood of young people during the hippie era. Romeo and Juliet were the sixteenth-century equivalents of the flower children in their philosophy, challenging the Establishment. So absorbed with the purity of the romance, and of the melody, was Phil that he learned the 'Love Theme' from the soundtrack on the piano and, in future years, would often be seen and heard playing it at rehearsals. When friends asked him why it was such a favourite, he replied that it reminded him of a major film that he had loved and lost. His friend, Peter Newton, sees Phil as 'a hopeless romantic!'

The irrevocable turning point for Phil between acting and becoming a musician came after he had been working in a fairly major part in a film called *Calamity the Cow*, which was planned as a Saturday morning television serial for children.

'Such as it was, I had a big part in this film, but whereas the other kids in the film were prepared to do anything to get on with their acting careers, I felt a little hipper than everybody else. Because I was a drummer/musician.'

Phil clashed with the director on the way he should act his role. 'I was playing the part of a sixteen- or seventeen-year-old and I wanted to play it like a seventeen- or eighteen-year-old. I had definite ideas different from the director. He wanted me to play it like a thirteen-, fourteen-, or fifteen-year-old, to appeal to the kids who would be watching it. We argued a lot.'

While the film was being made Phil went off on a cycling holiday, and when he returned, his part had been virtually cut from the film. 'I had mysteriously disappeared out of the story and came back at the very end of it. He'd had enough of trying to deal with me.' The conviction that would confront any artistic debate, with musicians all over the world throughout his life, was already apparent as a teenager.

He told the film director and his parents: '"I've had enough of this. I don't want to act. I really want to be in a band. So that's it." And I gave it all up, just as I was about to leave drama school. Mum and Dad were not at all happy about this, because rock 'n' roll was getting a bad press at the time. The image of the musician was sex, drugs and rock and pop bands were all over the *News of the World*.'

His parents despaired, also, because they saw him making substantial progress as a child actor. 'My dad was very proud of saying in the City: 'Clive's doing all right, doing his cartoons; Carole's ice skating at Wembley and doing very well; Philip's in the West End [on the stage]." For him to say that Philip had now left the West End and was in a rock 'n' roll group didn't feel comfortable.'

Since leaving his second stint in *Oliver!* Phil had become what he describes as 'a professional auditioner'. His mother recalls

that the weekly *Melody Maker* became his bible, and he vetted
the adverts at the back of the paper, notably the 'Musicians
Wanted' columns. 'That's what I did all day. And I never got
any of the jobs,' Phil smiles. He and Ronnie Caryl went for
an audition as a duo at the Marquee club, but were turned
away as inexperienced.

'I auditioned for Vinegar Joe [the band that spawned Elkie
Brooks and Robert Palmer] and for Manfred Mann's Chapter
Three.' Both rejected him.

Finally he got a job as the drummer with the Cliff Charles
Blues Band, traversing the country. 'Then I got wind of a group
that was being formed to back a black quartet, Four Tops style.
They were going to do the cabaret circuit.' This band was the
Gladiators and Phil joined it with Ronnie Caryl. With a fine
combination of teenage confidence and arrogance, Collins and
Caryl decided they were better together than staying in that
line-up. They left, and quickly secured a useful stepping-stone
accompanying John Walker, who had starred with his brother
Scott in the hit-making Walker Brothers. In this, they enjoyed
the experience and fun of working the Northern variety clubs
and were paid £40 a week each, the minimum which Phil had
set his sights on when he sat dreaming of success with Ronnie
in the Denmark Street café.

Either through his own restlessness or the natural split of
each group, he drifted from band to band, into such outfits
as The Charge, The Freehold, Zox and The Radar Boys.

Phil was still dating Andrea and Lavinia, but his emphasis
swung to Lavinia after he left school. Intent on becoming a
dancer, she attended lessons with an American woman, Molly
Molloy, at the Dance Centre in Floral Street, Covent Garden.
Phil would accompany her there and watch her dance to the
music of Tamla Motown and James Brown, before taking her

home to Acton. As he pursued his music career, Lavinia would make her mark in the troupe Hot Gossip, who appeared on BBC TV's *Top of the Pops*.

The historic events of 1969 contributed to Phil's next move. It was a year in which Richard Nixon was inaugurated as President of the USA; Concorde made its maiden flight from Toulouse, France; Charles Manson was arrested in California for the murder of actress Sharon Tate; and in Northern Ireland there was rioting in Londonderry after a civil rights march, precipitating the problems that would stretch across the next three decades.

Paul McCartney had married Linda Eastman and John Lennon had married Yoko Ono, and the slow, acrimonious dissolution of the Beatles had begun. One of rock's first supergroups, a tag that would mark the next decade, was born when Eric Clapton teamed with Ginger Baker, Steve Winwood and Rich Grech to form Blind Faith and stage a free concert in Hyde Park. And at 3.56 a.m. on 21 July 1969, Neil Armstrong and Edward 'Buzz' Aldrin became the first men on the moon, proclaiming 'One small step for man, a giant step for mankind'.

Next came a milestone in Phil's young career. It was called Flaming Youth. A keyboardist named Brian Chatto had been approached by Ken Howard and Alan Blaikley in London's Speakeasy club to put together a band, and since Chatto was friendly with Jack Barrie he asked if he knew any drummers. He suggested young, ambitious Phil Collins. After a rehearsal on the stage of the Marquee, virtually the promised land for Phil at that point, he and Ronnie Caryl joined the band, sharing the vocals alongside Chatto and Gordon Smith on guitar and bass. Caryl was featured on twelve-string guitar and bass.

At that time, Collins, Chatto and Caryl were rehearsing every day at Phil's parents' yacht club at Eel Pie Island.

Chatto invited Howard and Blaikley down there, and they were duly impressed.

Howard and Blaikley had made their mark as hit songwriters for Dave Dee, Dozy, Beaky, Mick and Tich and the Herd, featuring a strong guitar player named Peter Frampton. They called him the Face of '68. Howard and Blaikley also managed a kitsch group from Birmingham called the Honeycombs, who scored with a number 1 hit called 'Have I the Right?' Astonishingly, for this was the 1960s, the Honeycombs starred a female drummer, Honey Lantree.

With an eye for angles and gimmicks, Howard and Blaikley conceived a timely launch for Flaming Youth, whom they managed and steered towards a recording début with the Fontana label. Taking their cue from the moon landing, the songwriters let their imagination loose on eight songs about a spaceship leaving the burning planet earth. Moving Flaming Youth into the De Lane Lea studios in Holborn, where many top bands recorded, Howard and Blaikley financed the album and set a two-week deadline for Phil, Ronnie, Brian and Gordon to work wonders. They took forty hours to complete the songs, a very long time to record an album in 1969. On many nights after their sessions, Howard and Blaikley wined and dined them.

The result was a creditable and topical record entitled *Ark 2*. Released in October 1969, it was widely praised, especially by the *Melody Maker*, which named it 'Pop Album of the Month', eclipsing other releases in the same month by the influential American group The Band, Stevie Wonder, and the Small Faces. The paper described it as 'adult music beautifully played with nice tight harmonies'.

The pop weekly *Disc and Music Echo* called the album's theme 'a second Noah, the chosen few being rescued from earth and transported to another planet and safety ... there is some splendid music on this very good first album. Reviewing the single which was taken from the album, called 'From Now On', backed by 'Guide Me Orion', Penny Valentine warned of pretentiousness. But she concluded that Flaming Youth, in adapting the hymn 'Immortal, Invisible', 'have woken up to the fact that those hymns we were forced to chunter through at school, without feeling, are in fact extremely pretty with very good melody lines'.

Though launched in some style, with a big promotional party at the London Planetarium and a party at Howard and Blaikley's sumptuous house in Hampstead, neither the album nor the single took flight. The competition from other records was immense. On the album front, there was the Beatles' *Abbey Road*, Led Zeppelin's *Led Zeppelin II*, a much-heralded new band called King Crimson with *In the Court of the Crimson King*, and Pink Floyd with *Ummagumma*. New singles included David Bowie's evocation of a spaceship, 'Space Oddity', John Lennon and Yoko Ono's Plastic Ono Band with 'Cold Turkey', Joe Cocker with 'Delta Lady', and Stevie Wonder's 'Yester-me, Yester-you, Yester-day'.

Ark 2 was, however, in the vanguard of the new genre of 'concept albums', alongside such works as the Moody Blues' *Days of Future Passed*. Flaming Youth appeared at London's Lyceum ballroom with a twenty-piece choir and a huge orchestra including the Ray McVay Brass. Phil was, at last, mingling with musicians he had read about in the music press. At La Chasse club, Ronnie Caryl recalls, 'We moved into a slightly higher echelon of being hip young musicians.' The quartet bombed up and down Britain's motorways in a Ford Transit, playing the clubs, earning £5 a week each but ever hopeful. As they returned from one show, their van's engine blew up. As it billowed flames and black smoke, the musicians fled. Phil was the last to leave. 'Hey, I've got to get my shoes out,' he said as he methodically threw everyone else's possessions out after them. They were amazed at his coolness in the crisis, but Ronnie Caryl reflects now that such organizational flair was always typical. But the attitude of guitarist 'Flash' Gordon Smith soon irritated Phil. 'Flash would say: "Oh, I *can't* wear these socks!" And then he'd go on about his trousers. Well, Philip was the consummate professional and this sort of behaviour drove him mad.'

One night, Phil's best friend, Ronnie Caryl, also incurred his wrath. Flaming Youth were in the midst of a concert in a small hall when Ronnie jumped off the stage, went into the middle of the crowd and turned to face the stage, still playing. Backstage after the show, Phil was furious at what he saw as such casual behaviour. 'What the f . . . were you doing?' he challenged Ronnie. 'Hey, man,' his friend said, 'I was just checking the sound.'

Just as he had slapped Peter Newton's face at a school rehearsal, Phil went for Ronnie. 'If you do that again . . .' The two were nose to nose. Ronnie interrupted him: 'What, are you going to punch out another one of my teeth?' This, remembers Ronnie Caryl, referred to the occasion on which Phil had punched out one of his false teeth 'because I was drunk after a gig, not during it, and he thought that unprofessional. Oh yeah, he was quite volatile. I was nine stone and two years younger. He was very much the big brother of the situation. When it came to power games in the group, he'd call the shots because he was older and bigger.' Although fisticuffs were not a daily occurrence, 'He got very wound up about things.'

After about a year of personal tension and band frustrations, Flaming Youth collapsed. Before it did it had evolved into a free-form jazzy group, including Rod Mayall, brother of the noted rock leader John Mayall, on organ. Phil and Ronnie were starting to write their own songs and reacted against those of their managers. A big bridge had been crossed in this band by Phil, however. Indirectly, Ken Howard and Alan Blaikley had lit the fuse which prompted Phil to sing. 'Some of the songs were not that good,' Ronnie Caryl says. 'Flash, the singer, wouldn't sing them! Neither would Brian Chatto. I was only a fledgling singer then, so it fell to Phil.' Phil's response that if a job needed doing he'd do it illustrated an attitude that was to be crucial to his success in his later career.

The end of Flaming Youth signalled a disconsolate end to 1969 for Phil. His romance with Lavinia Lang crumbled. 'Lavinia turned him down,' says Ronnie Caryl. 'It was common knowledge. I remember one night when he rang me up and said: "You've got to take me over to Lavinia's. I've got to go and sort this out." And I had to get up in the middle of the night, drive him over in my little Morris Minor [Phil could not drive] and wait outside [her home in Acton] while he tried to sort out his love life. She was going with Barry Ryan, of Paul and Barry Ryan. She thought Phil was a drummer who would never get anywhere, and that was that.'*

Phil bounced back to Andrea Bertorelli, who remained Lavinia's best friend.

* Paul and Barry Ryan, a British singing duo, had a string of hit records in the late 1960s. Barry's solo record in 1968, 'Eloise', written by his brother, sold 3 million copies internationally.

'Drummer required'

Hyperactive, fiercely ambitious and talented beyond his age as a drummer, Phil Collins began 1970 with his optimism challenged. He knew he was a good player and was irritated by the rejections he had had at auditions; Flaming Youth had collapsed; and so had his romance with Lavinia.

Yet it was to be the year, and the decade, that began his route to stardom. His breaks came through his insatiable love of Tuesday nights at the Marquee club. He heard on the club grapevine that Yes, whose melodic strength so attracted him, were temporarily losing their drummer. Bill Bruford wanted time out to go to university. Phil buttonholed the singer Jon Anderson after a session, confirmed that the rumour was true, and asked if he might be considered. Jon invited Phil for an audition the following week. Strangely for such a punctilious person, Phil did not take up the offer. Perhaps he was overawed by the prospect of being judged by his heroes. Perhaps he had simply been turned down at too many auditions to face another test, particularly from Yes. Had he attended, Phil reflects now, there's little doubt that he would have got the job. He knew their repertoire intimately and, of course, had studied Bill Bruford's work at the drums, and its interaction with the band, with a zeal approaching fanaticism. He had hung on their every note.

Then, in the summer of 1970, aged nineteen, Phil received an invitation to play on the first solo album being made by George Harrison of the Beatles. The call came from a session 'fixer' who had heard on the musicians' grapevine that Phil was a capable young percussionist. Phil 'leapt in the air' and raced to the studio, thrilled to be in the company of the producing genius Phil Spector alongside George Harrison, Ringo Starr, Maurice Gibb of the Bee Gees, Billy Preston, Badfinger and Mal Evans, the Beatles' road manager. These were legendary names, working on the triple album that would be called *All Things Must Pass*.

Phil was asked to play percussion and was seated behind congas. Whenever Phil Spector called for the drums to be played, Phil remembers, 'I would play, figuring he meant me. Since I'd never played congas, my hands were getting some pretty bad blisters by the time half an hour had gone.' As Spector called out for different combinations of the musicians to play, including the drums from Ringo, Phil continued on the congas. 'About two and a half hours later,' Phil says, 'Phil [Spector] says: "Right, congas, you play . . ." My hands were almost bleeding by this time and he hadn't been actually listening to me at all. I had passed my peak by that point.'

When the album was released, Phil bought it, expecting to see his name alongside such luminaries as Eric Clapton, Gary Brooker and Klaus Voorman, famous names of the day who had played with George. But Phil Collins was not named on the album and his conga contribution was excluded. Phil was deeply disappointed.

He was still scouring the 'Musicians Wanted' adverts in the *Melody Maker* when one caught his eye: 'Tony Stratton Smith requires drummer sensitive to acoustic music, and acoustic twelve-string guitarist.' 'Strat', as he was known throughout the music industry, was a regular at La Chasse and at the Marquee. A former sports reporter with the *News of the World*, he had a keen ear for the new rock bands with fresh sounds that had mushroomed in the late 1960s. He ran a record label and managed bands. Phil saw him at La Chasse one night and asked him to reveal the name of the band behind his advert. Strat replied that the band was Genesis, on his lively independent record label, Charisma.

When Phil said he was interested, and told him a little of his experience, Strat checked with Jack Barrie, who had heard Phil in Flaming Youth and rehearsing at the Marquee. Barrie said he was a 'very good drummer'. Strat then told Phil that the decision was not his; he would submit his name and phone number to Genesis, who were auditioning.

Genesis had been formed, though without that name, at Charterhouse public school in the white heat of the Beatles revolution of the early 1960s. Peter Gabriel and Tony Banks were its forerunners, calling their group the Garden Wall before recruiting Mike Rutherford from another Charterhouse group called The Anon. In the autumn of 1966 they made a demonstration tape of their self-written songs and sent it to Jonathan King, a former Cambridge undergraduate who had scored a number one hit in 1965 with his composition 'Everyone's Gone to the Moon'. King was by then working for the head of Decca Records and charged with taking to the label some new talent.

He thought the sounds were too ornate, but promising. He did, however, feel that they had the genesis of something special, and that was the name he gave them. Elated to be asked to make singles, they made a few flops before they reasoned that their talents would be best displayed on an album. Their début on Decca, *From Genesis to Revelation*, was released in March 1969. It flopped. The association with Jonathan King ended but, undeterred, they recorded a new demonstration tape of their songs.

Securing a residency upstairs at London's Ronnie Scott's club, a showcase spot for new talent, they were heard by Tony Stratton Smith, who signed them to Charisma, a label he dedicated to new British talent.

Their second album, called *Trespass*, was, like their first, exploratory, and precipitated the departure of guitarist Anthony Philips and drummer John Mayhew. John was the third drummer to leave the band, and since Peter Gabriel had had early aspirations to be a drummer, the position was deemed crucial.

The advertisement that triggered Phil Collins's interest brought several hundred replies. It was high tide for young musicians as the emphasis in rock began to switch from singles to albums, allowing the players more time to show their virtuosity. The year 1970 brought the emergence of bands like Deep Purple, Free, Emerson, Lake and Palmer, and Marc Bolan with T. Rex. From America came the Jackson Five, and Simon and Garfunkel with *Bridge Over Troubled Water*. In Britain, the discernible shift from singles to albums brought with it a need for strong musicianship, which was to Phil's advantage.

Peter Gabriel co-ordinated the Genesis auditions, which took place at his parents' lavish house in Chobham, Surrey. 'Phil made his appointment through Mike [Rutherford],' Gabriel recalls. 'He said he had worked for George Harrison, but he didn't mention that it was the third tambourine part or similar!' Most of the others auditioned that day had arrived either on time or later. 'Phil, being Phil, arrived early, with his friend Ronnie Caryl.'

Phil's punctiliousness in arriving early was to prove an asset. He was asked to wait by the swimming pool while other drummers auditioned ahead of him. This meant he could hear exactly what he would be required to do, for the precise Gabriel had devised a twenty-minute audition that left nothing to chance. There were four specific tests, checking the player's capacity to learn as well as demonstrating rhythmic ability and a comprehensive knowledge of the drums. The songs were 'The Knife' and 'Stagnation', both from the second album.

When Phil's chance came, Gabriel immediately registered a big difference between his playing and that of previous applicants. 'I remember noticing him as he sat down on the stool. Before he even picked up the sticks, I thought: this guy can *play*. Because he had a confidence, a self-assurance I could feel. It was like watching a jockey get into the saddle, and instinctively knowing, from body language, that here is someone who knows what he's doing.'

Immediately Phil began playing, Gabriel, Banks and Rutherford knew that the audition was over. 'He was fantastic,' Gabriel says, adding that there was no doubt or discussion. There had been other good players, but their problem was that they displayed the stodginess of session men who were more interested in the money than in making good music. 'Phil was into the money, too, as everyone was. But we had the feeling that he also had the personality to become a band member rather than a hired hand.'

Joining Genesis hiked Phil's income by 100 per cent, to £10 compared with the fiver that he and Ronnie Caryl had been making in Flaming Youth. At least as important as the cash was the prospect of joining a 'happening' band with regular work. Says Ronnie Caryl, who auditioned for Genesis on the same day but was then a youthful prima donna and only worked for them for a week before getting the sack: 'We wanted to get into a group that played every day, and Genesis appeared busy every week from the back page adverts in the *Melody Maker*.' Caryl did not respond well to the musical demands of Tony Banks that might have secured him a job in the band. 'I don't think either Philip or I was particularly keen on the music of Genesis at the time. But Philip with his keen business sense, which I never possessed, knew what he was doing and got into it.'

Gabriel, too, reflects that Collins was not enamoured by Genesis's musical stance, and his coolness was to last for more than a year. 'For his first couple of months, he wasn't sure, and didn't seem to be locked in a hundred per cent. He thought we were a poor man's Yes, and there was always a chance that Bill Bruford might leave Yes. So for the first year or so he was a professional musician keeping his eyes open.'

Phil joined Genesis in August 1970. They still needed a strong guitarist when Peter Gabriel noticed an advert in the 'Engagements Wanted' section of the *Melody Maker*: 'Guitarist-writer seeks receptive musicians determined to strive beyond stagnant musical forms.' The advertiser, an original guitarist named Steve Hackett, was invited to see Genesis at a concert at London's Lyceum that Christmas. He had an audition, and joined soon afterwards. This was the band that would have a unique impact on the progressive rock movement.

The two new boys in Genesis first met at the Earls Court flat of Tony Banks, to prepare for a rehearsal. 'It was *de rigueur* in those days to have a jacket from Kensington Market, and Phil looked like he'd just come from there,' says Steve Hackett. 'I liked him immediately. He was very warm and open. "Hello, I'm Phil." He was so open-faced and affable, and had a bit of a beard and was thin. He looked like so many blokes of that era.'

Collins and Hackett, as the only non-public-school boys, felt no antipathy from Gabriel, Rutherford and Banks. But there was an unspoken division. In rehearsals, which began immediately Hackett joined, he recalls that 'extraordinary arguments would break out, such as "You swiped my wine gums at school back in 1961!" or "Yes, but you broke my ruler!" Events would be resurrected when things got heated. But, then, these guys had been together since they were about thirteen years old, so there had been a ten-year history that Phil and I couldn't possibly crack.' Peter Gabriel, recalls Hackett, although he had stood alongside Rutherford and Banks at Charterhouse, was 'less public school than Mike and Tony. Their accents were straight out of the Foreign Office. Mike had the same voice, delivery and manner as Prince Charles.'

Phil, totally unfazed by this, had not found the most natural of homes in joining Genesis. While the founders of the band were striving to invent something very different, Phil's musical education had been orthodox and his aspirations were more fundamental. At that time, he enjoyed the new breed of singer-songwriters who were making an impact, such as Elton John and James Taylor, while he had been soaking up the jazz at Ronnie Scott's club, learning from such inventive musicians as the Mahavishnu Orchestra, Tony Williams's Lifetime, Jack Bruce's band and US saxophonists Eddie 'Lockjaw' Davis and Dexter Gordon. In progressive rock, he loved The Band, the US outfit that had helped redefine rock's future. Steeped in rhythm and with a great hunger to learn from such sources, he took into Genesis, too, a remarkable technique as a drummer.

The other four men in Genesis were much less attuned to rhythm. Gabriel, with the futuristic character that would always mark him, was playing the new American sounds of Country

Joe and the Fish and Spirit; Tony Banks enjoyed Shostakovich and Sibelius, Mike Rutherford admired Joni Mitchell and Judy Collins, while Hackett was playing the records of Segovia and Buffy Sainte-Marie. Hackett recalls that he was initially wary of such disparate tastes and asked Phil whether they would ever be able to integrate as a band. 'I think we'll all influence each other,' Phil answered, confidently. But while the founding trio tended to dominate the songwriting, Phil's contribution to the band as a drummer, and as the man with an ear for the overall sound, became profound.

But Peter Gabriel felt, from Phil's first day in Genesis until his last, that the band was 'not his natural musical form'.

If the 1960s had been dominated by guitars, the next decade, in which Genesis was born, saw the rise of keyboards. Gradually a much less romantic approach was adopted by the music, as rhythm became king, and the massive sound of the drums, too, was born. Phil was in the vanguard of all that. Yet unlike scores of other top rock drummers, he brought a finesse to his playing. He had learned accentuation and punctuation from the records of Buddy Rich and singer Mel Tormé; he was able to suggest different phrasing to melodies created by the others in Genesis when they brought songs. He was not particularly influenced by rock 'n' roll, and did not favour the policy of the exhibitionist drummers who made dramatic points. More than push himself forward as a writer in the band, he preferred to take the songs of the others and make them swing, or even 'stutter', rhythmically. It was an immense contribution to a band that, even as it began, looked like becoming rather arty.

'I don't think there was any prejudice in the band. Gradually everyone would embrace other forms and want to know what the other bloke was on about,' says Steve Hackett. Soon, he was collaborating on a composition with Phil. Inspired by the Beatles' song 'Eleanor Rigby', Hackett wanted to write 'a straightahead song about a relationship'. He told Phil he loved 'Eleanor Rigby'. Phil suggested that instead of writing about an old lady, why didn't they centre on two old women who had lost their husbands. It occurred to Steve Hackett that Phil, unlike the others in the band, 'liked songs about relationships'. The first composition by Hackett for Genesis became 'For Absent Friends', which Phil sang on the band's third album, Nursery Cryme. Phil's vocal displayed a texture uncannily similar to that of Peter Gabriel. 'There were times you'd be hard pushed to know if it was Phil or Pete singing,' says Hackett. Released in November 1971, the album stepped beyond their début collection, but they still lacked focus.

Success came neither quickly nor easily. Belgium and Italy greeted their early records enthusiastically, but in Britain the band slogged round the campus rock circuit, sometimes to applause, but often to dispiriting indifference. One London promoter told them they should all return to whatever 'proper jobs' they were schooled to do, particularly with a Charterhouse education to boast about; one reviewer predicted that they would 'never make more than a second rate college band'.

This called for grit, something Phil, who knew about struggle and failed auditions, was much better equipped to find than Gabriel, Banks and Rutherford. 'He was much more comfortable than we were,' Gabriel recalls of the early years. 'He helped loosen us all up; he was much more comfortable within himself than we were. We all brought different things to the group but there was definitely a different way of behaving, from Phil, which I think helped loosen us all up.' Phil also used to attract more female interest than the others. 'He was the most sexually experienced of the group. It's always the drummer,' Gabriel says.

Tony Stratton Smith firmly believed in working his bands hard to build a strong word-of-mouth popularity. He sent

them to the US for a few dates in December 1972 to promote
their fourth album, Foxtrot. And in the spring of 1973 they
went back to the States for a full American tour. By then
Gabriel, hitherto just a worthy interpreter of the lyrics, had
undergone a startling change of persona on stage. The lyrics
of the band had attracted students who sat or stood, sombrely
taking notes to dissect in their colleges the next day. Suddenly,
Gabriel decided that more theatricality was needed, and he gave
Genesis, overnight, a monumental face-lift. He wore a red dress
and a fox's head as a mask.

Gabriel says now that he had 'dual motives' for his concen-
tration on theatrics in their stage shows. 'It was partly because
I was starting to feel some frustration with the lyrics by the
others which I couldn't relate to; and I wanted to get more
into story-telling. And the other reason was just to get noticed
with good old-fashioned rock 'n' roll gimmickry.' He sensed
that Phil tolerated it, was amused by it, but 'Although he had
a background in the theatre, I think he felt music should be
pure and unpolluted with any of that stuff. I think he could
enjoy it and admire it, but in its rightful place. And I don't
think he felt Genesis, or any rock group, was the rightful
place. But then, nobody in the band really liked my visual
stuff at the beginning.'

Derek Jewell, the Sunday Times jazz and popular music critic,
was to describe one of their shows around this time thus:

After two hours of music and mime, costume drama
and light-show, comes the ultimate coup de théâtre from
Genesis.

As menacing music crawls through the speakers, actor-
singer Peter Gabriel stands black-coated like a wicked
mad monk in an ancient creepy movie. Then POUF! (if
that's the word) an explosion blinds us. Through smoke

he moves heavenwards, on wires, still singing, making cycling motions. He is lowered, lifts a violet-lit tube before him, eye make-up glowing. Final chords crump, smoke belches, curtain falls . . . Genesis are interesting, ambitious, often moving, often funny. But they're limited still and, at times, chillingly reminiscent of what I've read about Berlin cabaret in the 1930s.

The friction in the band went unchecked, partly because by 1973 Genesis were on a roll to huge acclaim. Gabriel's gamble had coincided with the arrival in Britain of 'Glam Rock', with outlandish costumes and face make-up adorning such acts as Slade, Gary Glitter, the Sweet and Wizzard. 'It was really a big shock to everyone when I did costume changes and began jumping around,' Gabriel concedes. 'At first, Tony, especially, felt pretty uncomfortable and I don't think Phil liked it either.'

Phil remains diplomatic about the early 1970s in Genesis: 'I remember one tour, for the album The Lamb Lies Down on Broadway, where Peter couldn't get a microphone near his mouth because of what he was wearing. It didn't really matter because the audience by this time were in love with him. Mike and Tony were always happy to get the music across. Their view is if you're getting the music across, it doesn't really matter. But I always felt a bit frustrated that the music wasn't, I felt, being listened to. It was being watched.'

A video about the history of the band shows what Phil describes as '. . . a very telling bit from Italy. All of us were sitting there, Peter was the main one being talked to, and he had this strange haircut. You could sense that because everybody wanted to talk to him and he had to respond in a way that was demanded of him, there was probably a little bit of friction, which I didn't see at the time.'

Conflicts of ego remained buried and since Phil hates face-to-face confrontation, this suited him well. 'I think behind closed doors we all knew what was going on. It's just unfortunate that some of the songs that were credited to Peter were actually group songs; the lyrics that were credited to Peter were by two or three of the guys. That led to a bit of frustration.'

Chris Welch, rock journalist and Genesis chronicler, explains: 'At that time (the early 70s) quite often groups combined all their talents and a song would probably be written in the studio with three or four members of a group collaborating. In the end it was difficult to say exactly who wrote what. Sometimes, just for convenience, a group collaboration might be credited to one person.'

Genesis became, in Phil's words, a happy band with some terrible fights. 'There were never any major arguments apart from the usual bickering. We had a van that broke down all the time. I remember one terrible trip to Aberystwyth. We broke down three times on the way there, arrived too late to play, turned round and broke down twice on the way back. We then had three hours' sleep and drove to Plymouth. All bands in that period had their own stories like that. It was surprising that we didn't rip each other's throats out! But we got on great.'

At Christmas Phil would go with Ronnie Caryl to play at Butlin's holiday camp parties. He regaled his friends in Genesis with stories about how his father, who went along for fun, would enjoy seeing his son playing romantic music for the dancers, and even give instructions about what tunes to play and at what tempo. Phil said he enjoyed the exercise of playing for simple functions like those as much as playing with Genesis or Brand X.

In joining Genesis, Phil had faced a powerful triumvirate who were keenly aware of the uniformity of their social and educational backgrounds. The difference from Phil in chemistry was palpable. While Phil spoke straight from the shoulder, Gabriel, Banks and Rutherford were rather stiffer, more political, in their outlooks and responses. 'Phil was pretty straightforward about most things,' Gabriel says, 'and this was a great relief, because from our private education, we were remarkably equipped at not showing what we thought or felt about anything. I enjoyed that openness from Phil. He had no idea what our lyrics were about, sometimes. He would say that quite often.'

But Gabriel was very irritated by one aspect of Phil's character. 'He is non-confrontational. I think he purposely avoids confrontation. So when the three of us would have steaming rows, and especially Tony and me, Phil would hardly ever come down on one side. I used to get pissed off at him for that.' Gabriel considered Phil a kindred spirit 'in groove and feel for situations and I looked to him for support in some of those areas. But I got more support in the end from Steve Hackett.' The camps were usually divided, says Gabriel: 'Mike drifted into Tony's camp; Steve drifted into mine . . . with Phil sitting in the middle.'

Songwriting, one of the most satisfying and lucrative aspects of pop music, came relatively late in Phil's career. In the 1960s and 1970s, the big groups had dominant writing partnerships – John Lennon and Paul McCartney, Mick Jagger and Keith Richards – that discouraged contributions from their colleagues. Genesis was no different. Banks and Rutherford wrote to their own idiosyncratic formula and there was little scope for Phil. His soulmate Peter Gabriel, similarly frustrated, recalls that they tried to forge ahead together in their songwriting aspirations. But because Tony Banks was 'enormously possessive about his keyboards and wouldn't let us near them' during their spare time during sound checks, Gabriel and Collins would together go searching for a dressing-room which had a piano. Primitively, as a three-fingered pianist searching for chords, Phil sounded out Peter with a few ideas, and sang a little as he made a tentative move towards composing. Gabriel believed Phil deserved encouragement: 'He was very simplistic in his writing, but he is a naturally gifted musician who can pick up almost any instrument and make it sound good. I remember thinking he had a great natural voice. He was a more natural singer than I was. But he hadn't focused it at that stage; it was very American.'

With half a dozen albums in the early 1970s, Genesis romped to stardom as darlings of the new, analytical audience for rock. Sitting at the drums, applauded as the backbone of a sound he had helped to define, Phil Collins sometimes wondered if their lyrical stance was abstruse. 'But I had no ambitions to do anything other than play drums,' he says. 'It was the best job in the band, in my opinion.'

Tony Stratton Smith decided to relinquish the management of the band in mid 1973. The band was clearly fulfilling his hopes, and a live album which Strat had encouraged enhanced their stature. Strat felt that running his thriving record company was enough and he did not have time to devote to daily management. He passed the baton to Tony Smith.

With his father, Tony had a first-class pedigree in promotion of pop concerts. While at college, he had helped his father promote the first British tour by the Beatles in 1963; later, as he gained experience as a promoter for jazz and rock bands, the words 'John and Tony Smith Present . . .' adorned many posters for concerts around Britain. Tony innovatively staged the Who's ground-breaking rock musical Tommy at Sadler's Wells and became known to Strat by arranging Charisma Records package tours.

Tony Smith would help to steer Genesis to the top division of British rock. Since jazz was his first love, he had an immediate affinity with Phil Collins, recognizing in him an exceptional drummer.

Amid all this synergy, Phil's father died. Ten days before Christmas in 1972, Phil had arrived back from his first American tour with Genesis. Though his parents were happily married, they had what Phil calls a 'strange relationship'. Greville loved the country and, in his retirement, spent weekdays in Somerset where he had friends he had made during the war. June stayed in London to work and Greville returned to the family home in Hounslow at weekends. Phil recalls a phone conversation on his return from the United States in 1972, asking his father if he would be coming home for Christmas. 'He said "yeah." I said well do come, won't you, I want to see you at Christmas.'

Greville died on Christmas Eve. 'Apparently he had a history of heart troubles but never did anything about it,' Phil says. 'I see so much of me in my dad. If I see something wrong with me, I'm convinced it's going to go away. And if someone's ill or got a cold, I say: pull yourself together and get on with it; it's only a cold, for God's sake. So I tend not to complain about illness, and will it away. He did the same thing, but it killed him.'

Though he naturally mourned the loss of his father, Phil was able to sweep aside his inner feelings when work loomed. Early in 1973 Genesis reconvened for rehearsals. He mentioned his father's death to Mike Rutherford, and then it was on with the show. Rutherford told the rest of the band, after the rehearsal. Steve Hackett was astonished: 'He'd been working without a blip. You'd never have known such a thing had happened to him. I'd met his dad and their relationship was good and strong. But it was a funny thing with Phil; if he had a nervous breakdown he'd be able to do it with a smile; he wouldn't miss a beat.'

Throughout the formative years of Genesis, Phil had no serious girlfriend. Andrea Bertorelli's father had died in 1969, and after her mother's remarriage to a Canadian, Andrea went to live near her in Vancouver in 1971. She was twenty-two when, after a live-in relationship with a Canadian, she gave birth to Joely in Vancouver on 8 August 1972.

Phil and Andrea had not dated in the year preceding her departure to Canada. But he remained friendly with old friends from stage school, particularly Peter Newton, Sharon Campbell and Miriam Mann, who dated Andrea's brother John. 'Miriam used to write to me and say that Phil was missing me and wanted to write to me,' says Andrea. 'She asked why I didn't write to him.' Finally, Miriam urged Phil to write to Andrea 'instead of asking me to ask how she's doing, and asking me to send your love'.

Eventually, Andrea says, Phil did write. 'He asked me to go back to England and live with him. And I said no. I was involved with someone else at that time and I just didn't know what I wanted. I was young. I didn't take something like living with someone lightly. But I said to him I will be home later on in the year. Maybe we can hook up.'

In 1973, Andrea visited England with her one-year-old daughter. She met Phil a couple of times, 'but for whatever reasons, it didn't come together. But I realized how important he was to me.' Back in Canada she wrote to him 'and told him how I felt about him'. Andrea's mother, a determined woman like her daughter, encouraged the romance and had seen Phil as a potential son-in-law when they were teenagers, telling anyone who would listen: 'My Andrea is going to marry Phil Collins.'

After a British concert tour in the autumn of 1973, and a second American tour, this time under the aegis of new manager Tony Smith, in December Genesis returned to Britain.

Their star was now shining. In January 1974 the band packed London's Drury Lane Theatre for five nights. A hugely successful tour of Europe followed. At this time, Phil knew from the schedule of the forthcoming spring tour of the US that the band would be visiting Vancouver. He and Andrea had been corresponding and he mentioned the Canadian shows in a letter. Luckily, several dates were rearranged around the time of the Vancouver concert, meaning that Phil had about a week clear to spend with Andrea. 'That's when we put our relationship back together again,' she says.

Phil asked her to return to England with him and this time she agreed. But she wanted to stay in Vancouver until after her sister Francesca's wedding in May; she was going to be a bridesmaid. Phil took off to continue the tour and a week later he sent two plane tickets for Andrea and Joely to join him in New York for the Genesis concert there. 'He didn't want to wait until May to see us again.' They travelled to New York, and stayed with him until the tour ended in April.

After the death of her husband, June Collins had moved out of the family home in Hanworth Road, Hounslow. Initially she went to stay with Barbara Speake for a couple of weeks. But in that time, says June, Phil had 'filled the house with all the group. And I got to thinking that if I didn't do something about my house, it would deteriorate. I said to Phil: "Why don't you buy it?"' This never happened, but since June was intent on leaving the house for her own flat, Phil began looking elsewhere for a home of his own. Phil fancied the Surrey Downs, and he and his mother drove to Epsom. She paid a deposit, and from his still meagre income from Genesis he could afford the rent on a one-bedroomed flat in a large house at Sunninghill Downs.

When Andrea and little Joely flew back to Britain with Phil from the spring tour of the US, they moved into the Epsom flat. Phil, who was later to become the legal father of Joely, adopting her soon after his marriage to her mother, was, says Andrea, extremely caring and loving towards the child.

On a postcard to his old schoolfriend, Peter Newton, Phil had written excitedly: 'Have I got a beautiful lady coming to live with me . . . have I?'

'Why don't you let me have a go?'

Phil Collins had always been dynamic in his work, motivated and blinkered in his thirst for success. With its underlying tension and a style that was hardly natural for his musicianship, Genesis was not an easy band for him to stay aboard. But he had loyalty to his colleagues and maintained respect for their creativity.

In the autumn of 1973 their originality began to reap dividends. They released a critically acclaimed album called *Selling England by the Pound*. Surprisingly, for an album-based band, this yielded their first hit single. 'I Know What I Like (In Your Wardrobe)' was released in February 1974, becoming their sixth single released in six years of recording. It rose to number 21 in the British best-sellers.

Though he was far from being the leader, Phil Collins powered Genesis. 'It was more a matter of life and death to me than the rest of them,' he explains. After every performance, he would return to his hotel room and play himself a tape of the show they had just performed. 'And I made notes. I'd go through things with the sound engineer the next day about the gig the night before. I was the only one who did that. I'd occasionally drag Tony, Mike, Peter or Steve in to say: listen to this, it's great, or it's crap, or this needs to be worked on.'

He slipped notes under the doors of the others pointing out the deficiencies he had heard in the tapes: 'This needs to be done,' read his rejoinder. He was never the boss, he says, but 'certain people have the driving force in a band'. He and Peter Gabriel shared the function of 'pulling in the same direction, enthusiasm-wise. I was certainly not the musical leader. I saw my strength in Genesis, when it was a five-piece, as in being good at arranging songs and hearing a piece of music, and saying: let's try it like this. And they would admit that I was the best musician in the band at that time. But I was not a writer, and Tony, Mike and Peter's main thing was that they were writers. Their strength lay in the music that they wrote rather than the playing of it. My strength was the playing of it, and my enthusiasm. And a drummer's natural enthusiasm, if he's a good drummer, will normally pull the band along.'

He sums up his energy and drive with self-effacing modesty. 'I usually did the pulling. But what I pulled was probably more important than the pulling. If we stopped for a cup of tea and a sandwich, I'm the one who would say: "Ready? Let's go!" I'm the coach . . .'

Unexpectedly, the pivot for Phil Collins's life came in the spring of 1974, just as he settled in at Epsom with Andrea and baby Joely. Genesis went into a long period of rehearsal for what became a thematic double album entitled The Lamb Lies Down on Broadway. The project was conceived by Peter Gabriel. And it gave full rein to the singer's histrionic excess. The Lamb had been premièred in concerts, unwisely and prematurely, on their

American tour late in 1973. With his outlandish stage wear, Gabriel was suddenly to Genesis what Mick Jagger was to the Rolling Stones: the unchallenged visual focus. Despite the vital roles of foundation played by Banks, Rutherford, Hackett and Collins, this was Peter's show. And Phil felt uneasy.

When they finally completed the album for release in November 1974, Genesis embarked on a monumental tour. Visiting North America, Canada and Europe, they performed 'The Lamb' more than 100 times. The tour was quite a family affair. Andrea and Joely travelled to many of the concerts, as did the wives and girlfriends of the rest of the band members. But ticking away beneath the triumphant, theatrical concerts was Gabriel's time-bomb. The co-operative ethos of Genesis was shattered as he projected his baby, The Lamb Lies Down on Broadway, to critical praise and commercial success.

The startling apparition of Peter clad in a body-stocking, inside a whirling cage of snakes, emerging from a long inflated plastic tunnel as a warty monster, formed part of the decibel-high Genesis stage show. By spring 1975 the Lamb Lies Down on Broadway stage show reached Britain. Gabriel's work as its kingpin was widely applauded. The balance between visuals and sound was kept with skill, wrote Chris Welch in the Melody Maker. He heaped praise on Phil Collins: 'The precision and sheer intelligence of his work was a source of delight throughout a long and difficult programme,' he intoned in a review of the Genesis show at London's Empire Pool in April 1975. His roster of percussion had developed into a 'strangely personal layout, with the hi-hat as the fulcrum, with the snare drum increasingly taking on the role normally allotted to the tom tom'.

While the musical input had been from Rutherford, Banks, Collins and Hackett, the lead singer invariably gets the plaudits for such a work. After The Lamb established him firmly as the focal point in Genesis, Peter Gabriel decided to quit and embark on a solo career. He told manager Tony Smith in Cleveland, Ohio, during the US tour. No attempt to persuade him to change his mind worked.

In the curious psychology of Genesis, Peter was not resigning purely through ego, or to plan a career to outshine that of the band. Because he considered the band a coalition, he was actually concerned that his starring role would threaten the infrastructure of Genesis and that things could not be the same after *The Lamb Lies Down on Broadway*. His formal statement had some pithy asides on the Genesis that had evolved, however: 'The vehicle we had built as a co-op, to serve our songwriting, became our master and had cooped us up inside the success we had wanted. It affected the attitudes and the spirit of the whole band. The music had not dried up and I still respect the other musicians. But our roles had set in hard. To get an idea through Genesis The Big meant shifting a lot more concrete than before. For any band, transferring the heart from idealistic enthusiasm to professionalism is a difficult operation . . .'

He referred to the problems in his personal life that were known to the band at that time, adding: 'I had begun to think in business terms, very useful for an often bitten, once shy musician. But treating records and audiences as money was taking me away from them. When performing, there were less shivers up and down the spine. Much of my psyche's ambitions as Gabriel, the archetypal rock star, have been fulfilled: a lot of the ego gratification and the need to attract young ladies . . .' It was not impossible, Gabriel added, that members of the band would work with him on future projects and there was, of course, no animosity between him and the others.

Phil's restless frustration about getting the music right and being recognized for doing so was expressed in his interview with the *Melody Maker* in April 1975. 'The band is together and we're all happy. But there are frustrations and disappointments.'

One national paper devoted most of its review of the band to explaining that Peter's wife was the daughter of the Queen's secretary. 'It's a problem you can't put into words. I'm not pissed off. It's just that I find it incredibly frustrating to play, say, very well one night, not very well the next, and for people not to know the difference. I'd like to get booed on an off night!

'Of course it's a good thing that the show can get across by the visuals but a lot of people don't listen to the music. That's a bit of a drag. No, it's not jealousy. If it were, I'd feel it towards Peter and I don't at all. It's as big a drag for him as it is for us. I'd like to see Mike and Tony come out more. After all, they started the band for the songwriting. It must be frustrating for them when they write a lot of the music and get very little out of it.'

Peter Gabriel's last performance with Genesis was at St-Etienne in France in May 1975. At the end, he symbolically played 'The Last Post' on the oboe to the rest of the band. To many, including the musicians, it seemed more than a farewell from their singer. It seemed to spell the end of the band.

Phil Collins married Andrea Bertorelli at St Joseph's Roman Catholic Church, Epsom, on 27 September 1975. It was a small, family-and-friends occasion. Ronnie Caryl was Phil's best man. The two old pals played drums and guitar respectively at the reception, and people teased Phil that he couldn't even be torn away from the drums on his wedding day.*

Amid the celebrations, there was talk of the departure of Peter Gabriel from Genesis. Jon Anderson of Yes, who as a singer felt

* Lavinia Lang, Andrea's and Phil's close friend from stage school, did not attend the wedding. After their college years together, she and Andrea had drifted apart. Hot Gossip, the dance troupe which Lavinia had joined, was highly successful, and, featuring singer Sarah Brightman, scored a big hit single in 1978 called 'I Lost My Heart to a Starship Trooper'.

that Phil was something beyond a fine drummer, said to Banks
and Rutherford at the wedding reception: 'Why don't you just
get another instrumentalist? Phil's got a fine voice! He's your
man.' The idea fell on stony ears. To the leaders of the band,
the thought of their drummer becoming the vocalist was too
bizarre even to contemplate.

As he and Andrea moved back to their Epsom home, this
was a period of intense musical activity for Phil. Rutherford
and Banks pondered how to find their new lead singer, while
Phil was simultaneously busy playing drums in Brand X. He
had appeared during the past two years on random sessions by
several bands, sometimes to the consternation of his colleagues,
who had often been concerned, and sometimes irked, about
his frenetic schedule. 'We felt his energy was getting diffused
somewhat,' says Peter Gabriel. 'I think Tony felt more than any
of us that it was rather like the "another woman" syndrome.
It was a matter of loyalty. But that's Phil, that's always the
way he is. He's loyal to music and not to any one's music in
particular.'

Passionate though Phil had always been about music, his
workaholic behaviour might, in Gabriel's view, have been
used, unconsciously, 'as a means of avoiding the disturbing
stuff going on inside. You can use music and success for that,
as I have found. Being a workaholic means you make a lot of
sacrifices in more important aspects of life. I know that for
myself and I observe that in Phil, too. Sometimes it takes the
shake-up of a relationship to thrust you in on yourself. Like
me, he had internal stuff that needed dealing with. And I hope
he didn't continue to use work and success to avoid it.'

Brand X, however, was to be more significant and creatively
satisfying than most other work. An instrumental group, it
leaned towards freewheeling jazz with a fusion of rock. Phil
was joined by Robin Lumley (keyboards), Percy Jones (bass)

and John Goodsall (guitar) as they moved into London's Trident Studios to record their début album.

At one stage, when Genesis were in the same studios, Phil was 'doubling up', popping downstairs on some days to play with the musicians in Brand X who were preparing their album simultaneously. 'I only realized he was doubling up between two bands,' says Steve Hackett, 'when I bumped into the guys in Brand X in the corridor. They said Phil was downstairs with them. I said: Oh, really? I thought he was working with us.'

The freewheeling spirit of Brand X was a more natural home for Phil's work than Genesis. The structure of the two bands was totally different: while Genesis was orchestrated and bookish to a fault, Brand X was charged with spontaneity, young musicians using the band as a means of expression, unhindered by vocals. Phil enjoyed it, as they all contributed songs to their début album, Unorthodox Behaviour.*

Brand X was 'poles apart' from Genesis, says Phil now. 'It fulfilled another side of my playing which Genesis could not provide.' It was not a threat to the progress of the band. 'No, they didn't mind at all. I think everybody in the band saw that I needed to play more, needed to do more than was available to me in the band. And it could only bring other influences into the group, which was a good thing. Brand X was good fun to do, but it was the balance of the two that I liked.'

With a new wife and three-year-old daughter, Phil seemed to approach his work with even more intensity. 'We were very happy,' Andrea says. 'He loved Joely.' But she reflects that he was 'more detached than lovey-dovey' over kids; he had, she says, a rather old-fashioned, patriarchal attitude to

---

* Released in July 1976, when interest in 'fusion music' was increasing, Brand X's first album sold more than 100,000 copies internationally. American critics greeted it as Europe's best jazz album of its time.

child-rearing. 'I don't think he was that comfortable with children. Basically that was my job and my territory. His territory was his music.'

Stressing that she 'never married for money', Andrea recalls that money was tight even though Genesis were beginning their climb. 'We weren't well off and had to live within a tight budget. His per diem from the record company or whoever it was was not very big; he was driving a Mini like most of them in Genesis at that time.' The writing might have been on the wall for her from the moment she returned from Vancouver to be by his side in 1974: 'Within a couple of weeks he was touring. I didn't drive at that time, and I felt I was basically abandoned in Epsom.'

Brand X played its performance début at the London School of Economics in December 1975, beginning a schedule of much-praised shows, a crucial new era in Phil's life. 'He was driven, completely driven,' Andrea says in an admiring way. 'He was just totally focused on what he wanted right from the age of thirteen when we met at stage school. And he was going to get it no matter what. He was the most ambitious person I ever met. I liked that about him, actually.'

As Phil played the field as a musician, enjoying the contrast from his number one band, the problems in Genesis were unresolved. Steve Hackett, sensing the hiatus and wanting to assert himself away from the hothouse of Genesis, went off to record a solo album. Phil and Mike Rutherford went into the Kingsway Recorders studio to play on Hackett's solo début album, *Voyage of the Acolyte*. An odd atmosphere prevailed. Genesis was scheduled to make a new album and didn't have a singer. In the studio, Hackett reminded Rutherford of Jon Anderson's suggestion that Phil should be made the vocalist. Hackett later also mentioned this to Tony Banks. 'It didn't go down too well,' he says with an air of understatement. 'No, no, no. He's the drummer!' was their terse response.

Secretly, Phil hankered for the chance to prove his worth as Genesis's singer but seemed too diffident to come right out with it to Rutherford and Banks. His true feelings were revealed during a Brand X recording session. Bill Bruford, who was playing percussion alongside Phil, remembers that day in 1975: 'He said to me: "Peter Gabriel's leaving. We're auditioning for singers. They're all ghastly, and anyway I can sing better than most of them." And I said to Phil: "Well, why don't you sing then – and I'll play drums?"' It was an interesting insight into the oblique way in which Phil's mind often works. 'I think,' says Bruford, 'that he was floating the idea and wanted someone to suggest that he sang.'

In an extraordinary move for such a high-profile band, Rutherford and Banks had decided to advertise for a singer. This yielded about forty applicants, who were duly auditioned. Most of them failed for one of two reasons. Either they could not grapple with the complex Genesis songbook, which needed skills beyond vocal talent into the realms of story-telling; or, in the view of Rutherford and Banks, they were 'guitarists who sang' – a rejection that was to prove totally invalid as events progressed.

They had recorded all the backing tracks for their next album, which was to be called *A Trick of the Tail*, when the auditioning took place in late 1975. So the pressure to find a vocalist was great. Their frustrations peaked one day when a gravelly-voiced rock singer, totally unsuited to their sound, admitted that he found their melodies convoluted and confessed he felt 'uncomfortable'. 'We played it back to Phil next day,' Steve Hackett says. 'Mike Rutherford said to him: "What do you think"? Phil said: "I think it sounds fucking average. Why don't you let me have a go?"'

It was a golden moment. For beyond his ability as a drummer, and his thorough musicianship, beat the show-business heart which had been refined since he had entered stage school eleven years earlier. Ronnie Caryl had told him that singing would be a natural move. At home, Andrea had encouraged him to go for it, but she remembers being rebuffed on the subject by Rutherford.

In the studio, Phil duly sang one of the new songs, called 'Squonk'. 'He sang it through once,' Hackett says, 'and that was that.' In the next few days, Phil sang through the whole collection of songs which Rutherford and Banks had assembled for the new album. Phil had helped to write three: 'Robbery, Assault and Battery' (jointly with Tony Banks), 'Los Endos' and 'Dance on a Volcano', which were co-operative works by the band.

Easily and with a natural flair, Phil, hitherto only an occasional singer, made a strong impact as a singer on *Trick of the Tail*, which soared to number 3 in the British albums chart to become the most commercial of Genesis's eight albums by February 1976. Yet he still did not want to relinquish the drums. 'I thought the drummer had the best job in the band,' Phil says now. 'I didn't want to give it up.' The feeling was that singing was a 'job to be done', rather than a conscious, egotistical move to centre stage.

There was general delight at Phil's vocal work, however. Like many, Tony Stratton Smith remarked on the similar texture in singing displayed by Phil and his predecessor, and Rutherford, Banks and Hackett were relieved that the role had been filled successfully, even if it might be only temporarily.

As *Trick of the Tail* strengthened Phil's musical reputation, his wife fell pregnant. With a new baby due in the autumn, Andrea and Phil needed to move from the one-bedroomed flat in Epsom. They chose a small house in Ealing, where Phil set about the chores of decorating with gusto, and they moved in in the spring of 1976, just before Genesis took off for yet another tour of America and Canada. For this, a decision about the singer was essential. Almost by default, Phil had drifted into the role, and with no other candidate on the horizon, he got the job.

Told that Phil was to be the new singer, Gabriel was astonished. 'It all seems enormously obvious now, but at the time the others didn't think he could do it,' Gabriel remembers. 'And anyway, who would do the drums?' Gabriel was another who doubted that singing would fall naturally to Phil. 'That he would eventually write songs alone and have success as a solo artist seemed quite likely. But I didn't expect him to want the front position with Genesis.'

And then, later analysing the Collins character, Gabriel felt it all fell into place. Collins would have shrewdly perceived the role as a nursery for his vocal talents. 'It was his adolescence as a singer,' Peter reasons. 'He took on an existing job and could then find his feet and see what he actually wanted to do. Because, while he is a risk taker in some areas, he is extremely cautious in others. This was quite a safe way of becoming a front man. It was with songs he knew. Although it could have gone wrong, when he was put out there and under pressure, he knew what to do. That came from his stage school days. He was born with it; he was very comfortable in front of an audience.'

The key position of drummer was filled by Bill Bruford, whose brilliant work had powered Yes and King Crimson, and who had been one of Phil's early heroes. 'He was going to the front and didn't want the sound to fall apart,' Bruford says. 'He was a bit uncertain how the drumming would sound, but anyway I only saw myself as a journeyman helping Genesis over a difficult period.'

Although Phil had had the roar of the greasepaint in his bones from the age of fourteen, he did not consider the role of Genesis singer to be a full-blown show-business function. 'It was a giant leap,' reflects Bruford, 'but he saw it as entirely musical and pragmatic. He didn't say: "Well, I'll be the *singer*," with a swagger of the shoulders. A job needed doing and he was a worker. Nobody else could do it, and he could. I didn't detect a bit of ego in his move.'

Interviewed on the announcement of his joining Genesis, Bruford said: 'I'd played with Phil in Brand X; I've been over to his house and we altered the course of percussion together in an afternoon over a cup of tea. He's very like me, y'know. When he was telling me he couldn't find a drummer for Genesis, I said: "Why don't you ask me, you fool? I'm not doing anything."' They rehearsed together at the Una Billings School of Music.

In his formal interview with the *Melody Maker* on 13 March 1976, Phil said of the arrival of Bruford: 'We were at a loss to find someone to replace Peter Gabriel, so I decided to come upfront and that left us with the problem of finding someone I respected enough to stand and watch play the drums. Bill seemed an obvious choice. We won't be using Bill for recording, however. We're still a four-piece group. All this doesn't mean I've stopped drumming for ever. Quite a few of the pieces we'll be doing are split into two parts and I'll be playing on the instrumental sections. There will be some points where Bill and I will both be percussing.'

Phil's nervous début as the front singer was at Hamilton, Ontario. Bruford seemed a perfect choice as the new drummer, his humour and professionalism fitting in perfectly and giving Phil confidence. With Gabriel gone, the band placed more accent on the light show, and there was a conscious effort to camouflage the departure of the theatrical lead singer. Phil faced a tough first night: a member of the audience stood up throughout the concert, dressed like Gabriel in bat wings and a cape. 'In those days audiences must have been very polite because apparently nobody asked this guy to sit down,' says Steve Hackett. 'He was as much a show, from beginning to end, as the band was. He stood up for the entire gig.'

After a successful US and Canadian tour, Genesis returned to a British tour, and five nights at the Hammersmith Odeon in June. An anonymous visitor to one of these shows was Peter Gabriel, who sat watching the concert with both positive and negative feelings. 'When you have put a lot of effort into creating something, there's a tenderness. It's like watching someone with your ex-wife. You feel a little territorial, even if, like me, you felt you've made the right decision [to leave].'

Gabriel had not told them he was going to see the show because 'that might have freaked them out, especially Phil. For the first part I thought he was doing incredibly well and seemed comfortable. But there were one or two places, like in "Supper's Ready" or "The Lamb", where there is a lot of emotion, and he was playing with the voice on "Supper's Ready" and I remember being pissed off at that. He was putting in little decorative things and I was thinking: Fuck the decoration, deliver the message!'

Genesis's first appearance in Britain without Gabriel was highly charged and greeted with scepticism. 'For fans,' reported Chris Welch in the *Melody Maker*, 'it was a nerve-racking, breath-holding moment as they bounded on stage . . . and the new boy, Bill Bruford, began to probe at his kit. Across the stage was another kit with an empty stool. Then came the man who would soon fill it, the man who was to stun the audience with his presence and energy. Phil Collins. For it was Phil's night. The drummer who was secretly a singer all along bounced up front and took over where another equally commanding presence had left off.'

Bruford played kit drums throughout Phil's vocals and then, when Phil returned to his drums, the pair either worked in unison or Bill added tonal or rythmic effects. 'There were no flashy drum solos.' The band, glowed Welch, dispelled any hankering for the past. They received a five-minute standing ovation.

Phil's stage personality, while informed by his experience as a child actor, carried none of Gabriel's excesses. For him, the music had to be the key attraction, and any visual impact, or comedy, was a bonus for the audience. 'When I took over,' he reflects now on the old Genesis, 'I said, "I'm not going to do any of that [dressing up in outlandish costumery], I don't mind singing, but I don't want to do any of the other." So I just stood there and sang. And I became something different from Peter. I became more of a mate next door, and a mysterious traveller. I just used to tell jokes, funny stories. Peter did, too, but they were of a different kind.' The emphasis switched to appearing ordinary, accessible, and Phil's easy blokeish personality paid dividends. While, as he noted, people had hung on Peter's every word, with him it was different. The music carried the message more powerfully.

In mid-tour, Phil spoke about his insatiable hunger for work outside the parameters of Genesis. The workaholic was partly born of a need to play in all-music situations where, unlike with Genesis, there was no diversion of theatricality. 'I'd like to do more sessions with other bands,' he told the *Melody Maker*. 'In Genesis I'm not pushing myself more than sixty per cent and with other bands I can get out the other forty per cent.' When the 1975 British tour was over, 'I'm going to have a blow with another band. I don't stop! But it's hard on my lady and little girl when I'm away so long.' He spoke of the session the previous year for David Hentschel, which was released on Ringo Starr's record label, 'and I've done his next LP which is a film score and I did a few things with Peter Banks for his new version of *Flash*. Between Genesis's American and European tours, I did an LP with a bass player I met who used to be in the Liverpool scene. We just had a blow at Island studios. I like playing with other bands because it keeps me fresh.'

Andrea considers that becoming the singer with Genesis forced upon Phil a huge transformation. 'It was a big responsibility but it was also something that was unexpected. He basically felt that when he was drumming, that was as good as it was ever going to get. And he was a brilliant drummer. I love Phil when he plays drums, way better than when he's singing; that's what attracted me to him.' The turn of events threw the focus on to him quickly: 'Previously, people had wanted to interview Peter. Now it was Phil, Phil, Phil.' And it changed him, she says. 'He became very egotistical, suddenly, not in a good way. I think that his taking over the vocals in a way wrenched him away from me and the kids. Because now he had more to gain, in some ways.'

Successful though they were, Genesis had been regarded as a bunch of unwelcome iconoclasts by many of their contemporaries in music. And Bill Bruford, who had been one of Phil's earliest inspirations, was among the cynics when he joined. Widely regarded as one of rock's most proficient and tasteful drummers, he considered joining Genesis, albeit temporarily, a pragmatic demotion.

In Yes and King Crimson, his two previous bands, there had been a snobbish attitude towards Genesis. 'They were regarded as latecomers to the progressive rock, or art-rock, movement, a bit second-hand.' He was confused about joining the band: 'I wasn't sure I wanted to be there. In Yes and King Crimson, which I loved dearly, I had a lot of input, helping to shape the sounds, so that joining Genesis, where I was expected to play as a hired gun, was a comedown. I was a brat, far too forthright with my obnoxious views, telling them what they were playing was rubbish. I didn't understand, like American musicians do, that if you are a hired hand, you have been paid partly to shut up. An opinion wasn't wanted. I have been apologizing for this at every Christmas and birthday party since and they've let me off the hook. I felt no emotion about the band and not having any creative input made me a very sour character to have in Genesis.' Phil was, says Bruford, 'extremely patient' with him.

Bruford's fairly light style at the drums concerned Phil a little. 'I wasn't the perfect drummer for Genesis. My ambivalent attitude about being there showed. I didn't play as heavily as Phil would have liked and perhaps I fiddled about with the music too much.' As for the internal dynamics: 'You'd put Tony and Mike on one axis and Phil as the stranger,' says Bruford. 'He was the unusual one in the band, the bundle of energy. That might be doing Mike and Tony a disservice in the writing department, but all bands are a collision of characters of some sort. The tensions in Genesis were OK compared with most of the maniacs I've seen in this business. If people weren't fighting by the end of the night, in other bands, they were doing pretty well. Genesis was a gentlemanly organization, extremely nicely run, very generous.'

As the birth of his child loomed in the autumn of 1976, Phil Collins had never been so busy, or on such a 'high'. Accepted as the new singer, he joined Genesis for the preparation of their ninth album, which was to be called *Wind and Wuthering*. Then came another big hiccup. Bill Bruford resigned, having always said it was a temporary relationship with music for which he felt no affinity. Phil's choice for his successor was inspired by his love of black music: Chester Thompson, a high-pedigree drummer from Baltimore, Maryland. Phil wanted to feature in two-drum workouts, and Thompson had experience of this, having played in the bands of Frank Zappa, Weather Report (a Collins favourite) and the Pointer Sisters. With subtlety, in this writer's opinion, Phil had effectively assumed the leadership of the band, though he and Rutherford and Banks would deny it. As the drummer and the singer and a co-writer of songs, he had marginalized the founders of the band, who, for all their musical talent, seemed content with anonymity. As Peter Gabriel sailed away to a successful solo career, Phil commanded Genesis, propelling it rhythmically and projecting it visually.

Immediately they completed their American tour, the band travelled round Europe to reassert themselves without Gabriel. Phil's stage persona and accessibility proved a big hit. Returning to Britain for a pause in Genesis work, Phil played several shows with Brand X. Then the band planned to go to studios in Holland to record the *Wind and Wuthering* album, before going back to London for nine days of rehearsal for a British tour.

Andrea and Phil's child was due at the beginning of September, and the trip to Holland was scheduled to start just a few days later. 'The doctors gave us September 1st,' says Andrea. 'The band planned to leave on the 3rd, so we could have a few days together after the baby was born and then off they'd go. But the baby was two weeks late; I had to be induced.' Genesis held up their departure for two weeks and baby Simon was born at Queen Charlotte's Hospital, Hammersmith, on 14 September 1976. 'The day I came out of hospital Phil went to the airport,' Andrea says. Although he returned intermittently, and was good, she says, at phoning her from the road, 'I didn't see him for weeks. And it continued like that for the next three years. That was what happened to us; it didn't ease off.'

It was against this background of Phil's work schedule that his marriage began to disintegrate. On New Year's Eve, 1976, in the kitchen at their new house, with three-month-old Simon and four-year-old Joely, Phil had told Andrea that Genesis simply had to crack America wide open the next year. That would mean a tour of forty-five cities during February, March and April.

Phil says that Andrea announced that if that happened, he should not expect the marriage to survive until the same time the following year. Andrea denies she delivered such an ultimatum. 'I said: "Oh no, I can't *do* this. I don't think I can make it if you go away for another year." I desperately needed help at that time. His whole attitude was: stop whining; he basically wasn't interested in my problems.'

Confirming that he was away within a couple of weeks of Simon's birth for seven weeks of recording *Wind and Wuthering*, Phil says: 'I felt that when I was there, I was always there. But I was a musician, with all that entails. So it's hard to keep the hours of a bank clerk if you're a musician.' Phil's mother adds ruefully: 'It always seems to me that she *knew* he had to go on tour, when she married him.'

Two more years were to elapse before that pivotal conversation in their kitchen could be seen to have marked the beginning of the stormy end of the marriage.

While many artists felt passionately about their music, Phil was different. 'He is absolutely *defined* by his work,' states Bill Bruford. 'He would be very anxious about record sales, asking if they were in any way worse than they were last week or last year. I would imagine he's not a happy man to be around if, for example, a record sold nineteen million compared with the last record doing twenty million.'

So it was that on the day after his epochal conversation with Andrea, Phil went to work. Genesis were the stars at the re-opening of the London rock venue the Rainbow on 1 January 1977. This marked the début of Chester Thompson, triggering an explosive and a unique two-drummers performance at certain points in the show. Chester arrived into a band in which Phil was already singing, 'But he made it clear to me that he didn't intend to give up playing drums so it was pretty key to him that he found someone like me who could function in that situation,' Chester recalls.

In February the band triumphantly set off on the tour which Phil had told his wife was essential to 'break' the band in North America: a three-month, forty-five-city tour of North America and Canada, returning to Britain for three sell-out concerts at Earls Court in June.

If the ghost of Peter Gabriel had been truly vanquished with Phil's massive contribution, other problems occurred in this mercurial band at this peak of its success. Steve Hackett quit later that year. The eloquent guitarist had been agonizing over his decision for two years, since Gabriel had left, and finally, he felt his songwriting and means of expression within the band were stifled, and that the band had gone on to autopilot. On the day he decided to quit, Genesis were mixing a live album. 'I phoned Mike Rutherford, the politician in the band, and said: "Would you just tell everybody that I've left?" I didn't want to go to them individually and be talked out of it.' The same day, Hackett bumped into Phil Collins in Wardour Street, Soho. 'I said: I won't be turning up today; Mike knows all about it. Phil gave me an incredulous look. We were very brief with each other. My departure had nothing to do with my relationship with Phil, personally or professionally. I have a tremendous fondness for him and his talent.'

Hackett's resignation came as the band won the award for 'Best Live Band' in the *Melody Maker* Readers' Poll. 'The problem has been plaguing me for a long time,' he told the paper. 'By the time we got to the last album, *Wind and Wuthering*, I felt the challenge within the band had really diminished. We were in the position then where we could play for ever and there was no challenge at all. It seemed to be always a foregone conclusion that every time we stepped on stage we would go down beautifully . . . it was taking a lot of spontaneity out of playing.'

Mike Rutherford, who switched from bass to lead guitar on Hackett's departure, said the band 'will carry on as we always do. We fight on to a fresh challenge.' He explained that problems had come to a head at the end of the American tour. 'When people leave, it's quite exciting,' said Tony Banks, 'because the people left have to broaden out and try and encompass the roles of those we've lost.' They were in no hurry to find a replacement. People continued to call in asking if they were still seeking a vocalist, even though Phil had by then settled in. 'I get that all the time,' Phil said. 'Even on the last tour, people asked: "Have you settled in as a singer yet?"'

Bearded and with a receding hairline, the Collins of the 1970s seemed a self-effacing figure. He was always modest about his abilities and about Genesis's successes. 'As a band we've been around quite a long time and it's good to spread into different directions,' he said in the wake of Hackett's resignation. He added enigmatically: 'We will go on the road again, but if we didn't and just became a recording unit, kept the name and occasionally did concerts, that would be good, too.'

A whiff of the band's hunger for American success – which would precipitate a personal crisis for Phil – came from Tony Banks at that stage. 'We always say we're going to slow down and end up working harder than ever. In the States we're still a growing group, certainly not peaking at all. *Wind and Wuthering* sold twice as many as *Trick of the Tail*, which sold far more than any of the others. The problem with America is the old single hit, which we're not very good at producing.'

Hackett's shock departure, announced in October 1977, merely strengthened the resolve of Collins, Rutherford and Banks to demonstrate that Genesis was bigger than the sum of its parts. For live concerts they hired guitarist Daryl Stuermer from Milwaukee, but as they entered the studios again in Holland to record their next album, there was a tacit admission that the old order had been changed. They called the album *And Then There Were Three*. This seemed to bring a shift in emphasis and approach, and suited more the warm melodicism that would characterize Phil Collins's voice and songwriting. Released in the spring of 1978, it featured a lilting hit song which lifted Genesis, and the freshly poignant voice of Phil Collins, to new heights. 'Follow You, Follow Me' became their biggest hit single in Britain, rising to number 7 in the charts that March. It stayed in the lists for thirteen weeks. Even more crucially for the band that was targeting the vast American market, 'Follow You, Follow Me' became their first US hit, reaching number 23 in the *Billboard* Hot Hundred.

Phil's career was in orbit. But this continued to exacerbate the simmering tension in his domestic life. 'Basically his lifestyle changed once he became the singer, with all the media attention that was put on him,' Andrea reflects. 'So that obviously affected us. Whether I couldn't adjust or didn't adjust, or whether he couldn't adjust or didn't, I will never know. We were both very young. But the result was that it created a gap between us. Because I had to spend more and more time at home with the kids, at the time he was having to spend more and more time away from the home, and becoming a rock star. So we were both going in these opposite directions.

'We loved each other, but there was this polarity going on. So something had to give, one way or the other. And it did. I couldn't leave my kids. He was good when he was at home. He would take Joely to school and pick her up; when he was at home he was part of the family. We used to cook together. He would vacuum and tidy. He was a cleanliness freak, and helpful. When we were together at home it was good.'

The diary of a band scaling the heights was as relentless as it was successful. After starring at the open-air rock festival at Knebworth, Hertfordshire, in front of 100,000 fans, Genesis with its vast armoury of equipment was among the big bands of the 1970s that were in danger of becoming more famous for their bombast than for their music, a factor that partly provoked the back-to-basics attitude of the punk rockers. America, though, carried no such cynicism towards success. Towards the end of 1977, Genesis unveiled their plans for the coming year. In 1978 they would play twenty concerts in America in the spring; the same total in Europe in May and June; fifteen open-air and stadium dates in America during July; ten open-air festivals in Europe during August and September; twenty-five more concerts in America in September and October, and a six-date tour of Japan in November. This was to be followed by the recording of a new album, for which they would need to write fresh material.

'There is little doubt,' intoned the artist and writer Pete Frame, a rabid fan from their early days, 'that some or all of Genesis will be dead from exhaustion by the end of 1978.'

'Have you met Eric?'

The rollercoaster success of Genesis was unstoppable as they steeled themselves for the huge world tour. Money was on the horizon, although it was coming through slowly from world sources. When Tony Smith took over management of the band in 1973, they were in debt to the tune of £150,000. Five years on, their future secure as a hit album followed each tour, they were solvent. And, with no real dissent in the band, they were also supremely confident of a golden future.

It was time for these international troubadours to put down some roots. Mike Rutherford and Tony Banks headed for country homes in Surrey. Phil was told, like them, that he could now afford to invest in decent-sized property, although the size of the mortgages daunted them all. For Phil and Andrea this was perhaps a palliative to the difficulties in their marriage caused by Phil's workload.

The couple began looking at properties in the Richmond and Twickenham area, near where an integral part of Phil's boyhood had been spent at the yacht club. When they failed to get the house they fancied, Rutherford and Banks suggested that Phil should consider a home farther afield, perhaps near to them both in Surrey. It would help to create a nice band-family atmosphere. Phil and Andrea decided on Old Croft, a £100,000 seven-bedroomed house set in five acres of its own grounds in the picturesque village of Shalford, Surrey. They added a tennis court and swimming pool, and the house seemed an idyllic base in which to raise two children. The family moved there in the late spring of 1978.

In May and June, Phil was engaged in the three-week European tour, which was swiftly followed by the grinding schedule of trails round America and Japan. Andrea says that while she loved the beauty of Old Croft, 'The difference between us and the rest of the band was that the others didn't have children at that stage so their wives could go on tour with them. I was stuck by myself in the middle of nowhere, taking Joely to school and raising Simon. That was a big stress on me. Moving there was a bad move, a big mistake for me.

'It got to me. How was I supposed to find the emotional strength to raise two children alone? I was cut off from my family, isolated in the country. It was one thing to be alone during the day, taking care of the children and the house and the dogs and all that. But to sit on my own at night was lonely. I was not out partying.' Nor, she states, did she have a wide circle of friends. Andrea adds: 'Everyone I knew at the time did not have kids, so I was basically out of the loop. I was very much alone, out of sync with my peers. Phil was never there; it was very difficult.'

Phil has usually dealt tersely with the roots of this billowing marital strife. 'My first wife just didn't understand what I needed to be happy, which is work,' he declared after the divorce.

*   *   *

By the late 1970s, the country area where Phil and Andrea lived had become known as the Rockbroker Belt. However, Phil was totally unaware of the fact that as well as his Genesis mates many city boys in the same business were living close by. His affability in London music circles, by contrast, made him many friends who keenly respected his steady climb from semi-professional status to the top job with Genesis. Phil Collins had truly paid all his dues, and could claim a grounding in the theatre, too. Among his coterie of close friends was John Martyn, the respected singer-songwriter-guitarist who also counted Eric Clapton as a colleague. Phil was later to produce Martyn's album, and Eric Clapton guested on the highly rated 'Glorious Fool'.

One day in 1978, Martyn was visiting Collins at Old Croft. 'Listen, have you met Eric?' Martyn asked. 'No,' said Phil, intrigued. 'Well, he only lives down the road,' Martyn revealed. 'You should get to know him, because he's living so close and he's such a nice bloke.' Ewhurst village, where Clapton lived with his wife Pattie, was a mere two miles from Shalford. 'That would be great,' enthused Collins, recalling to Martyn that the guitar virtuoso was 'an old hero of mine. I used to play all his Cream songs in my school years, things like "Cat Squirrel", "NSU" and "I'm So Glad".'

So began one of the richest and most fruitful friendships in Phil's life. He was initially in awe of meeting such a legend, and was also a fan of Pattie, whose first husband had been George Harrison of the Beatles.

The first visits by Phil with John Martyn to Clapton's home had aspects of tragicomedy – the tragedy being that this was bang in the middle of Eric's worst period of alcoholism, when a bottle of brandy a day was the norm and when Pattie was in despair. Sometimes, when Phil arrived, Eric would be in bed asleep, having passed into an alcoholic stupor, and Phil would play snooker with Pattie until he rose to join them. The comedy aspect of their early meetings was that Genesis was a name scarcely known to Eric, and he had to be told privately that Phil was actually the drummer with a very successful band. Pattie smiles now: 'When John Martyn said: "This is Phil Collins," it meant nothing to me. And I hadn't *heard* of Genesis.'

The run-up to Phil and Andrea's marital split had begun by this time. When Phil was touring America, Andrea says, she felt 'lonely, isolated and depressed' and had an affair with someone who was helping to renovate the house. 'I realized I had made a dreadful mistake and told Phil when he returned home for one week. He was supportive at first, but we were constantly rowing at this point because of all the stresses on our relationship.' Andrea, Joely and Simon were scheduled to go with Phil on the week-long tour of Japan in November, but this was cancelled by Phil, according to Andrea.

On the Japanese tour, Phil was in the doldrums. And against the background of their fractured relationship, Andrea's aunt had died. When Andrea's mother arrived in London from Vancouver to attend the funeral and witnessed the embattled state of the marriage, she suggested to her daughter that she return with her to Vancouver to recuperate. This Andrea did in January 1979, taking Joely and Simon with her.

Joely Collins was six years old when all this was happening. 'I knew something was wrong,' she recalls. 'I didn't like my school, and those were really weird, bad-vibe times living in Old Croft.' Her parents had tried to protect her and Simon, as much as they could, from the tensions. 'But you can only really hide so much. My dad's got a wicked temper, too, and he can be pretty scary when he's irate.

It's not super-vivid, but in my gut I knew that this was not right.'

Then began Phil's shuttle flights to and from Vancouver, his desperate attempts to retrieve his wife and children from Canada and bring them back to England, his statements to Mike Rutherford and Tony Banks that he might go and live in Vancouver, or leave the band. This was the period of domestic chaos which planted the seed for that breakthrough album, *Face Value*.

Phil's friendship with Eric and Pattie Clapton grew, vitally, during this period of solitude. While Eric was beleaguered by drink problems, Phil was despondent about his marital break-up and the departure of his children, and they gave each other solace. Clapton was gradually realizing that his new friend was a splendid drummer, and he and Pattie went to see him appear with Brand X at a concert at Guildford Civic Hall. 'I phoned as many of our friends as possible to make sure that they went along to support him,' says Pattie, who still had little idea of Phil's status. Forty Clapton friends attended. 'Backstage, the number of people who recognized Phil and knew him threw me slightly; I thought he was just our friend who lived nearby and played drums in this band called Genesis.' Eric, six years Phil's elder, and grounded in blues music, respected the solid musical values which Phil brought to his work.

Even in these difficult months, Pattie recognized something special in Phil: 'It was too early to predict he would be such a success, but there was something about him that made me feel he deserved it. He was full of good, ambitious energy.' One time when he was visiting the Clapton home, she cut his hair. 'He had long, rather thinning, beautiful blond locks that I decided had to go, shortly after we met. He seemed willing, but might have been absolutely terrified.' At the snooker table

and in conversations with her, Phil spoke of his sadness at
the departure of Andrea. 'I realized,' says Pattie, 'that he was
deeply unhappy and he felt he had made a great mistake by
being constantly on tour without her, and this was the reason
for the split. I just felt I wanted to make it better for him
somehow.' On one occasion she tried a bit of match-making,
introducing him to a friend, the daughter of the man who ran
the pub near the Clapton home. 'Miranda was a wonderful
fashion designer; she was on her own and so was Phil. But
she was very ambitious and Phil was very ambitious. They
enjoyed each other's company but they were not really right
for each other.'

However, an important connection, and male friendship,
stemmed from Phil's regular visits to Clapton's home, where the
American singer-songwriter Stephen Bishop was in residence. A
year earlier, Eric had been in California and played guitar on a
track on a Bishop album entitled *Careless* and a fast friendship
developed; in 1978 Bishop visited England to promote his
album, and stayed with Eric and Pattie. 'You should meet
my friend Phil,' Clapton told Bishop. 'He's a great guy and
a great drummer.' He played Bishop a video of Genesis. 'I
thought the music was just weird,' the latter recalls. 'I didn't
really understand it. But I did notice in the video that Phil
was obviously a great drummer.'

Pattie introduced Stephen to Phil when he popped round
one day. 'Hello, I'm Phil Collins, I really love your work . . .'
was Phil's opener to the American, who, like the Claptons,
was unaware that he was an established musician. Phil was,
in Bishop's memory, 'really thin', possibly showing the effects
of worry over his personal life. Later, Phil would confess that
he had known all Bishop's albums through his wife Andrea.
He had told her he didn't like it, but that the music grew
on him.

The following year Stephen Bishop was again in London, accompanying his girlfriend, the actress Karen Allen, who was filming *Raiders of the Lost Ark* and starring opposite Harrison Ford. 'I kinda wanted something to do; I got bored, being there for a month,' says Bishop. Although he had completed his new album, which was to be called *Red Cab to Manhattan*, it needed, he felt, a bit of an injection. Bishop asked Eric to arrange a band for him to record two of his compositions, 'Little Moon' and 'Sex Kittens Go to College'.

Clapton duly got together a unit that included himself on guitar and Phil Collins on drums for the recording sessions at Air Studios, London. 'I had never played with Phil before and wasn't sure how it was going to go,' Bishop says. 'We improvised and goofed around on "Rhythm of the Rain" and "Hit the Road, Jack". And boy, it was fun. I thought Phil was just a rocker drummer but he really showed me how he could do just about anything, such a wide variation of styles. Wow, this guy was good, an incredible drummer.'

The bonding of Eric, Stephen and Phil was to develop personally and professionally in the years ahead. As Phil began the decade which delivered him to individual popularity, he began a custom that would endear him to his friends. Postcards, and later faxes, bearing news and wit and good wishes, would arrive unexpectedly from Phil as he lapped the world. Some would be signed off by a hastily drawn self-portrait of himself flailing away at the drums. As time went by, Phil became known among his friends as King of the Faxes.

In 1980 Genesis released their album *Duke*. In the run-up to it, Phil had played to Rutherford and Banks some of his songs that would form his solo venture. As a collection, these sounded too personal for a Genesis record, and the band took from various songwriting sources, never from one man. They did, however, decide to feature on *Duke* two Collins compositions which came from his 'diaries in song', relating to his domestic strife. One was 'Please Don't Ask', which he regarded as one of his most personal, introspective compositions. The second Collins song on *Duke* was 'Misunderstanding'. Proving that he was the most commercial writer in the band, this gave Genesis their second American hit single, rising to number 14 in the *Billboard* Hot Hundred in June 1980. It stayed in the charts for eleven weeks. In Britain, the record reached number 42.

Phil's professional star was therefore shining brightly at precisely the time his marriage was collapsing. When he and Andrea returned from Vancouver after the attempted reconciliation in April 1979, he went alone to Shalford while she moved into rented accommodation in Limehouse Close, Ealing, with Joely and Simon. His touring and studio work continued unabated in the spring of 1980, and when he was in London, he collected the children from Andrea in Ealing and took them to Shalford. Sometimes he arrived with them at the Clapton home, once for a fancy dress party and on another occasion to see the local lions owned by a woman deep in the Surrey countryside.

The 'reconnection' which Andrea claims happened between her and Phil occured in the late autumn of 1980. 'We spoke about putting our relationship back together again. Because we still loved each other. But, of course, he went away on tour about a week after that conversation! I couldn't go. I stayed with the children. Maybe I should have gone. There was a lot at stake, really. And while he was on tour, he met Jill.'

The 'cracking' of the American market by Genesis was well under way when the band embarked on their tour there to support the *Duke* album. They generated another hit single from the album ('No Reply at All'), which reached number 29 in the American charts. As always, the conscientious Phil phoned

Andrea regularly throughout his travels, chatting happily to his kids, until that fateful night when he didn't call and Andrea instinctively knew there was another woman on the scene.

The inevitable tension between Phil and Andrea when they met at weekends reached Joely, who says: 'Jill was staying at Old Croft with my dad and we were in London. It was weird because I don't think my dad wanted my mum and Jill to ever meet. He kind of played the mediator and it was very strange for me because my mum would have to wait in the car to drop us off [at Shalford] or Jill would have to wait in the car to drop us off at my mum's place [at Ealing]. And it wasn't a super-open and friendly situation. My dad had control of it. I remember coming home and sometimes there would be the odd little tiff between my mum and dad. I'd have to tell them both to shut up because "I don't want to listen to it."' It was 'really horrid because at seven or eight years old when you're tender, and although you're growing up, you're still very, very dependent on your parents'.

Phil's marriage to Andrea proceeded inexorably to divorce, and the decree nisi was granted in 1981. Andrea states that the value of Old Croft was put at £120,000 and she received half of that; with it, she bought a three-bedroomed town house at 25 Hollingbourne Gardens, Ealing. Lawyers finally agreed a settlement figure of £100,000, she states, making her total figure £160,000, plus maintenance and child support.*

It was in that Ealing house that she first heard *Face Value*. 'I think Phil gave me a cassette after he'd finished in the studio. I didn't hear it until everybody else heard it.' She felt hurt; the songs touched her. 'Very much so, because I loved him. I didn't stop loving him but I just couldn't live with him any

---

* Phil has since also bought Andrea, Simon and Joely a home in British Columbia, Canada.

more. I didn't like him. So I think my heart was broken, too. It wasn't that he was the one suffering while I was off having some affair. I suffered an awful lot. To have a marriage and to separate from someone you love, to have to relocate yet again with two small children; it was a lot.'

When Phil went on BBC Television's *Top of the Pops* to sing 'In the Air Tonight', he took with him a bizarre prop. On top of the piano, in full view, was a large paint-pot with a brush sticking out of it. Even in the zany world of pop, this seemed bizarre. The millions watching British TV's biggest pop show must have been bewildered. But, sitting at home in Ealing, Andrea was in no doubt that the paint-pot was Phil's coded message to her, 'implying decorator, implying affair, implying that was what had happened to our marriage when that wasn't what happened at all. I felt particularly insulted and I felt it was unnecessary. It was personal and it was private. I didn't lie to him. But it was personal and he should have kept it to himself, especially since it was taken out of context . . . he didn't take any responsibility. That hurt me more than anything, caused me a lot of pain. I spoke to him many times about those kind of comments and he just basically said: "I'm allowed to do whatever I want. It's artistic licence." '

To anyone who knew the inside story, the paint-pot was a symbol, however brutal, of what had provoked the *Face Value* album. To others, like Pattie Clapton, it showed that Phil had at least, despite the trauma of divorce, retained his sense of humour.

Phil had always been a rabid fan of British comedians and American humorists. In his teenage years, Tony Hancock, Peter Cook, Dudley Moore and Frankie Howerd were among his favourites, and Hancock records would often feature as family Christmas presents to him. By the time Stephen

Bishop became friendly with him, Phil had gravitated towards American comedy, and to Bishop's surprise launched into a fine impression of Steve Martin.

Genesis's record label, Charisma, also featured the Monty Python team, and the band had once played five-a-side football with members of Python. Phil was a keen student of the laconic humour of John Cleese, who by 1981 had starred in the TV series Fawlty Towers. Phil's world concert première of 'In the Air Tonight', and indeed his first solo appearance anywhere, was to be on a London charity show hosted by Cleese. The catalyst to Phil's historic first performances as a soloist was Martin Lewis. Garrulous, voluble and a bundle of demonic energy, in 1981 he was limbering up to promote his fourth and final concert to aid Amnesty International. The series had been a comedy-based success, with artists of the calibre of the Beyond the Fringe team, Peter Cook and the Python team anchoring the first three shows. For the third show, Lewis had asked Cleese if he might augment the comedy with some music. 'Do what you want', said Cleese, who was fairly contemptuous of rock. In what can now be seen as a precursor for the international MTV series Unplugged, Pete Townshend appeared solo for the third show, called the Secret Policeman's Ball, singing with just acoustic guitar his compositions 'Pinball Wizard' and 'Won't Get Fooled Again'.

For the fourth and final show, basking in the glory of the early successes, Lewis was a man possessed with excitement as he set about attracting rock stars to appear alongside John Cleese at the Secret Policeman's Other Ball. The shows were set for the Drury Lane Theatre for four nights from 9 September 1981. Sting quickly agreed to do his first solo show away from the Police. Eric Clapton said he would appear, but would need to bring a mate to help. Martin Lewis was sceptical. Who? 'Jeff Beck,' said Clapton. That was OK. Donovan was signed up. So was a newish rock artist who protested that he had never done a charity performance in his life because at that time he felt they could be a waste of time, were unlikely to change the world or make any impact. His name was Bob Geldof. Then Lewis, who had bypassed all the artists' managers, phoned Phil Collins.

Introducing himself, he said: 'I'm doing another *Secret Policeman's* . . .' Phil interrupted him instantly. 'Oh, I'll do that,' he said. Lewis had a sales pitch prepared about Amnesty, Clapton, Sting and John Cleese. 'But I didn't get any of that out. I found out later that one of the things he was most keen about was that he was a huge comedy devotee and the thought of meeting John Cleese on the same stage as the Pythons was very attractive to him.'

'What would you like me to sing?'

'It would be wonderful if you could do "In the Air Tonight",' Lewis suggested.

'Well,' Phil said, 'I've never done any of this before. I've never been on stage on my own before.' Having agreed to do the shows, he became nervous. 'I'd like to bring someone with me,' he said. Having already capitulated to Clapton, Lewis was worried again that the simplicity of the show might be threatened. A rule for all the artists was that they brought strong songs and communicated them without amplification, in their rawest form with no embellishments.

Phil's extra man turned out to be Daryl Stuermer, the guitarist with Genesis. 'Being greedy, I wanted two hits,' Lewis says. He asked Phil if he would perform, solo, 'In the Air Tonight', followed by the Genesis hit 'Follow You, Follow Me'. 'There was a silence, and he said: "I've got something else; don't worry, I'll come up with a second song."'

Asked to do four nights, Phil said that because of prior commitments he could not, but would do two, on Friday 11 and Saturday 12 September 1981. He arrived, jittery, on the first night. Lewis was less than attentive; Billy Connolly was there with Pamela Stephenson and the paparazzi were in pursuit, sensing a marital split for the Scotsman from his first wife. 'Phil repeated that he had never been on stage as a solo musician in his life. Stadiums in the States with 20,000 people, which Genesis played, were fine as there was a lot of noise and he could crack jokes. But this would be him alone at the piano. He was more than apprehensive.'

For the great moment, Martin Lewis had ordered, with considerable panache, a nine-foot Bechstein grand piano. When it was wheeled out on stage to follow Sting's appearance, everyone close by had their mouths agape. There, atop the beautiful piano, was a large paint-pot with a wooden stirring stick inside it.

Julien Temple, who had been hired to direct the filming of the concert, ran up to the stagehands ordering them to get the paint-pot off the piano. Lewis, having checked with Phil, said no, he wanted it left there, although he didn't know why, and didn't want to risk the insensitivity of asking at that point what it meant. 'Having been in the business for ten years I knew better than to query the foibles of a pop star who wanted a paint-pot on his piano. I thought it was some kind of joke, maybe a talisman.'

Seen now on video, Phil's début of his special song was a rare moment of chilling energy. He began tentatively, but built the tension with a performance worthy of a soul singer. Daryl Stuermer played exquisite counterpoint guitar; and while Sting had done well with hits like 'Roxanne' and 'Message in a Bottle', Phil knocked dead the audience of just over 1,000. Next he performed 'The Roof Is Leaking', from the *Face Value* album, with Stuermer switching to banjo. This earned the same reaction from a crowd that had come partly for the comedy in the programme; the rock stars had been expected originally to provide a bonus. Phil had hit the most personal, emotional moment of the night.

He left the stage aglow. 'Was it all right?' he asked Martin Lewis. 'Wonderful, and you know it,' said the promoter. 'He knew he had blown people away.'

A curious blip marred the all-star finale of this exceptional concert. John Cleese had been in a bit of a dark mood throughout the music performances from the cream of the rock field. Though they comprised only a quarter of the bill, Cleese felt Collins and company had hijacked the concert. 'He was angry with me because he thought the music had upstaged the comedy,' says Martin Lewis.

When Clapton, Collins, Beck, Donovan, Bob Geldof and all the musicians occupied the whole stage at the finale to sing the rousing Bob Dylan classic 'I Shall Be Released', John Cleese had to find a way through to the microphone at centre stage. In the film, he can clearly be seen pushing Phil aside to clear a path for himself. It does not appear a jocular prod, but rather peremptory. Phil was undoubtedly taken back; he retreated to the back of a sea of artists singing the song. A more fitting gesture by Cleese would have been to thrust the star of the show to the front to enjoy his well-deserved applause.

An artist hoisted to the level of Phil Collins, who had triumphantly succeeded Peter Gabriel and then delivered such an impactful individual album, might have gone solo. There was no precedent in rock for such an achievement as *Face Value* by a band member. But neither Phil nor Genesis entertained any such notion. Indeed, Phil believed Steve Hackett had acted hastily in leaving the band simply because he wanted to stretch; he could, Phil said, have easily done solo work in tandem with the band.

'It never crossed my mind,' says Phil, when asked whether he considered leaving in 1981. 'We'd lived in that situation when I had done Brand X. I had two concurrent careers and we had done solo projects. Steve had done a solo project. Mike and Tony were doing theirs. There seemed no reason. When people said: are you in Brand X or Genesis, I said: I'm doing both! I'd already made a point of saying I'd do as much as I could that's as different as possible, because it's all adding to something. Therefore, I would continue to do the band. I had no wish to leave the band. I knew it was going to be possible to do both so it never really became an issue. I never even thought about it.'

Phil's solo breakthrough came at a time when it could not pose a threat to Genesis, declares manager Tony Smith. Had it come earlier in the band's career, it would have broken the band up, he feels, adding: 'The main reason Peter left the band was because of the lack of ability to get his writing published. They were limited to one Genesis album every eighteen months or so. And there was so much writing within the group at that time, between Peter, Tony and Mike especially, that it wasn't enough of an outlet. And they couldn't deal with the idea, and nor could Peter, of having a solo album separate from the band. And it's true to say that the band's identity at that point was bound up with Peter's own identity. So it would have been a lot more difficult. And they were young and they wouldn't have been able to deal with it.

'When Phil's record came, it was a different time. They had survived Peter Gabriel leaving, so as a band they felt much stronger as individuals and they had proved there was life after Peter Gabriel. At that point Tony and Mike had decided they needed to deal with this problem of not having enough of a writing outlet anyway. And they had by that time released solo albums. So they couldn't say: we can't do solo albums, therefore no one else can. Psychologically they had got their outlets and let their steam off.'

There was no jealousy that Phil's album was by far the most successful solo outing. 'Phil was the singer,' points out Tony Smith. 'His was a much more commercial album. The voice is a lot easier to sell. There were all sorts of ways you could justify it, if you are sensible, and by that point in their lives they were older, more mature, and felt secure with their own position in the band. So it didn't become a problem for them. They always said that the moment they stopped enjoying it in the studio, they would stop. And every time they made a record they had a great time. So provided everybody gave each other enough space there was no reason why the two things shouldn't carry on together.'

Nevertheless, such elevation of Phil brought a palpable change in his confidence. While his nature would preclude conceit, 'He gained confidence as a writer, clearly,' says Tony Smith. 'And within the group, it became more of an equal partnership. Because until then, to be honest, the band was run by Tony and Mike – and Phil was there as the drummer and singer. It was very incremental, not an overnight thing at all. *Face Value* was a hit but not a monster hit. It was the first time in our experience that in some territories it outsold Genesis records, including Peter's. It was a big record, but incrementally; it didn't happen overnight.'

Phil's changing status in the band was also gradual. 'It wasn't like for the next record he turned round and said: Right, chaps, now I'm in a different position. He grew confident, started to have more input into writing. One thing he did discover in doing *Face Value* was the difference between singing his own lyrics and someone else's. He could sing his own lyrics better; I remember that being a bit of a revelation for him.'

That creative revelation of performing his own material was

very important to the evolution of Phil Collins. 'I was always having to sing songs about things I knew nothing about,' he told me. 'And I'm being our worst critic here. "All in a Mouse's Night" was a song I had to sing. Tony and Mike were great at writing "ideas songs". But while it's great to write them, to sing them and get behind them, putting emotion into a song about a mouse and a bit of bread is very hard. And I started to get really frustrated about that.'

'It wasn't until he did his own record,' says Tony Smith, 'that he realized that Tony and Mike, when they wrote lyrics, did not write as singers. So they would put them in the wrong key, or they'd write the lyric before he'd sung it. And suddenly they'd record the track in a certain key, and of course then it was difficult to sing. Whereas Phil's approach was to write and sing the lyric as he wrote. So suddenly, he could sing these songs a lot easier than he could sing the Genesis songs, which was a revelation for him.'

Phil's new-found thrust changed his vocal style, and his commanding influence changed Genesis perceptibly. Each record would change slightly, with the pervading soulfulness of Phil's singing adding lustre and warmth to even the most drab material. There was also the growth of Phil's winning personality. From Artful Dodger to accessible rock star, and respected musician, his chameleon-like rise was appropriate for a new decade that in the wake of the vacuous punks needed fresh and intelligent personalities.

The success of his solo album was to benefit Genesis tangibly, too. With new confidence, Phil joined Mike Rutherford and Tony Banks in the studio in the summer of 1981 to make their next album, and suggested that the band's evolution should include some punchy brass work. Always a fan of the raunchy American sounds of Earth, Wind and Fire, Weather Report, Kool and the Gang and the Ohio

Players, Phil believed that Genesis could use some input from that sphere.

Tom Tom, the arranger, and the Earth, Wind and Fire horns gave a sizzling new edge to the Genesis sound released in 1981 under the title of *Abacab*. Spurred by Phil's correct deduction that the band needed a transfusion, this broke the mould for Genesis, stretching their audiences and record buyers into a wider range. Their sound more pacy, the songs more melodic, they scored a number 9 hit single with the title track in Britain, while in America the album found them a fresh, hipper crowd who gave them four hit singles from the vibrant collection.

If he needed it after his *Face Value* triumph, Phil was now installed as a first among equals in the band he had joined as a drummer. He remained quietly modest in interviews at that time, saying he wanted to lift Genesis away from people's preconceptions. There was an unexpected gratuitous sideswipe at other major bands: 'They have put us in the bracket with Yes, the Moody Blues, Pink Floyd and Emerson, Lake and Palmer and Jethro Tull. And we've always been a bit more conscious of the songs . . .'

Where Andrea had found Phil's workload impossible, Jill seemed to thrive on it. Nearly two years into their live-in relationship, they seemed inseparable and she played a full part in his working life, fielding business calls and helping with his itinerary. And his pattern of packing in as many sessions and production roles as he could continued. In 1982 he played drums on the solo album by Led Zeppelin singer Robert Plant, *Pictures at Eleven*. He produced the noted album *Glorious Fool* by John Martyn, which featured Eric Clapton. And then he got a call from Thomas Johansen, the Swedish promoter who presented Genesis concerts, saying that the singer Anni-Frid Lyngstad (Frida) of Abba wanted to get in touch with him.

The cropped red-haired singer in the hugely successful group requested a meeting with Phil to discuss a solo project. She flew into Britain and visited him at the newly built Genesis studios, the Farm at Chiddingfold in Sussex. She told him she had identified strongly with *Face Value*, playing it every day for months on end. Planning her own solo work, she decided that Collins was the only producer for her.

Phil recalls: 'She said: "I love what you do and I think you'd be sympathetic to what I want to do because I'm just in the process of going through a divorce and I, like you, was on the other end of it." So I said yeah, this would be good fun. We went to Abba's studios [Polar, in Stockholm] to do it. I took a band of my mates and we had about eight weeks there and it was wonderful.' Flying in from the USA, members of Earth, Wind and Fire augmented Collins regulars Daryl Stuermer, Mo Foster and keyboardist Peter Robinson. The engineer was Hugh Padgham and Frida sang one of the *Face Value* tracks, 'You Know What I Mean', which was special to her.

Phil's sure touch ensured that the album that resulted, *Frida: Something's Going On*, bore no relationship to the distinctive Abba sound. He duetted with her on one track, 'Here We'll Stay', and there were songs from Stephen Bishop, Bryan Ferry, Rod Argent, Russ Ballard and Giorgio Moroder. Although neither he nor she could replicate the stark power of *Face Value*, Frida's début was a stirring and therapeutic album by a fine singer who had not written any of the tracks but had chosen, with Phil, songs that came from the heart. The album was not, however, a big commercial winner. At a listening party at the home of Stig Anderson, Phil recalls the Abba manager saying as the record played: 'Ah, there are no singles!' This proved incorrect. The track 'I Know There's Something Going On' rose to number 13 in the USA, stayed in the charts for twelve weeks, and was a modest British hit. But the album failed to ignite.

While he was in Sweden, Phil felt inspired to get down to planning his own next solo collection. It was daunting, because, as he recalled, he 'did not have the same emotional kick in the ass' that had inspired his début. He would have to write from a different perspective. This time he would be more disciplined, setting himself a time limit of, say, seven weeks, rather than the sprawling year's work that consituted *Face Value*. Returning to Old Croft, he went to the eight-track machine, called in Hugh Padgham as assistant producer and engineer, and set to work on the album that was to be called *Hello, I Must Be Going*, which was completed at the Genesis studios at Chiddingfold with mixing again done at the Townhouse in West London. Released in the autumn of 1982, the album bore the title of Charlotte Chandler's biography of Groucho Marx, who was Jill's godfather.

Even with Jill by his side and his career in and out of Genesis rocketing, this second album continued to raise the spectre of his separation from Andrea, which was now absolute. The album revealed Phil's mixed emotions, set off by his air of resignation in the opening track, 'I Don't Care Any More':

> You can tell everybody about the state I'm in,
> You won't catch me crying, cause I just can't win,
> I don't care any more.
>
> Well, I don't care now what you say,
> Cause every day I'm feeling fine with myself
> And I don't care now what you say,
> I'll do all right by myself.

In 'Don't Let Him Steal Your Heart Away', a coded message to Andrea who was now settled in Vancouver with her new man, Phil said:

Don't pack my suitcase, I'll be back,
Don't take my pictures off the wall,
Don't let him change a thing, cause I'll be back,
Just tell him to pack his things and get out of your life,
Just give me one more chance; I'll show you I'm right.

There were other direct commentaries on the past, a strange over-the-shoulder repetitiveness for so thrusting an artist. One track was called 'Do You Know, Do You Care' (in this Phil made his début as a trumpeter), and others included 'It Don't Matter to Me'. The album had a lusher sound than *Face Value*, and he felt the songs fitted his mood at that point because, as he told me, the lawyers had moved in by the time he was writing, and there was a feeling of hurt and bitterness laced with 'it's over', contrasting with the despondency that marked *Face Value*.

For the album's keynote song, however, there came a stroke of irony. Phil always loved the optimistic lyrics of his beloved black music: the themes of 'Don't give up' and 'You're a winner' and 'Everything's gonna be fine.' As he set about writing the song called 'I Cannot Believe It's True', he tried that approach. But this failed. 'I tore the lyrics up. I felt so self-conscious singing them that I went back and wrote some more lyrics that were really downers, which actually related to getting this letter from my wife's lawyers asking for more money. The figure was going up and up and up and up and I opened the letter and I couldn't believe my eyes.' The song became 'I Cannot Believe It's True'.

For all its craftsmanship, *Hello, I Must Be Going* was creatively treading water. By failing to turn the page and depart from the dominant theme of his 'Divorce Album', Phil was virtually offering a sequel to *Face Value*, continuing the introspection but now lacking the incisiveness which carried the first collection.

Even the spread of photographs inside the gatefold sleeve, complete with snaps of Joely and Simon and the adoring gaze of Jill, was repetitive in its visual approach. The album cover showed a wistful Phil in profile. On the front of *Face Value* he had stared out at the world full face. Phil denies that the album was a retread of his début, insisting that he had worked hard to avoid just that. The lyrics, however, spoke volumes.

There was one upbeat track on the album. The Supremes smash from 1966, 'You Can't Hurry Love', was delivered by Phil in a joyful style, the irresistible sound of the Tamla Motown music he always loved helping the album with its touch of fun. On the sleeve, Phil hand-wrote: 'Motown, we salute you.' Even the lyric seemed to allude to his partnership with Jill.

Settled in Canada when this second solo album was released, Andrea heard the songs with astonishment and a mounting fury that has still not abated. 'I was trying to get on with my life. I was with Mike [her partner Mike Fleming] and wanting to put it all behind me. When the first album came out I thought that would be the end of it. When the second came out, and those songs on the Genesis album, I was just horrified and angry.* I didn't understand why he wasn't writing incredible love songs for Jill. I didn't understand that; or why he kept going on about us when he didn't even give us a second chance. To go on and on as long as he did was very mean of him. He didn't care about my feelings. He kept re-opening the wound.'

She was especially angry about the song called 'Don't Let Him Steal Your Heart Away'. 'I found it very humiliating, because talking about me and another man is no one's business and it was exaggerating a small incident [the affair] which never really

* This refers to the songs 'Please Don't Ask' and 'Misunderstanding', which went on the Genesis album, *Duke*.

amounted to anything. And I remember phoning him and being really angry and he said: "You can't prove the song's about you. I could be writing about anybody. It's called artistic licence. I can write what I want." And he slammed the phone down.'

She adds: 'I wasn't going out of my way to hurt him or talk to the press about him. He didn't allow me to get on with my life. He just kept going on and on and on about something which I personally found very painful. Since he hadn't given us the opportunity to try again, I don't know what he was still whining on about, and that's the truth.'

Replying to Phil's statement that the tone of some of his lyrics reflected the fact that lawyers had moved in, Andrea says: 'When you get divorced, you have to have lawyers. We separated in 1979 and were not divorced until two years later.' She claims that any delay in settling was not her fault. 'He tries to paint me as a gold-digger and it bothers me. People take the lyrics of his songs literally and they simply aren't true. The only thing that's true is that we broke up. Everything else is basically down to him and the way he wanted to put that across, artistically. But it's not very accurate . . . I don't think he took responsibility for why the marriage broke up, which was because he was never there. Even when he was not with Genesis he chose to play with other people. It was like that became more important to him than his family. So it was him that really abandoned us. And I'm angry that he blamed me for everything and never took any responsibility himself.'

While *Face Value*'s cover had been in black and white, he chose blue and white for *Hello, I Must Be Going*. But, departing from the faceless image of Genesis, Phil again presented his face, this time in profile, as the striking cover. His handwriting adorned the entire sleeve again, right down to the credits. But such stylishness could not camouflage a flawed concept. And he paid the price commercially.

The first indication that the album might hit difficulties came when Tony Smith flew to New York to play it to executives of Atlantic Records. 'I remember sitting there and after every track they were saying: "Oh yes, that's nice." And I could see them visibly wilting as the record went on, because they were looking for the hit single. And it wasn't coming. "You Can't Hurry Love" was the last song on the tape that I had. When that came on, it was as if someone had opened all the windows in the room and the sun was shining in.'

The US record men's reaction proved to be the same everywhere: if that album had not had the Supremes oldie on it, it might well have stiffed. 'It did not have an "In the Air Tonight" on it, a career single, on it. "You Can't Hurry Love" saved it commercially. It was a classic second album syndrome, even from a mature artist. It wasn't as good as the first,' says Tony Smith. In sales performance, the album would always lag behind Phil's future releases. People remembered it mostly for its curious title, which somehow summed up the impish humour of the man.

The first single taken from *Hello, I Must Be Going* was 'Thru These Walls'. This could only reach number 56 in the UK charts in October 1982. But Phil was rescued handsomely by his cherished Tamla Motown. 'You Can't Hurry Love', destined to be a perennial radio favourite, hurtled to the number 1 position in Britain in December 1982, giving him his first chart-topper. In America, it reached number 10. On both sides of the Atlantic, the record stayed in the chart for sixteen weeks.

With Jill by his side every step of the way, Phil embarked on his first solo tour in December 1982. He called the tour, quirkily, *Phil Collins in Concert with the Fabulous Jacuzzis and the One Neat Guy*. The strain of this long tour across America and Europe threatened his vocal chords, but he survived and enthused about his independence. It was strange, he said at the time, to get up in the morning and find a different set of faces in the hotel lobby when on the road. 'But what I'm doing now is more important to me than anything else. I dabble in Genesis and I dabble in a bit of production. But myself, that's my thing.' Imagine a circle, he said, with him in the middle and reaching out doing all these different things. And one of them was Genesis. Although he always swore loyalty to the band, there was often a sideswipe about the lyrics he had to sing. It was great, he said, to be able to sing songs like 'If Leaving Me Is Easy', which he meant, compared, for example, with 'songs about bread bins, that I don't write'.

The tour's success reflected the perfectionist who would in the next ten years grow into one of the world's hardest-working and most respected artists. Phil's command of the stage, and his demonstrative way of introducing his musicians, was utterly different from the aloof persona of Genesis in concert. His warmth and enthusiasm were contagious. Analysing himself, he said that the better the touring show became, the more he panicked and wanted to improve it. Instead of relaxing and enjoying it, he tended to become more tense as a result of the success. Such tension probably explained his voice problems. He felt they came either from his heavy working schedule, or from the stress of being on the road alone without Genesis. It was certainly a psychological tiredness that he felt, since he played the drums less in his own show than on a Genesis tour, and consequently felt less physically exhausted from singing.

He told an American interviewer that he wanted to consider buying a pub. He enjoyed serving drinks at his local, in Sussex, mingling with 'very normal people; keeps your feet on the ground'. He reiterated his belief that he was the 'injured party' in his divorce from Andrea, and said he was not sure if he

wanted to remarry. He was living with a woman and didn't
want to ruin it by getting married. 'I've got a fantastic son,'
he told the US magazine *The Record* in March 1983. 'And my
daughter is also fantastic but she's my daughter as opposed
to my son and she was by my wife's previous engagement.
It would be strange for me to have another son, considering
how much I think about mine, you know, not having his dad
and stuff. That's what hurt me more than anything else when
we broke up.' But he conceded that it would not be fair on
a mate to say he did not want another family, because that
undermined any confidence in emotions. But having just got
over a divorce, he was 'holding on for a little while yet'.

'I was thinking of flying her out . . . do you think it would be OK?'

Jill Tavelman's earliest days with Phil Collins had been like a rock 'n' roll fairy tale. Shortly after meeting her in 1980 in the Rainbow Bar and Grill in Los Angeles, Phil had either lost or mislaid her telephone number, and called the Rainbow to ask the staff to track her down. When he eventually reached her, he asked her to join him on the Genesis American tour.

'What do you think? This guy wants me to go on the road with him?' Jill asked her best friend Megan Taylor. 'Go! Why not?' her friend enthused.

Phil had also sought approval for his actions. Daryl Stuermer recalls: 'Phil told me he had met this girl [Jill] and said: "I was thinking of flying her out, having her come on the road with me, do you think it would be OK?" I said, "Why are you asking me if it would be OK? If you like her, of course, it's up to you."' Stuermer adds that Phil's marriage to Andrea had already started to fall apart at this time. When Jill joined Phil the three of them would hang out together. 'Sometimes Phil would want to get some rest and then Jill and I would go to the hotel bar for a drink. It was a nice time. In the beginning they were like kids together, having a lot of fun.'

For Phil Collins, sending for Jill was untypical behaviour. He has always been the precise opposite of the philandering rock star. The 1970s had bred the international groupie industry, but it never attracted Phil, who always sought a firm relationship. The invitation to Jill to join him on his travels was based not just on personal magnetism but on his lifelong need for a soulmate. When he left town, she had given him a perfect gift, a book on his favourite American comedian, Steve Martin. As their relationship deepened when she joined the Genesis tour in Houston, everyone who knew Phil realized that it would be no quick fling. From the start, it seemed a love match.

Jill Tavelman, a pert and pretty blonde, was born on 9 April 1956 in Beverly Hills, the only daughter of a Jewish father, Jack, and a non-Jewish mother, Jane. Jill has one brother, also called Jack. Since childhood, Jill had been used to show-business company. Her father owned an outfitter's store in Beverly Hills that was the equivalent for celebrities in town to Savile Row in London, and stars like Groucho Marx and Milton Berle were among his clientele. Marx was Jill's godfather, and Phil was given the great man's cigar humidor with the initials GM on it. Jill had grown up in an environment where money was not a problem; at the time she met Phil, she had more money than he had.

When they met, Jill was studying to become a teacher in a junior school, but she gave that up upon moving to England. As they settled into a blissful relationship at Old Croft, friends remarked on the astonishing closeness of the couple. The big difference between this relationship and Phil's marriage to

Andrea was that Jill, who was not tied by children, wanted to go everywhere with him.

Like anyone encountering Phil at home, Jill had to become accustomed to a uniquely domestic man. He was meticulous about his clothes and the general tidiness of the house. Megan Taylor, who visited them occasionally to stay, saw Phil's obsession with cleanliness: 'His idea of a project for the day, a thrill, was to clean out the kitchen drawers. He could spend all day doing that. We would go and shop at the supermarket in Guildford, come back, decide who was going to cook dinner, and Phil would yell at us because there were crumbs on the floor. He put a rubber mat around the sink and counter area because he could not bear to watch people preparing food and making a mess. He would sweep up the mat and we would torture him, saying: "Phil Collins! Sexy Pop Superstar Sweeps the Rubber Mat in his Kitchen! If the Fans Knew!" If Phil saw a layer of dust anywhere, adds his pal Ronnie Caryl, he would immediately have a J-cloth in his hand. And Daryl Stuermer describes him as 'the kind of guy who, if you were staying at his house, could suddenly wake you up because he's vacuuming.'

The other members of Genesis and their wives were not initially welcoming to Jill. A young woman from California arriving in their clannish Surrey milieu was treated coolly. 'The wives were askance when Jill from Beverly Hills appeared in his life,' says Bill Bruford. 'She had to prove herself a genuine character; there was a degree of suspicion, typically British.' This resistance melted when they saw that as with everything in his life, Phil meant business. Even without the Genesis friendship, Phil and Jill were quite happy alone, and when they were together, in the view of Megan Taylor, they were 'joined at the hip'. Margaret Banks and Angie Rutherford gave Jill a cool time, says her friend Megan. 'Jill thought it was because they were English and she did not know how to battle it.'

As his career and that of Genesis climbed, the early 1980s found Phil, with Jill bringing him personal happiness, at a perfect moment in his life. His family visited regularly, and every summer Joely and Simon would come from Canada to stay, initially for a couple of months. Old friends like Ronnie Caryl and Peter Newton, and Alun Owen, the scriptwriter who wrote the Beatles' *A Hard Day's Night*, were regular visitors. His interests beyond music were mostly comedy. He adored *Monty Python* and played Tony Hancock tapes in his car. A friend might say they had the new cassette of the Two Ronnies (Barker and Corbett). 'Quick, drive over and let's hear it,' Phil would respond. His first two cats were named Corbett and Barker, to be followed by cats called Martin (in recognition of Steve) and Hancock (as in Tony).

The cat family had been initiated by Jill when Phil was away. At first, Jill and Megan were concerned that Phil might not like having animals in the house, because of the inevitable mess. 'A dog would have been too much,' says Megan, reinforcing Phil's horror of untidiness.

Something else it took Megan a while to get used to was Phil's natural demonstrativeness. She remembers introducing one of her boyfriends to him 'and on the third or fourth time they met Phil gave him a hug. My date asked me: "Why is this guy hugging me?" and I said, "It's just Phil's way. He's just like that."'

Phil enjoyed an occasional Sunday afternoon at the local pub. He enjoyed his days in his studio, brainstorming about his next direction in music. By night, he was a video enthusiast. He would watch several movies each night, including such classics as *Our Man in Havana*, and study the nuances of Alec Guinness's

Phil Collins (in top hat) as the Artful Dodger in the 1965 production of Lionel Bart's *Oliver*. Also in the cast were theatre school chums Jack Wild (on Phil's right) and Arthur Wild (in front of Phil). For Phil, the West End role led to a confrontation with his headmaster.

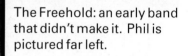

The Freehold: an early band that didn't make it. Phil is pictured far left.

Genesis around 1974-5. Left to right standing: Mike Rutherford, Tony Banks, Steve Hackett. Front: Peter Gabriel, Phil Collins. *(Harry Goodwin)*

The bride and groom. Phil and Andrea on their wedding day with Andrea's daughter, Joely, outside St Joseph's Catholic Church, Epsom, 27 September 1975. *(Andrea Collins Collection)*

Portrait of the musician as a young man - with hair. *(Harry Goodwin)*

Two ladies who played a prominent role in Phil Collins's life: his first wife Andrea, left, and Lavinia Lang, her best friend, pictured in 1967. *(Andrea Collins Collection)*

Fun and games with Dad. Joely and
Simon with Phil when Genesis were
touring Canada in 1983 or 1984.
(Andrea Collins Collection)

A family Christmas in Sussex dressed in Victorian attire. Phil, Jill, Joely, Simon and Lily in 1991. *(Andrea Collins Collection)*

Jill Collins on the day of her wedding to Phil, 4 August 1984. The groom cried during the service.

(Left) Among the guests at Phil and Jill's wedding party were Tony Stratton Smith, sporting a red carnation, and Julian Lennon, seated front left.

With Sting at the Live Aid Concert, Wembley, July 1985.
(Rex Features)

(Opposite page: top) Phil in 1986 during a break in filming an interview with Martin Lewis for American TV. *(Timothy White, Martin Lewis Collection)*

(Opposite page: bottom) Playing snooker with Martin Lewis, 1986. *(Timothy White, Martin Lewis Collection)*

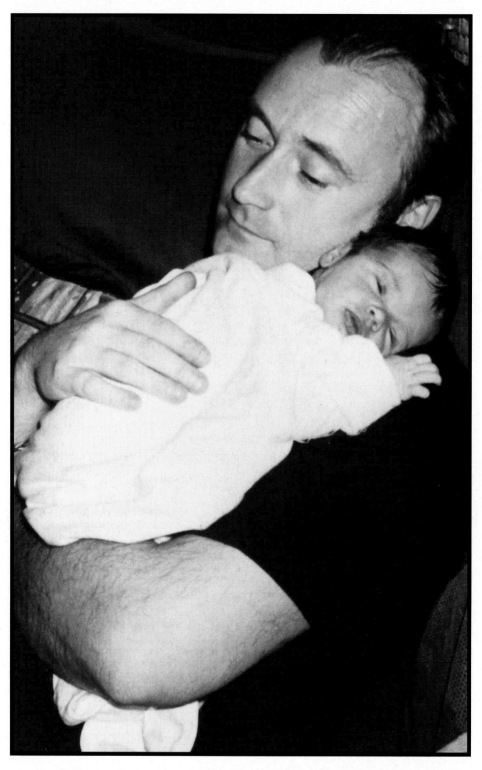

Newborn Lily with doting dad, March 1989.

Royal rocker with wife Jill and daughter Lily talking to Prince Charles and Princess Diana at a Prince's Trust Concert. Both couples were later in the news at the same time with marriage problems.

Phil and Jill at a Music Therapy fund-raising lunch.
Pattie Clapton is under the hat. *(David Koppel, Pattie Clapton Collection)*

Storytime: Lily and Phil on a plane.

Lily the fairy dressed for
a Halloween party.

Phil with Megan,
Jill's best friend and
godmother to Lily.

All smiles: Phil and Jill in the Florida sunshine.

With actress Julie Walters at the Cannes Film Festival, May 1987, for *Buster*.

Proud dad: Phil and Joely in Los Angeles for the Grammy's, 1991.
(Andrea Collins Collection)

Phil, the inveterate faxer, sends get well wishes to the author, August 1996.

Dear Ray,

Word has just reached me over here that you are in hospital, and that you are 'under the weather'! I just wanted to let you know that we were thinking of you, and hoping that you'll find the strength to get back on the tracks again soon.

Tony had told me that you weren't too well recently, so I hope all will be well and that we'll see you again shortly.

In the meantime our thoughts are with you.

All our love

Phil & Orianne

Drummer and kit, 1993.
(Paul Massey, Rex Features)

Best mates: Phil Collins and
Eric Clapton at the Royal Albert
Hall, February 1991.
(Richard Young, Rex Features)

It was love at first sight when Phil met Orianne, the young interpreter
assigned to his party on a European tour in 1994.
(Richard Young, Rex Features)

At the Mandela Concert at the Royal Albert Hall, July 1996.
(Richard Young, Rex Features)

Phil today. *(Guzman)*

work closely. He absorbed every Peter Sellers film and loved stories with strong romantic themes.

The first hint that Phil might one day return to acting came through Martin Lewis, with whom Phil had struck a rapport during the *Secret Policeman's Other Ball* concert. The film of the concert, starring Phil's exceptional performance of 'In the Air Tonight', had done well round the world. By the end of 1982, Lewis had relocated to New York, but at Christmas, just before he left London, he got a call from Phil. They found they shared an enthusiasm for the humour of Woody Allen, Steve Martin and Tony Hancock. Impressed with the way Lewis had taken a small benefit show and spread it around the world, Phil spoke of his love of comedy. Lewis said that since he wanted to get further into producing comedy films, perhaps he could help. 'Well, I'm very interested; you know I used to be an actor when I was a kid,' Phil said. 'I really want to do acting and comedy; I think it's something I should do and could do.'

Lewis envisioned Phil as the next Dudley Moore. 'He had that cheeky chappie, impish humour. He was the artful dodger. I mentioned an idea I had for a film set in the 1960s, two con men in a Beatles merchandising deal. He loved it. I asked if I could use his name in trying to pull it together. He said: "Absolutely. We could be doing some stuff together, Martin." ' In New York, Lewis conferred with Ahmet Ertegun, the Atlantic Records chief who was a big fan of Phil's work. He agreed with Lewis that film was a natural step for Phil. Lewis then began socializing with Phil during his US tour in January and February of 1983.

'They were soppy in love,' observes Martin Lewis of Phil and Jill. 'They couldn't be separated; you never saw Phil, it was always Phil and Jill together.' Meeting Phil on the road, Lewis, a rock business veteran, was taken aback by such visible closeness. 'In San Francisco, I said to Jill: "Do you want to go for a bite to eat while Phil's at the sound check?" She said no, she'd be going with Phil. At three o'clock, she was off with him, and by his side throughout, backstage, watching from the seats while they did the sound check. She would hang out in the wings and the moment Phil stopped, she would wander over to be with him. She seemed like part of him; it wasn't like a puppydog and master, more like two puppydogs. That's what they wanted to be. I never understood it; for Genesis shows, Mike Rutherford's and Tony Banks's wives came out for major gigs. But Jill was everywhere! I remember thinking it was a recipe for disaster. I thought a couple should spend some time apart, to refresh the situation. But I never heard a cross word between them and I spent a considerable amount of time with them at that stage.'

The film idea had not become an urgent project in Phil's mind, which was just as well. Martin Lewis says he met resistance: 'It was tough to sell it. First, I was new to America, secondly, I was living in New York and not in Los Angeles, and thirdly I was an Englishman.' The film never happened, but the friendship of Phil and Martin continued.

Phil's short fuse, which had been apparent on his way to the top through letters and phone calls to critics, did not diminish when stardom arrived. At least three examples of Phil's impatience were noted by Martin Lewis. In 1983, they met by chance when they sat alongside each other at a Sting concert at Wembley Arena. 'Sting had invited friends, like Phil, to go and see him backstage afterwards. Normally, these stars are in laminate heaven, with "Access All Areas" passes. But we couldn't find our way backstage; I was wandering around with Phil and Jill and thought he would know his way around, but here was a major star as geographically challenged as me.

I could see Phil's frustration; he was easily irritated by such things.' Lewis was used to such situations, but Phil was affronted and agitated as he was blocked by security staff. 'We are expected!' he rasped.

In New York in the spring of that year, Martin Lewis hosted a visit for Phil and Jill to see the Broadway show 42nd Street. In the box, there were tall people sitting in front of Phil, Jill and Martin, who tried to persuade them to move to one side to improve their view of the stage. 'No, this is where we're sitting,' they answered. 'Phil was so angry at such inconsiderate behaviour.' The short fuse was in evidence again: 'He was furious with these people; they did not recognize him; he showed his fury without getting into a battle.'

Another difficult scene occurred as the night wore on, when the trio adjourned to Manhattan's Russian Tea Room. 'It was summer and Phil was wearing a nice shirt but no jacket. They would not allow him to sit down without a jacket, and went off to the cloakroom where they kept jackets for such occasions. He was a bit irritated by it.'

This might have been the inspiration for his next album title, No Jacket Required. Phil, Jill and Martin Lewis were enjoying their meal, Lewis teasing Phil that he might be remembered as the most significant musician in Britain since Honey Lantree, the drummer with the kitsch 1960s group the Honeycombs; and even better than Dave Clark, drummer-leader with the Dave Clark Five. Phil was enjoying such banter when another diner walked over to the table, wanting to talk to him. 'He introduced himself as the owner of an up-market store selling leather jackets and clothing. Phil was polite but firm: "Nice to meet you; I'm having dinner with friends." The man persisted. Would Phil sing at their sales convention in return for a load of money? For the second time that evening, Phil snapped. "Would you leave us alone?" he said, ending the man's interruption abruptly. Totally justified in the face of such an intrusion, Phil was 'very snappy', Lewis remembers. 'He went from first gear to fifth without passing through two, three or four.'

New Yorker Virginia Lohle, who runs Star File, a showbiz photographers' agency, recalls another occasion when Phil lost his cool: 'There was a party at Bishop's Salt, a swanky restaurant in Manhattan, and Phil and Jill were there. As they were leaving one of the photographers backed into Jill and literally knocked her out of the way to get a picture of Phil; Jill fell to the ground, she just went sprawling on the sidewalk. Phil, who up to that point had been absolutely delightful and was good with photographers, rushed to help her, started screaming and went after the man who'd knocked Jill down. His reaction was really, really intense. It was the only time I've ever seen Phil Collins angry.'

The official engagement of Phil and Jill delighted everyone who knew them both. It happened formally backstage at the Hammersmith Odeon after one of Phil's solo concerts in 1983. His mother and Barbara Speake were among those celebrating. Jill and Megan went out excitedly to choose a ring. Despite Phil's love for Jill, Megan Taylor doubts whether he wanted to get married so soon after his divorce from Andrea. But Jill was eager to get engaged, says Megan.

Phil's extraordinary energy at that time charted the career that would elevate him way beyond Genesis, into record production as well as solo success. He played on sessions with Pete Townshend and produced Strip for Adam Ant. And during the marathon Genesis tour of the USA across 1983 and 1984, he created a classic that was also his first piece of work for film. The route to it was full of politics and intrigue.

The eminent Hollywood film director Taylor Hackford had established a reputation for powerful songs in his movies. A rock aficionado, he had taught a class in history of rock 'n' roll at his college at the University of Southern California. He had produced a lauded film with Chuck Berry called *Hail, Hail, Rock 'n' Roll*, and in 1982 he had produced the acclaimed *An Officer and a Gentleman*. Experimenting with the title song towards the end of that film, he paired singers Joe Cocker and Jennifer Warnes on the love theme of the movie, 'Up Where We Belong'. It topped the American chart. The song won an Oscar for 'Best Song' and the music was used by Continental Airlines as their theme song. Starring Richard Gere and Debra Winger, *An Officer and a Gentleman* reaped two wins and six nominations in the Academy Awards.

This fired Hackford's enthusiasm for powerfully sympathetic music for his next movie. Set in Los Angeles, and starring Jeff Bridges and Rachel Ward, the film was to be called *Against All Odds*, and would reflect the changing nature of the city, its hardness, and its slickness as a trend-setting capital. When Atlantic Records was set as the label to release the soundtrack, Hackford checked their artist roster. Phil Collins was his first choice for the theme song. Securing him was not going to be easy, however.

When Hackford met Tony Smith for his first overture, he sensed a concern. Genesis, having ridden the storm of Peter Gabriel's departure, was then touring America with Phil Collins at the front, but there was an unspoken worry that he might pull away and go solo after his record success. 'What Tony Smith was basically saying to me was: you are asking me for a Phil Collins song at a time when Genesis is alive and well . . . I can't really talk to you about Phil doing something.'

Hackford persisted, and it was agreed that he should fly to Chicago to a Genesis concert to see if Phil was interested. He met him after the show. 'He was exhausted; he had worked out and was completely drained. He could easily have played the rock 'n' roll star, saying he was too tired. But I was struck by how attentive and attuned he was to the subject. I gave him some footage of the movie and said I was looking for a hard ballad.'

As the tour continued, Smith phoned Hackford to say Phil had a raw tape of something which might work. Under the pressure of the tour, Phil did not have enough time to come up with a completely new melody and lyric, so he cast around to his previous work. At the time when he was preparing songs for *Face Value*, he had written something called 'How Can You Sit There'. 'But I had one too many ballads and it was my least favourite, so I shelved it,' Phil told me. 'I said: "I can't write on the road." Now I can, but then I couldn't; I didn't have the right instruments to carry around with me for songwriting. And I said, "I've got a song, if it's good enough, I'll write some words for it."'

The raw demonstration tape was sent to Hackford in Hollywood. Phil was at the piano with a very rough vocal. 'I immediately said I liked it and the song could be developed, but the song had to be called "Against All Odds",' says Hackford. It would feature at the end of the movie, when the man walks away from the woman and she expresses all her inner feelings. When Hackford insisted that the title had to be 'Against All Odds', Phil said: 'Well, *maybe* I can do it.' He was, says Hackford, a little resistant. 'Actually he kept stringing me out. This was to play with me. But as he criss-crossed the Midwest on tour, he sent the finished demonstration tape, bearing the lyrics, to Hackford. Phil's professionalism had won through any stubbornness or tiredness to provide a song full of potential. 'I OK'd the song. It was really good,' says Hackford.

All this had been done without the knowledge of Doug Morris, the head of Atlantic Records in New York. On hearing

of the project, he was concerned that Phil's role as the lead
singer in Genesis was being diverted to something of a solo
nature, even though Atlantic released both Genesis and Phil
in the USA. Coincidentally, Hackford bumped into Morris on
a flight from New York to Los Angeles and won him over,
persuading him that the song would enhance not merely his
movie, but Phil Collins's career.

Next, Phil told Hackford that he would love to work again
with Arif Mardin, whose brilliant touch with strings had
made 'If Leaving Me Is Easy' such a favourite of his. This
was geographically difficult, as Hackford's deadline loomed
and Phil's touring schedule continued across the States. When
Phil arrived in New York, he set to work with Mardin recording
the backing music with a full orchestra. He then went on the
road again, visiting a studio in Los Angeles to add his vocals
and insert the exceptional drum break that punctuates the
record. Hearing this happen, Hackford said: 'I watched the
hair on my arm rise; it satisfied the chill factor. I knew we
had a great record.'

Next they shot a video, again under strained circumstances
as Phil traversed the US. Hackford was impressed with Phil's
application to every logistical problem that beset their work
together. 'Instead of being temperamental, he just got on with
it. He belted it out with a power that was terrific; he conceived
the song; went to work with Arif Mardin; he'd seen the film
in one city, wrote it in another, laid down tracks in various
cities and then mailed it all to me. I put it in the film and
the rest is history.'

'Against All Odds (Take a Look at Me Now)' roared to the
top of the American charts in Billboard on 21 April 1984. In
Britain it reached number 2. It was a massive breakthrough
in the US, since Phil was still not particularly well known as

a solo act. The bizarre irony of this fact came home to him in an astonishing way.

When the Academy of Motion Picture Arts and Sciences asked him to sing his Oscar-nominated number 1 song at their annual awards ceremony, which was telecast coast-to-coast, the affable Phil jumped immediately, rearranging his US tour dates to ensure that he would be in Los Angeles for one of the biggest accolades of his life. But he never received a call to confirm the booking.

As the date neared for the show at the Dorothy Chandler Pavilion on 25 March 1985, Paul Cooper, vice-president of Atlantic Records, wrote to the Academy to underline the correctness of having Phil sing his song, and asking for details. He received a letter saying that 'the spots have already been filled'.

Kathy Orloff, publicity chief for Columbia Pictures, which released the movie *Against All Odds*, told *Daily Variety* magazine that when she spoke to Oscars producer Gregory Peck she reiterated the enthusiasm of Phil Collins to sing his hit. 'He didn't seem to know who Phil Collins was,' she said. Indeed, in correspondence relating to Phil, he was named as Phil Cooper.

Gregory Peck told *Daily Variety*: 'We know Phil Collins and we admire Phil Collins. It's just that we decided early on that we would not be using five recording artists. It's pure showmanship; we want variety.' Peck told the *Los Angeles Times* that the Academy's function was not to promote record people, and they preferred to use film people. Phil's experience as an extra in *A Hard Day's Night* and on the London stage as a boy actor was apparently ignored.

Finally, on the big night, Phil sat in the audience and saw his big song lip-synched by Ann Reinking. 'He was very upset,' remembers Martin Lewis, who was there. 'They thought people would switch off their televisions because nobody would know who he was. But it was virtually unheard of for the performer of a hit song nominated for an Oscar, not to be invited to sing it themselves at the ceremony.' The award went to Stevie Wonder's 'I Just Called to Say I Love You' from the film *The Woman In Red*.

Phil remembers the feeling of delight, however, at the phenomenal worldwide success of a song he wrote on the road, something he had never attempted before. The geographical difficulties of Phil recording his vocals in Los Angeles while producer Arif Mardin added the strings in New York represented, to a triumphant Taylor Hackford, 'a textbook case of designing a song to fit a film, designing the lyrics to reflect what the film is about, and having the title of the song be the title of the film.' The song helped the film's success, as it was played on radio internationally.

A mere eight months after that snub from the Academy, Phil Collins was back with what would become one of the hallmark performances of his career. The song 'Separate Lives', written by Stephen Bishop, raced to the top of the American charts on 30 November 1985; in Britain it reached number 4. Phil duetted with US singer Marilyn Martin on this song about a shattered relationship, and it would become his special ballad moment in his concerts.

Bishop wrote the song about the traumatic break-up of his three-year relationship with the actress Karen Allen. 'I really loved her and missed her when we split. I was at the Parker Meridien hotel in New York and she called me and said: "How you doing?" I said to her: "You have no right to ask me how I feel." That became the anger line in the song.'

The song, though a fiercely personal commentary on Bishop's collapsed romance, might have been tailored specially for Phil Collins's first marital split and for the ensuing years. In fact,

Bishop had written the song for another Taylor Hackford film, called *White Nights*, and Bishop considered it his catharsis. While Karen Allen had judged it to be a song about love, he insisted it was a song about anger.

That characteristic hardly punctuates any of Phil Collins's work, but the urgency and emotional power of the lyrics attracted him when Bishop played him a demonstration tape in England. Arif Mardin and Hugh Padgham were drafted in as producers, and a sensitive American singer, Marilyn Martin, sang the duet with Phil. Phil originally intended it for the album that would be called *No Jacket Required*, but there was a surfeit of material for the record. Released as a single, it proved to be hugely commercial.

'Stephen wrote it because he, like I do, tends to write good love songs when someone has just walked out,' remarks Phil wryly. But as the years unfolded and 'Separate Lives' became a vital part of Phil's repertoire, fans around the world believed it was not only written by Phil but was a doleful commentary on the stormy romances in his life.

On stage, 'Separate Lives' is a musical and theatrical highlight which brings the house down. Though he did not compose it, Phil seems to invest every ounce of believable emotion in the heart-torn lyrics about love gone wrong. Marilyn Martin never sang the song live with Phil; singer Brigitte Bryant was the first duettist, and Phil and she believed they struck such empathy that he promised never to repeat the exact duetting formula with another singer. When in 1995 he toured the world, his backing singers Amy Keys and Arnold McCullen sang it with rare power. It will remain one of the most important songs in Phil Collins's armoury.

Such success would never allow Phil Collins to coast. International stardom as a singer was now established, but in many

ways he remained the drummer in Genesis and Brand X, or
an enthusiastic producer of other artists' records. In 1984 he
had been asked to produce an album called *Chinese Wall* by
top US musician Philip Bailey of Earth, Wind and Fire. At
the Townhouse studio in London, Phil met for the first time
the experienced bass guitarist Nathan East, who would figure
strongly in his future music. 'I'll never forget how special it
was to play bass along with his drumming for the first time,'
says East. It was a creative success but fraught with tension in
the studio. 'Bailey had asked Collins to produce the record,'
East recalls, 'but we'd finish a take and Bailey would ask me
what I thought. It was uncomfortable for me because Phil was
in the control room saying: "Well, you know, I'm just the
drummer. I'm not producing this record." I stepped in and
tried to be a peacemaker between Phil and Phil.'

Phil Collins was peeved by the early atmosphere in the
studio, which was 'a bit iffy', but Nathan East recalls that he
desperately wanted it to be a great record. Bailey was, after
all, co-lead vocalist with one of his favourite bands. Finally,
says East, 'We all put our heads together to make a winner
out of it.' The result was a spectacular surprise. Towards the
end of the sessions, realizing the album lacked a commercial
kick, Collins, Bailey and East co-wrote a haunting song called
'Easy Lover'. Released as a single on which Collins and Bailey
duetted, this quickly sold a million, reaching number 2 in the
American chart in December 1984. In Britain it reached number
1 in March 1985. Both album and single were very successful
throughout Europe. Phil Collins had another winner.

When Bob Geldof planned the international Live Aid concerts
in Britain and America to help the starving of Ethiopia, he
gathered an astonishing array of rock stars to play free. For
the concert, on 13 July 1985, Geldof sought a special twist

that would help get the charity talked about. Phil had already helped by playing drums on the multi-million-selling single 'Do they Know It's Christmas', and Geldof knew that he would find it hard to resist the almost outrageous plan to appear at the Live Aid concerts in both London and Philadelphia – courtesy of Concorde.

Phil went for it. In mid-afternoon he appeared at the Wembley Stadium concert singing 'In the Air Tonight', before being joined by Sting for 'Long, Long Way to Go'. Then, after joining Sting on 'Every Breath You Take', Phil raced from the stadium to Heathrow airport *en route* to Philadelphia, arriving there at 7 p.m. He was greeted by friends Eric Clapton and Robert Plant before jumping on stage to sing 'I can feel it coming in the air tonight, oh Lord . . .' Phil had given the two concerts a link, a uniformity. It was a remarkable example yet again of his tenacity and energy.

Shortly after Live Aid, Phil was at home and answered the door to a stranger. The man explained courteously that he needed £8,000 for a worthy cause. Most rock stars faced with such a request, however plausible, would apply the rule of either ending the conversation abruptly or referring the problem this represented to their manager or minder. But Phil invited the man into his home. 'I didn't know him from Adam,' Phil recalls. 'I loaned him the £8,000 and he paid me back two years later, which is what we agreed on.' The incident reached the pages of the *Daily Mirror*, however, prompting shoals of letters addressed simply to 'Phil Collins, Surrey'. Many of them seemed genuine pleas for help and Phil wanted to take them seriously. His secretary Annie Callingham took on the job of filtering such requests.

His social conscience had made him a vital founder member of the rock star fraternity that gathered to help the Prince's

Trust, launched by Prince Charles, and it was in his work for the Trust that the dominant characteristic of Phil Collins, total involvement in every corner, came into play. He applied a 'hands on' approach, visiting Caister, Norfolk, for the Trust's gathering of unemployed teenagers, and seeking to provide a therapeutic method of encouragement and stimulation.

'It was a week of sport and work and leisure, and with all these kids from different cities under one roof, it's a potential time bomb,' Phil says. They did not believe a star of Phil Collins's status would go to encourage them. 'The visible effect you have when you meet them and then you perform for them, and the boost and uplift you get when you meet them, because they don't actually believe you are going to be there, makes you want to do it. It would be easy to delegate but that wouldn't work. It only works if you are there. You make the point of trying to make the effort.'

Phil's involvement with the Prince's Trust had begun around 1983 with a phone call from George Martin. 'George and Pete Townshend were getting together a group of musicians for the Prince of Wales for a gala evening at the Pavilion Theatre. They had Townshend, Gary Brooker, Robert Plant, Kate Bush, Jess Roden, and asked would I be the drummer, and I said yes. Jethro Tull were playing and I was going to be their drummer as well. It was the first I'd heard of the Prince's Trust, which had recently been formed. I met Prince Charles and Princess Diana briefly. There was another concert at the Albert Hall with Imagination and Paul Young, and I was invited along to play a few songs at the piano and again I met the Prince and Princess, and Genesis also did a show for the Prince's Trust. Then I got a phone call from the chairman of the Trust, who said Prince Charles wanted me to become a trustee. I said, of course, I'd be flattered. I went to meetings every three or four months.'

The rock world's support for the Prince's Trust ballooned to a headline-grabbing series of events in the 1980s. The hierarchy of rock, including Paul McCartney, Elton John, Eric Clapton and many others, joined Phil as figureheads. Spectacular concerts took place, with all profits donated to the Trust, and Phil was as active as anyone. Remembering the early days, when he was asked to pull Clapton and Elton in to the first shows, Phil says: 'Now it's beyond that because there's corporate sponsorship.'

As he mingled with the royal family, notably the Prince and Princess of Wales, the progress from Artful Dodger to Royal Rocker was complete.

'I'm not a sex symbol'

Even to their coterie of friends, who considered it a marriage made in heaven, there was something bizarre about Phil and Jill's isolation, their apparent need for no company except their own. Joined at the hip, they made determined plans to avoid socializing unless it was necessary. Thoughout their marriage, their friends remarked on this most exceptional rock 'n' roll union.

'If they ever had any tension in their marriage, it was because Phil wanted her to be everywhere with him, and sometimes she did not want to go,' says Megan Taylor, Jill's best friend, who lived at Loxwood sporadically. 'Some people got jealous, saying: "We don't see much of Phil or of Jill." But if one of them didn't like the partner of one of their individual friends, that was that. They weren't going *anywhere*! And since it was rare that they both liked two members of a couple, I can count on the fingers of maybe two hands when they went out to dinner with anybody.'

Together they regularly enjoyed eating at a Thai restaurant in Guildford. Very occasionally friends of the level of Eric and Pattie Clapton would join them there. House visits were also exchanged. 'But Jill and Eric didn't really get along, so it was easier for Phil to go to his house alone,' says Megan. When the quartet did meet, they often played pool, snooker or cards. 'Jill was really competitive and played to win, and Eric is very competitive and hates to lose. So they went through stupid situations. Someone would say: "Why don't you let Eric win?" Jill would reply: "Why should I?" It was not the greatest foursome; Eric was not at his best. Jill made it work because she knew how much Phil adored Eric,' Megan adds.

In Eric's drinking days he would get through a bottle of brandy a day and sometimes Phil used to help him. Now and again Phil and Jill would meet Eric at his local pub in Ripley High Street, and Phil remembers driving one of Eric's Ferraris back to his home when the guitarist had had too much to drink. Foursomes together at Eric's home inevitably ended with Eric and Phil watching TV or playing records and the girls in the kitchen, talking. Each curious about the other's musical tastes, Phil and Eric would play each other records. 'I remember taking *Abacab* round and playing it, and before that, *Duke*, just to see what he thought,' says Phil. 'Suddenly he put on *Layla* and we listened to the whole double record.' (The title song, which Eric had written for Pattie when she was still married to his friend George Harrison, took its title from a Persian tale of unrequited love.) Stevie Wonder's version of 'Ave Maria' was, Phil recalls, regularly on Eric's turntable.

Strangely for a couple so entwined and presenting a united front to everyone, Phil and Jill appeared to have had little in common. 'She was not interested in what he was interested in. She had no interest in the Prince's Trust,' Megan continues. 'Phil would go off with Prince Charles on those retreats and she would pass.'

Megan and Jill shared a passion for spending lavishly when

they were on the road with Phil. 'We both came from rich families and would buy everything in sight.' An endearing characteristic of Jill was demonstrated when Megan became short of money: she would scale down her purchases so as not to embarrass her impoverished friend. 'She was very sensitive in that way. But you had to play the game in other ways. She was incredibly possessive of Phil: no one had to go near him if she wasn't around. No woman other than me got within a thousand miles of Phil! As for someone attractive: no chance! They were possessive of each other.'

There seemed to be a strand in Jill's make-up that wanted to foster the friendship of the musicians and road crew on tour, while preserving her and Phil's distance. 'She would go to the concerts and buy presents for everyone on the tour.' Such warmth and generosity of spirit contrasted sharply with Jill's wish to cocoon Phil from other women. The irony of this is that Phil is the opposite of the rock 'n' roll philanderer and a central core of his make-up is that he is a one-woman man.

'I am a very loyal person,' he avers. 'I have never taken advantage of stuff on the road. Some guys can't wait to get out of the house so they can go and sleep around. It's never really interested me because I've always felt, well if I'm doing that, maybe she's doing that; so I'm very loyal.'

Jill's weekly forays to antique fairs in the Guildford area and to sales at Sotheby's left Phil cold. 'Jill's not mean but she's not generous in ways that used to drive him crazy,' Megan recalls. 'She would go into an antique fair and bargain someone to death.' At this, Phil would be 'dying' from embarrassment.

Phil did not try to stop her, 'but it came to a stage where there wasn't anything to do together'.

Precision is the central characteristic of Phil Collins. On the road, he packs his own suitcase – he values his clothes and folds each shirt and suit immaculately, carefully placing tissue between each one. He has always been that way. 'When Eric Clapton got him on to Versace clothes, Phil really respected his ability to be able to afford it,' says Megan Taylor. But whether an item of clothing cost £50 or £500, he is appalled to see it treated badly. 'It's not in his nature to buy something and throw it on the floor!' When any member of his road crew told him of a difficulty in packing a case as they trailed round the world, Phil did not understand. They should develop a routine, set aside time, and pack properly, in his view. It was the only way he knew. 'Phil's closet was always perfect, immaculate,' Megan adds. 'He could not perceive why anyone should want to be a slob.'

Keen though she was on rock 'n' roll, Jill's musical tastes were more radical than Phil's. She adored Led Zeppelin (her idea of heaven was when Phil toured with Robert Plant, and she loved it when he worked with Eric); she liked music with an edge, like the Rolling Stones and Lou Reed. The melodic material Phil liked to play around the house was soul, jazz and Tamla Motown. Friction occurred when Jill tried to get involved in any aspect of Phil's career. If, for example, she took an interest in an album or singles project, any suggestion she made was squashed, says Megan. 'It became so frustrating. Jill never ceased to think that Phil had a beautiful voice, and wrote great songs. But she began to get frustrated with having any suggestions rejected.'

Despite any difficulties between Phil and Jill, it remained unthinkable that they should be separated geographically. The first time came, predictably, through Phil's work. In 1984 he was asked by Eric Clapton to produce his next album, *Behind the Sun*, released in 1985. It was to be recorded at George Martin's Air Studios on the island of Montserrat in the West Indies.

For Phil, this was an honour. For Clapton, it demonstrated confidence that his friend had such musicianship and original ideas that he would improve upon his last two rather sluggish albums.

Surprisingly to Phil, the demonstration tapes Eric played him showed that he was going to make an autobiographical album, and a highly charged one at that. Eric and Pattie's marriage was creaking, and this was reflected in the songs, which were mostly about unrequited love. One song in particular, 'She's Waiting', was likely to give Phil food for thought. As Eric explained later, it was all about how Pattie was waiting for another man to love.

The invitation to Phil to produce the album came by an unorthodox method. 'Eric left a message on the answerphone,' he recalls. 'He said, "I wonder if you fancy coming over because I want to ask you about producing my album." I was completely taken aback. I'd grown up listening to Eric's albums and it was a shock to realize I'd gone from being a fan to being asked to produce . . . I went round and I wasn't quite sure whether I'd be able to do it or not.'

In Montserrat it took several weeks to put the album together. 'Eric and I got really close,' says Phil 'it was a very enjoyable time.' Unusually, Jill did not go along. 'Eric and I agreed beforehand that it would be just blokes.' It was the longest that Jill and Phil had been apart.

Phil, weaned on the music of Cream and in awe of Clapton's guitar work, felt acutely the responsibility of being charged with 'refreshing' his friend's music. In his view, Clapton had sounded a bit jaded on *Money and Cigarettes*. Eric credits Phil for his introduction to the synthesizer. 'It took me a long time to pick up on the coming of the synthesizer,' he says. 'It crept up on me through the use of keyboards, which came about through my working with Phil. When he came on as producer,

my recording sound changed. Phil wanted to produce an album
that would show lots of different sides that hadn't been heard
or seen before.' They finished recording the album in a month
and spent a month mixing it. 'By today's standards that's quick,'
adds Clapton. Towards the end of their time together in the
studio, Clapton recalls 'getting a bit loose, mucking about'.
Phil admonished him. 'The only other person who's ever
done that to me was Pete Townshend,' he told the author,
adding that 'Both he [Townshend] and Phil are professionals
of the old school.' Phil wrote some of the lyrics on 'Never
Make You Cry', which Eric described as his favourite song on
the album.

'I was surprised to be asked,' says Phil. 'I thought a love
song is the one kind of song you would normally want to
do yourself, but Eric didn't want to, or couldn't. He had a
chorus and I was to write the verses . . . I spent a lot of time
and a lot of love and a lot of energy on Eric's album, and I'm
very pleased and very proud that I did because I love him very
dearly as a person, I really do. He's the kind of guy who if
I don't speak to him for a while when we do speak he will
understand why. Last year I felt I had to have a conversation
with him and I felt the longer it went the more difficult it
was going to become. He came to the show and liked it and
was going to come back and play with us but that night Rose
[Clapton's grandmother, who raised him] died. I called Roger
[Forrester, Clapton's manager] to find out how he was and
he said I should call him. I did and he said: "You're always
there for me, you know, I want you to know I love you for
this."' When Clapton's son, Conor, was tragically killed, Phil
and Keith Richards of the Rolling Stones were the first to make
contact with their distraught friend.

After completing *Behind the Sun*, Phil and Eric went off in their
separate professional ways. Phil was disappointed to learn that

the record company was not entirely happy with the album, and felt he had let his friend down. 'The comments I heard were "Where are the guitar solos?" ' remembers Phil. 'I said, well, these are his songs. If he actually writes songs that he doesn't want to put guitar solos on he doesn't have to have a guitar solo. The response was: "There are no singles. He's in the market place with Duran Duran now." I said, I'm sorry I don't understand this. This is his album, what he wants to do. Anyway, they took him back into the studio and did three other songs. I was a bit disenchanted with that.'

Phil moved on to work on Philip Bailey's album *Chinese Wall*, on which he spent three or four months, which spawned the hit single, 'Easy Lover', but because of his disappointing experience with the Clapton album he was having second thoughts about record production. 'I did those albums almost back to back and I thought: I don't know about this production thing, because I'd been used to delivering something and saying, this is me, you put this out (and the same with Genesis) and suddenly it was: "No, there's no singles, no guitar solos." I thought, I don't know if I like producing.'

He was, however, persuaded to collaborate with Clapton again. 'Eric asked me if I'd do another album with him and we said, this time we'll do it in America, in LA, so the record company can come down and get involved and let us know [what they were thinking] and they did. Tom Dowd was involved, which I guess gave the record company a little bit of confidence because they thought: "Well, Tom did *Layla* so he's going to know what he's doing." '

The album was *August*, released in 1986, which became a massive international hit. 'Every time I hear it I think, it's good, didn't we do well?' says Phil. 'It had some great stuff on it. It wasn't a blues album, it wasn't an Eric Clapton wailing guitar solo album, it was Eric and his music in a modern setting. "Behind the Mask", for example, was a hit single in England.' (It reached number 15 in January 1987 and stayed in the charts for eleven weeks.) But once again Phil had doubts about whether producing was his true métier. 'I thought, do I want to spend four months of my time doing this, producing an album, choosing the songs with the artist, babysitting, recording it, mixing it, cutting it and then you [can] end up with someone sticking a pin in a balloon.'

In March 1985 Phil's third solo album, No Jacket Required, had been released. Rolling Stone commented: 'The sly craft and warm, low-key humor of his solo records and his resourceful production jobs for Philip Bailey and Frida make his ascension seem inevitable. He goes and gets his audience with hard, clipped rhythms and brash horns that epitomize white R&B bounce, and he holds them with unexpected melodies.'

The album, which entered the charts at number 1 in the UK and topped the US album chart for seven weeks, included four songs which went on to reach the top ten in the American singles charts; 'One More Night' and 'Sussudio' hit number 1 in Billboard's top forty list, 'Don't Lose My Number' made number 4, and 'Take Me Home', number 7. In Britain 'Sussudio', 'One More Night' and 'Take Me Home' all made the charts. 'Sussudio' hit number 12, 'One More Night', number 4 and 'Take Me Home', number 19.

Constantly striving to break new ground musically, Phil's foray into dance music had resulted in 'Sussudio', another song which was to become a permanent favourite with Phil Collins fans. He explained that he wanted to write a dance song simply because it was something he hadn't done before. He listened to some of his favourite dance tracks 'and thrashed about on the keyboard until I got something that musically excited me'. The title, 'Sussudio', he says, came 'off the top of my head. I tried to find a real word to fit the rhythm but couldn't so I ended up having to invent a word.'

Like the previous solo albums, the cover for No Jacket Required featured a striking portrait of Phil on the front, while inside he solicitiously thanked those who had helped him, including Simon and Joely. He also publicly acknowledged the new lady in his life with 'thanks to Jill for being so patient'.

For the world tour to promote the album, Martin Lewis received a phone call from Tony Smith. They were making a video for a TV special and maybe this was the time to get Phil's comedy acting career off the ground. Would Martin come up with a gag that could run throughout, between the songs. Lewis duly brought into the project the actor-comedian John Bird, a seasoned writer who had been in the vanguard of the British comedy scene. Together they concocted a character named Bill Collins, a doorstepping brother of Phil who would be making mischief trying to cash in on his brother's fame. 'Basically, it was a slice of the Artful Dodger. I spent weeks honing it; as well as being a great video it promised to be a great showcase for Phil's comedic talents on camera. Phil fell in love with the idea,' says Lewis. 'Then one day Tony Smith called me up and said: "No, we're going in a different direction." I didn't want to spoil my relationship with Phil so they never realized how upset I was.'

Phil's warm-to-tepid relationship with the irrepressible Martin Lewis reached its nadir in July 1986. An American composite album featuring John Lennon, Pete Townshend, Simon le Bon and Phil Collins needed an accompanying television special, and Lewis was hired to put it together. The film was called Playing for Keeps, and Lewis had to get interviews with all the celebrities. 'I bombarded Phil with letters and irritated Tony; they had had it up to their necks with this project, had given it a song, and now would we all go away.' They reckoned without Lewis's nerve and verve.

Lewis flew to London and then to Birmingham, where Phil was playing alongside Eric Clapton. After great pressure Phil agreed to a short interview of fifteen minutes at The Farm in Sussex. 'I got my crew in three hours early; when Phil arrived I gave him a clock and said he could keep time with it; this was a clock advertised in *Private Eye* that went backwards. He was so guarded in the interview. I had to make him say the tacky line: "Hi, I'm Phil Collins. I'm *Playing for Keeps*! It's what you need to succeed!!" He hated it. I softened it by giving him toys to play with; I actually got Phil Collins with a kid's toy drum round his neck, banging it briefly. He played with toy money on camera; I filmed him playing snooker.'

Lewis had ensnared his old friend, but at some cost. 'I had been this film producer who was going to take him to Hollywood when he first saw me. Now I was down to being a shyster TV producer putting a toy drum in his hand. I suppose he thought this was not going to turn him into the next Charlie Chaplin. The problem with Phil and me was that we were both the Artful Dodger, and I was more the Artful Dodger than he was. This episode shifted my relationship, but it was very affectionate.' Lewis would continue to look for movie opportunities for Phil.

The up-beat tone of *No Jacket Required* and Phil's new interest in dance music was attributed to his new-found happiness on the domestic front. After being together for four years, Phil Collins and Jill Tavelman had married at Guildford Register Office on 4 August 1984 with a blessing at their local parish church in Shalford, in the company of Eric and Pattie Clapton, Jill's friend Megan Taylor and Phil's manager, Tony Smith. Pattie was matron of honour, Tony best man and Megan maid of honour. Barbara Speake and June Collins were also there. So, too, were Phil's children, Simon and Joely. Joely, twelve at the time, remembers it as 'a fun wedding. I had a great time,' she says.

Among the wedding presents was an unusual gift from Phil's old chum from schooldays, Ronnie Caryl. Wrapped in brown paper and labelled 'Only to be opened in dire emergency', the parcel contained a 'survival kit' of Spam, beans, cheese and pickled onions – food the two friends regularly enjoyed as youngsters when they catered for themselves. Caryl was impressed by Jill. 'I thought she was wonderful. She was used to Hollywood and show business and whether it was Don Johnson on the phone or me or Prince Charles or Richard Branson she dealt with everybody the same. She'd take care of things while Phil was upstairs working. I thought they were a great couple.'

Super-sentimental Phil cried when 'Morning Has Broken' was played at the church service. 'We teased him about that for ever afterwards,' recalls Megan.

At the reception back at the house, Gary Brooker, writer and singer of the classic Procol Harum hit 'A Whiter Shade of Pale', with whom Phil and Eric and George Harrison had worked on his solo album, *Lead Me to the Water*, started the music rolling. He played piano and Phil began playing drums. Eric Clapton played guitar and Mo Foster was on bass. Daryl Stuermer and Chester Thompson joined in and Robert Plant sang. 'I played at my first wedding and I got severe stick for it so I thought I'd better not play for too long,' says Phil. 'I think I played three or four songs.'

Stephen Bishop remembers Julian Lennon also being among the 200 or so guests. 'Phil really liked my song "Separate Lives" and wanted me to sing it', says Bishop. 'I said: this is a wedding, Phil, won't it be kind of weird?

And I remember Jill said, go ahead, sing it, it's a good song.'

Marquees had been set up in the back garden, with a special one for the children. 'It was very important to Phil that Simon and Joely enjoyed themselves,' Megan remembers. 'Phil played. Various people got drunk and had their little differences. Everyone was having a great time. It was a wonderful day. I think Phil was extremely happy, and so was Jill. Then they went off on honeymoon to some country hotel where the door wouldn't lock and they had to push a chair in front of the door; it was like *Fawlty Towers*.'

Unlike Andrea, Jill appeared to be unfazed by Phil's devotion to his career. She travelled with him on tour and when he was in the studio got used to being alone. 'Phil almost gets in the way when he's around,' she told *Rolling Stone*. 'I have to tell him, "Don't sit in my favourite chair . . ."' In the early days of the marriage, according to Megan, Phil claimed to be 'deliriously happy'.

Against this backdrop of domestic bliss his musical career forged ahead. In 1986 *Rolling Stone* readers voted Phil Collins the second most popular artist of the year (Bruce Springsteen topped the poll, Sting was number three, Bob Geldof four and Madonna five), and in 1987 Phil announced at the Cannes Film Festival his latest project: he was to star in the film *Buster*, based on the real-life story of Ronald (Buster) Edwards, one of the Great Train Robbers. As a potential movie star Phil Collins held all the aces. He had looks, of proven appeal to women, he could sing and he could act.

Phil claimed he was attracted to the script because it was primarily about the love story of Edwards and his wife, June, rather than the robbery. It was the romantic element that appealed to him – and also the fact that the part of June would be played by Julie Walters, of whom he was a big fan.

He'd played a cameo role in an episode of the US television series *Miami Vice*, as Phil the Spiv, in December 1985, but this was to be his first major acting part since Lionel Bart's *Oliver!* The portents were good; those in the know saw Phil as 'a natural for the screen, in the manner of Bob Hoskins'.

The *Los Angeles Times* saw Phil's involvement as 'an unusual casting move' on the part of producer Norma Heyman and director David Green, reminding its readers that thirty-six-year-old Collins was doing pretty well financially at the time, having been reported as earning $30 million in 1985 as a rock star. 'His world tour with Genesis (15 countries, 5 million people) supposedly brought them a paycheck of $15 million . . . each,' its reporter gushed. Having already cast Julie Walters as June, Green says he 'agonized' over who to cast as Buster. 'One evening my wife and I were at home in Hertfordshire and she called me in from the kitchen. "Come and watch this," she said. "This is Buster" . . . it was Phil in *Miami Vice*. It took me five minutes to agree: "There he is." The next day I rang a friend, Pete Rudge, and said, "I've got to get a script to Phil Collins fast. What's the best way?"' Rudge directed David Green to Phil's manager, Tony Smith, whose reaction was: "It sounds perfect, send it over." 'Phil read the script and loved it and I went down to see him in Sussex. We got on well and he committed to it. Boom . . . we had a movie.'

The film was shot in England and Acapulco and, as was her custom, Jill accompanied Phil to Mexico. Phil told the journalist David Wigg, in the *Sunday Express Magazine*, that he and Jill were now keen to start a family.

Green says that Phil was 'a joy to work with. It's easy for a director to say: "My stars are wonderful," but I have worked with some pretty big names and they have not all been as wonderful as Phil Collins. He was enthusiastic, willing to learn and had no pretentions. He was up to the challenge of stretching himself. In the music world he was king and in the TV and film world he had done a little bit and now he was ready to step up on to a bigger world stage. He worked very hard and had real acting talent. On the second day of the shoot, when he and Julie [as June] were sitting in their house, prior to the robbery, talking about the misery of their lives, I thought, "There's a real actor there," and when I saw the rushes afterwards I thought, "He's really got it."' Phil's co-star Julie Walters agreed. She told David Wigg: 'I would love to do another film with him because he's so easy and good – he really is an actor.' She said despite being a rock star she'd found Phil to be 'unpretentious and not at all posy'.

The 'real' Buster Edwards acted as technical adviser on the film and he and Phil became friends. Meeting Edwards after a Genesis concert at Wembley, Phil was touched to be told: "You've got me down, apart from the clothes; I was a nattier dresser than you are." Says Phil: 'Buster and I hit it off straight away. We discovered we had a lot in common. He was very embarrassed with women, as I am; I'm not a natural chatter-up at all.' Looking back now, Phil says he has fond memories of the film 'but I have problems with it . . . I didn't ask questions about the script because I didn't know what questions to ask. I made the part my own but I said pretty much what was on the paper. For example in Mexico, when Buster and June's marriage is breaking up, I slap her and Buster said: "I would never do that, I would never hit my Juney." And I smoked right through the film because I thought in the sixties he would have smoked but when I met Buster I found he didn't. People said I played him like a lovable rogue, an artful dodger, but that's what he was like.'

When Edwards died in December 1994 Phil did not attend the funeral, but he sent flowers, and as mourners including

Bruce Reynolds and Charles Kray entered St George's Chapel, Phil's version of 'A Groovy Kind of Love' from the film *Buster* was played over loudspeakers.

Buster had a royal première at the Odeon, Leicester Square, on 15 September 1988 in aid of the Prince's Trust. Princess Diana was said to be a Phil Collins fan and it was rumoured that the Collinses and the royal couple exchanged Christmas cards every year. The soundtrack album of *Buster* brought Phil three more hit singles. 'A Groovy Kind of Love', a cover of the Mindbenders' 1966 hit, was number 1 in the British and American charts and stayed in the lists for thirteen weeks. In America, 'Two Hearts' and 'Another Day in Paradise' also topped the *Billboard* list and in Britain 'Two Hearts' reached number 6 and 'Another Day in Paradise' number 2.

At first Phil had said he didn't want to have anything to do with the music for *Buster*, 'but David Green and Norma Heyman said, "Even if you don't want to do it, you must have contacts – please put us in touch with some people." I tried George Martin and Pete Townshend. Pete had done *McVicar* and George wanted to do it, but the film people thought George wasn't as big a name in terms of a singer, though I felt he would know exactly how the sixties [the period of the film] felt. Then I thought about the other side of the sixties, if it's not the Beatles it's Motown for me. I'd met Lamont Dozier on a gig. When I was touring he'd come backstage and I'd got his autograph because he was a big hero to me. I got in touch and asked him if he fancied doing some music for the film. He said, "Yes," and he came to Acapulco where we were filming the last two weeks of *Buster*. He came with these demos. One was 'Loco in Acapulco', which we ended up doing with the Four Tops, and one was 'Two Hearts', which wasn't called 'Two Hearts' at the time. It didn't have a melody and it didn't have lyrics but it had this great rhythm track which was just like Martha and the Vandellas. Within the weekend that he came to Acapulco I'd gone to him with some lyrics that I'd written to his song. It all happened very quickly. I sang them to him and he said, "This is great," and I did a demo in my studio and sent that to him and he said, "Now you're stuck with singing it because this is your song now." I love that song very much.'

Phil's performance as an actor was also well received. Reviewers described his portrayal of the villain with a heart of gold as 'charismatic', and Phil travelled the world promoting the film. He talked to the press in Britain and Europe, spent a week in New York and a week in Los Angeles, and then moved on to Austrialia and Japan. He wanted to help the film as much as he could, he explained. Journalists regularly referred to him as 'Mr Nice Guy of the international pop world', an epithet that was to haunt him for the rest of his life.

The way Phil launched himself into publicizing the film with such zeal impressed David Green. 'He was more than an actor, he was part of the team. He launched himself into publicity with gusto, wrote music for the film ('Two Hearts' was nominated for an Oscar), went to the Academy Awards and sang 'Going Loco Down in Acapulco' with the Four Tops. The album [of Buster] did very well and the video still sells.'

His proud daughter, Joely, joined in the popular acclaim. She thought her father's performance 'really good', she says. 'I bawled my eyes out when I watched him in Buster. I saw it as a start in his film career. I forget sometimes how big he is.'

In a business not particularly known for the co-operativeness of its leading lights, Phil Collins is acknowledged as a diplomat. When his American record label, Atlantic, held a fortieth anniversary bash at New York's Madison Square Garden in

June 1988, Phil was among the celebrities brought in to perform. All around him artistic temperament was causing problems behind the scenes, while he simply stated: 'I'm here to do whatever Atlantic wants me to do.' And what they wanted him to do, it transpired, was more than most. His schedule, according to *Rolling Stone*, had him playing a solo version of 'In the Air Tonight' at 1.45 p.m., introducing Keith Emerson and Carl Palmer immediately afterwards, performing 'In the Air Tonight' again at 8.20 p.m. to open a live broadcast of the show, then introducing La Vern Baker; introducing Robert Plant an hour later, donning dark glasses for a duet with Sam Moore on 'You Don't Know Like I Know' soon after 10 p.m., performing a twenty-minute set with Genesis around 11 p.m., and at midnight introducing Led Zeppelin.

A perfect pointer to Phil's workaholism about this time came from Steve Hackett, who bumped into him with Jill on a Concorde flight from New York to Heathrow. Phil casually mentioned his busy schedule and Hackett smiled, remembering the intensity with which his former pal in Genesis always worked. 'Phil,' he asked, 'do you have a life outside music these days?' 'No,' came the reply. 'I don't. I don't really have time for anything else.'

In the view of Ronnie Caryl, Phil's tunnel vision of his own life and especially of his career has meant that he knows 'very little about other things. His attitude to things is that of a cocooned person. Because he doesn't get out and about very much. In twenty years, he'd read two books, *Second Chorus* by Humphrey Lyttelton and *Owning Up* by George Melly. He's read *Second Chorus* fifteen times! There was no time for reading during the years with Genesis and getting his solo career going.'

In the 1990s, however, Phil became an avid reader of biographies.

*   *   *

Phil has always recognized the requirement for an artist to promote the latest product. When a new album comes out he sets aside several weeks for press interviews. 'I have to do it,' he says. 'When you make a record you open a can of worms; you have to do all the promotional stuff, you have to make videos. Do you just let the record crawl out or do you let the world know?'

His manager, Tony Smith, confirms Phil's total involvement. 'He wants to know every single detail, all the figures, but he leaves it [the running of the business] to me. He's interested in the figures and the sales but it's almost like a way of keeping score. He's not actually interested in the money. Money never has been a motivator; it's come along with success and is more a way of keeping score. He's a showman to the nth degree, and yet in his private life he wants to live a quiet life. He would be very happy if he wasn't noticed.' Tony Smith muses that Phil may be embarrassed by the adulation he receives on stage. 'What makes a great performer is interesting,' he opines. 'Great performers have to be insecure in their personality because they want to be loved by everyone and they want it reaffirmed all the time. It's Phil's fragility that makes him endearing to people, absolutely,' he theorizes.

To Pattie Clapton, Phil is 'a very dear, sweet person I absolutely adore'. When asked whether his success was predictable she told the author: 'I always felt there was something very special about him. I was not surprised when I saw him emerge as a big star, I felt a tremendous pride for him.'

When asked to analyse his appeal himself, especially his appeal to the women in his audiences, Phil is uncomfortable. 'I hate to say it because it sounds so trite, but I think its the little-boy-lost/mothering instinct. Obviously I'm not the traditional rock god. Women don't think of me as that, I'm not a sex symbol or some good-looking rock singer, I think they think: "Oh, I could sort him out, I could take care of him."' He is sensitive to criticism about his height – 'I'm five foot eight, which is average in England. In America they call me short because they're all giants' – and his hair: 'I've had this hairline, and my son and my daughter, Lily, have it a bit, since I was a boy. It's obviously gone farther back and got thinner. When I'm asked what I am going to do about my hair I say, "Why should I do anything about it?" I'm not vain. I have an ego, I like to show off on stage I suppose but I'm not vain, not really.'

Phil's ordinariness has been much commented upon over the years, especially in the American press. The *New York Times* once dubbed him 'the Alfred Hitchcock of Rock'; *Rolling Stone* called him 'Pop music's Cabbage Patch Kid', and *USA Today* described him as 'an everyday kind of guy', adding, with some bemusement, '. . . teenage girls have begun rushing the stage as if he were a blowdried poster boy instead of a 15 year art-rock veteran who looks like Dad.' Phil has said himself that he 'established an image without having an image. If you haven't got an image you can't be affected by images or trends changing. You're always there, just running parallel with whatever fad is in,' he adds.

However, in some ways Phil Collins is a paradox. He wants to be anonymous – but conversely he can feel surprised if nobody recognizes him. His friend Ronnie Caryl recalls Jill telling him of the night they stopped off in Richmond to pick up a takeaway pizza. Phil in his baseball cap passed unnoticed and was amused but quite taken aback.

In the eighties everything seemed to be going right professionally for Phil Collins. In 1981 his début solo album, *Face Value*, was number 1 in the UK chart. In 1982 'In the Air Tonight' won 'International Hit of the Year' at the Ivor

Novello Awards, he had his first UK number 1 single with 'You Can't Hurry Love' in 1983, and the following year, 'Against All Odds (Take a Look at Me Now)' topped the American charts for three weeks. In the 1985 Grammy Awards Phil won the 'Best Pop Vocal Performance, Male', award for 'Against All Odds' and the song also brought him the Ivor Novello Award for 'Best Song, Musically and Lyrically'. 'One More Night', 'Sussudio' and 'Separate Lives' all topped the American charts. He continued mopping up awards in 1986, including 'Best British Male Artist' and 'Best British Album' (for No Jacket Required) at the BRIT Awards, 'Best Pop Vocal Performance, Male', 'Producer of the Year' and 'Album of the Year' (for No Jacket) in the Grammies, and 'Most Performed Work' (for 'Easy Lover') at the Ivor Novello Awards.

At the 1987 ASCAP (American Society of Composers and Publishers) annual awards ceremony he swept the board. He was honoured as composer, producer, performer and Genesis front man, picking up seven awards. The following year he dominated the proceedings again as songwriter of the year, having scored the highest number of US performances in the previous twelve months among members of the Performing Rights Society, whose works are adminstered by ASCAP. This was for 'Against All Odds', 'In the Air Tonight', 'Invisible Touch', 'Take Me Home', 'Land of Confusion', 'One More Night', 'Throwing It All Away' and 'Tonight, Tonight, Tonight'. With remarkable understatement, Billboard commented: 'Phil Collins has come a long way since he stepped forward from behind his drum kit . . .'

In 1989 'Two Hearts' brought Phil his seventh US number 1 hit record and was named the 'Best Song Written Specifically for a Motion Picture or Television' at the Grammy Awards. The Ivor Novello Awards voted it 'Best Film Theme or Song'. Buster was 'Best Film Soundtrack' in the BRIT Awards. 1989 also saw Phil co-producing and playing drums on Stephen Bishop's new album, *Bowling in Paris*; singing and playing on Eric Clapton's 'Bad Love', to be included on his *Journeyman* album, and drumming on 'Woman In Chains' on the Tears for Fears album, *The Seeds of Love*; and playing the part of Uncle Ernie at two performances of the rock opera *Tommy*, with the Who, in Los Angeles and London for charity, as well as recording his fourth solo album, . . . *But Seriously*, another co-production with Hugh Padgham.

One of the tracks, 'Father to Son', dedicated to Simon, concluded:

> I'll always be with you don't forget,
> Just look over your shoulder I'll be there,
> If you look behind you, I will be there.

Another of the songs on . . . *But Seriously* was 'Another Day in Paradise', a composition spawned by Phil's social conscience. He cites two incidents particularly as motivation for the work, on which he was joined on vocals by veteran singer David Crosby. 'I was in Rio with Genesis and at the end of Copacabana beach is this shanty-town on a hill, homes made of corrugated iron and wood with no running water, no electricity, overlooking the beach. We went to a record company party at a million-dollar apartment and from the balcony you could see this shanty-town so close by. To be amidst that wealth with such poverty so near, I will never forget that image. The other image I have that always pops into my mind, and which really prompted the song, was when I was in Washington. We were driving from the airport to the hotel and there was snow on the ground, and we passed the White House and Capitol Hill, which were beautifully lit, and as we approached traffic lights I noticed there were lots of black folks on the pavement. There were so many of them I asked, "Is this a demonstration or something?" and was told, "No, this is where these people live." At one end of the street was the Capitol dome and at the other, these grilles with hot air coming out and people sleeping in boxes in the snow. I remember thinking: "I can't believe this." It was the first time I'd really become aware of homelessness, although I know that cardboard city [in London] has been there for years. People who live in these places don't really see it, they drive through and after a while they don't notice it any more; it takes a visitor to see what's going on.'

Writing the song, he says, came easily. 'It was one of those times when you put your hands down on the piano and start playing something and start singing something and that's it, it's easy once you know what you've decided to write about and you've got a melody and a first verse. After that it's easy to write the second and third verses.'

If writing 'Another Day in Paradise' assuaged his social conscience, it didn't, admits Phil, immediately change his own behaviour. 'Having written the song and recorded it and gone to the studio in Tottenham Court Road to cut it as a single, I was leaving the studio with Hugh Padgham and as I crossed the street a woman with two kids said to me: "Give us a quid, guv." And I didn't do it! I walked on! I thought, "What am I doing?" I couldn't stop then, it would have been more embarrassing to turn around. I thought: "I just wrote this song and I did exactly the same as the guy in the song." He walks on embarrassed to be there, doesn't look round, starts to whistle. I was that person in the song . . . I'm as guilty as anyone else,' he told the author. But his conscience was obviously severely pricked by the incident and since that time if he sees someone needy when driving he will wind down the car window and give.

He recounts with obvious delight the influence the song has had on others. 'I was doing a radio programme in America on a promotion tour for the record and a woman rang up and said: "One evening there was a tramp in our garden going through the rubbish and my son (a little boy of six or seven) looked out of the window saying, "Dad, Mum, there's someone in the garden." I rushed out, ushered him away and my son ran after me and said: "No, no, Phil Collins would like you to give him some food. That's what Phil would do." '

Phil credits the song with triggering his own increased involvement with charity. 'I didn't really think about getting involved in homeless charities when I did the song, but when it was a big hit and I did the video I started to get involved. We did a tour with the National Coalition for the Homeless.'

Ever the consummate professional, Phil enthusiastically promoted the album . . . But Seriously and the single from it, 'Another Day in Paradise', making trips around Europe in a private jet cramming innumerable radio, TV and press interviews into the few hours he was in Amsterdam, Rome, Frankfurt, Milan or wherever. . . . But Seriously became the fastest-selling album in UK chart history and sold over 17 million copies. The homely pictures on the sleeve notes included a snap of a baby – Phil and Jill's new daughter, Lily, born on 18 March 1989. Pattie Clapton went to visit Jill and Lily in the hospital in Guildford where Lily was born.

As often as was practicable, where Phil went Jill and now Lily went too. 'Phil was very happy with Jill,' says Pattie. 'I thought she was a nice girl and when he first brought her over to meet me he was obviously besotted with her. I really admired the way she travelled with him because it's not easy.' Interviewed in America on a world tour in 1990, Phil told USA Today: 'If I was away from Lily on this tour I would have missed half her life so far.' And when all three turned up for the Grammy Awards party in New York, 'Phil's little treasure', as Lily was dubbed by the media, stole some of the limelight. While Phil, who had eight Grammy nominations, faced the television cameras, Jill read stories to Lily and it was duly reported that Lily 'looked adorable in a round black hat with bow, green kilt, white blouse and a little heart-shaped handbag'.

'Lily had her first birthday on the road in Brisbane,' Phil recalls. 'At ten months she was in Japan when we started the 1990 tour and she came everywhere with me until she started school.'

. . . *But Seriously* was a monster hit, but for Hugh Padgham it marked a big blip, a break in his relationship with Phil and not a happy finale at that time. 'It was me who had pushed quite heavily to get a selection of musicians in, more like the first album. If you look at the first album, there was more variety of musicians than on the middle two which I did with Phil. For . . . *But Seriously*, I tried to get Phil to entertain the idea of using one or two more, to add some different sounds. He was happy, but also kind of reticent.'

Padgham co-produced and engineered . . . *But Seriously*, feeling less inspired than on the first three albums. Perhaps their relationship had deteriorated, professionally; it was, he reflects, probably his fault that he did not say more, 'because I felt that he would not agree with me anyway'.

It boiled down to Padgham's restlessness with Phil's chosen safe route. Hugh felt that to contrast with such obvious winners as 'Another Day In Paradise' and 'I Wish It Would Rain Down', Phil might have pushed himself, musically, and taken a few risks, perhaps in jazz mode.

But such a conversation never occurred because, for all their empathy, the two men had never become true mates. They were closer on the first two albums, Padgham said, 'before he became a pop star, the housewife's darling', which was anathema to Padgham. 'I don't know if it was what he expected, but it certainly wasn't what I expected. It wasn't what I wanted. I'm not saying that stopped me from being matey with him; we always had a very professional relationship in that he kept his private life to himself. If he had invited me to dinner I would have gone, sure, but he never invited me. In the ten years I knew him I probably went round to his house a couple of times for tea.'

Padgham had experienced Phil's piledriving style, too. If Hugh was five minutes late in arriving in Sussex for a recording session, Phil would get agitated. 'When we'd stop working to eat supper, the minute he put his knife and fork down, it was: "Come on, let's get back to the studio" . . . and I didn't feel I was allowed even a five-minute breather. Maybe it was Phil's workaholism combined with not being happy. It was like a factory and a machine, and I took exception to that. But I didn't really speak out when perhaps I should have done.

'The bigger stars are more committed than the others . . . which is why they are bigger stars. That can happen in a nice way, and in not so nice a way, because with some people who have a single-minded ambititon, it doesn't matter who they shit on, on the way. I'm not saying Phil is like that. Phil would be, by his own admission, a workaholic, which is one very good reason why there have been two marriage break-ups. It is difficult for the other half, no matter how much you love each other, to keep relationships going on the phone.

'We had a good time in the studio in the early days. I didn't have a great time on my last album with him [. . . But *Seriously*]. But that was my problem, not his. When I first met him he was relaxed, the cheeky chappie next door. By the time we were on the fourth album, everything was taken a lot more seriously. Thanks to Phil I became a full-time record producer and was off doing Police and later I was with Sting. Working with Phil launched my career, I'll be in his debt for the rest of my life. I love the guy dearly.'

If . . . But *Seriously* was an apt title, reflecting as it did Phil's new approach to his music, it also, some of his friends thought, described his attitude to life in the early nineties. Some who knew the old, ebullient Phil noticed a darker person around this time. 'He was very charming, just like the old Phil, but some of the humour had gone from him,' says Bill Bruford, remembering meeting him at Mike Rutherford's home. 'I cracked a couple of old jokes that didn't work; a certain light had gone. He seemed to be on another planet.'

Phil, in Bruford's opinion, carries the cares of the world on his shoulders. 'And he feels that he has a responsibility for setting the world right, in return for all his success. It must be frighteningly lonely being Up There. He's probably surprised himself. I thought that for two and a half seconds I ought to try to remind him of the time when life wasn't quite so serious. But it didn't really work. He's paid quite a price, with two divorces. I have no advice for him other than: it's only rock 'n' roll. I can't speak highly enough of him and would wish him to be happy with his success.'

Few, however, could have guessed that the person who would put the sparkle back into Phil Collins's life would be his old flame from theatre school, Lavinia.

'I know a lot about relationships'

Lavinia Lang, Phil Collins's sweetheart from his teenage years, had never been far from his thoughts in the twenty years since they officially split. 'I thought of her very often,' he says. The passion of that first love had not entirely dimmed through two marriages. When she ended their romance, he was a struggling drummer whose first band had collapsed. Two decades on, he was an international superstar. They were to reunite in a scenario more dramatic in real life than fiction.

By 1992 Phil felt his marriage to Jill was faltering. 'More things were starting to bother me about the person I was living with, but there was no tangible evidence of the marriage going downhill. I think in some respects I was just losing contact. All the reasons you live with someone, stay with someone, stay married to them, were gradually being lost. There were signs that maybe it wasn't as special, or wonderful, as it used to be. Her answer to that was: well, things do change and you can't expect things to be like the first date every day. Of course I realize this. You have to bend and be flexible to make a successful marriage. But ultimately, because you only get one chance at life, you have to be able to feel comfortable.'

Phil's first wife, Andrea, played a crucial role in orchestrating the reunion between Phil and Lavinia that catapulted him to notoriety. In Vancouver in 1992, Andrea met the actress Olivia Hussey, whom she had not seen since her theatre school years when Olivia had starred in *The Prime of Miss Jean Brodie* on the London stage; Andrea and Lavinia had had small children's parts in the show. Filming in Vancouver, Olivia told Andrea she was now living in Los Angeles and that she had reconnected with Lavinia. This news intrigued Andrea, who jumped at the chance to renew a school friendship.

Olivia duly gave Lavinia's Los Angeles phone number to Andrea, who rekindled by phone from Vancouver, in many enthusiastic conversations, the rapport of their teenage years and beyond. The two women also corresponded, exchanging pictures of their children. They spoke of their time at stage school together; and of their children; and Lavinia (now married with two children) invited Andrea to go with her to England to attend her sister's wedding. Inevitably they also talked about Phil.

'Have you ever seen one of his concerts?' Andrea asked in one of their regular phone chats.

'No, never.'

'You should go. I could probably get tickets for you. He'd love to see you. He hasn't seen you for so long and we're all old friends,' Andrea told Lavinia.

By chance, Phil was on the road as she spoke. His tour had just hit Vancouver, and Andrea, Joely and Simon went to his concert there. Andrea had a shock for Phil.

'Guess who I've been in touch with! Lavinia! She lives in LA!'

Phil was flabbergasted. He recalls his reaction: 'Good God! I'm through LA all the time and she's never once come to the show. I know she's happily married with two kids . . . when you speak to her next, just say: "Why don't you go to the show? Why have you never been?"' A concert at Dodger Stadium in Los Angeles was on the itinerary.

Andrea saw little point in being the messenger between them. 'I said to Phil: "Look, rather than me be the middle man, why don't I give you Lavinia's number? I'll ask her if it's OK. Then you can arrange where the tickets and backstage passes are going to be picked up."'

Phil takes up the story: 'I rang her up from Vancouver, because I was there playing. And she came on the phone and said: "I knew it was you." And straight away there was electricity. So I said: "I just wondered whether you wanted to come to the show. I haven't seen you for twenty years." So she said: "Sure. Can I have three tickets, because there's a great friend of mine who's a big fan and I want to bring my husband, and I'll come."

'So we get to LA and I call Sheryl [Gordon, one of Phil's assistants]. I ask: Has Lavinia picked up her tickets yet? Sheryl said: "She's come down; she looks lovely." Actually, I didn't even know what she looked like. I said: I haven't seen her for twenty years, I don't know. Sheryl added: "She only took two tickets because her husband can't come." I said: OK. Is she going to come back and say hello afterwards? She said: "Yes."

'We did the show and in a way I'm looking . . . I have seen a picture which Andy showed me but I didn't really know what she looked like. Anyway, I see two people arrive somewhere after the second or third song and then leave after about an hour. One looked enough like Lavinia for me to think that it was her. And I thought: She came late and she went early. That's the end of that.

'But Tony [Smith, Phil's manager] came up to me afterwards and said: "That was a fantastic show. That was one of the best shows we've ever put on in LA. There was something about it tonight. It was just different." I guess subconsciously, this was it: I was saying to Lavinia: this is what you have missed . . .

'I came back off stage and of course this was LA so I had Jill there; her best friend Megan; Jill's mother; all the guys in this band that I use were there as guests. Steve Gadd, my hero. Kevin Costner and Danny De Vito's partners were there and when Kevin Costner came in, we met between the hospitality room and the band room. I wanted to meet him. So I am saying to Danny [Gillen, Phil's personal assistant]: "Is there any sign of Lavinia? I can't believe she'd go without saying hello."

'So Sheryl and Danny were both on the lookout in the hospitality room. It was very crowded. I was talking to Kevin Costner and then over his shoulder I see this vision of such a special person. And she looks absolutely incredible. She is beaming. It wasn't the person I'd seen in the show; she'd been there from the beginning. She'd seen the show. And straight away, my reaction was: how the fuck do I get rid of Kevin Costner? Which was funny because this was a person I wanted to meet. But now, how can I manoeuvre this?

'We were between two big rooms. Half were my friends and people like Jill's mum, and half were other guests who wanted tickets and passes but I didn't actually need to see. We were in this confined part. And Lavinia came between me and Costner and I said: I'll be in, in a minute, to say hi. And I was totally blown away by the effect that she'd had on me. So I said to Costner: Listen, come with me. We'll go in the other room. And I briefly spoke to him and then I went up to her and I

said: I can't believe this. You look fantastic. I'm so pleased to
see you. And apparently, she said to her friend: "You hold
my bag because I want to have both of my hands free for
this." And she gave me her dad's phone number, because I
was very close to her mum and dad. We talked for a while
but I felt embarrassed because it was so obvious; I had to get
away. Stephen Bishop was there so I went and sat and talked
with him. I didn't spend much time with Jill, but then that's
the way it usually is at those things.

'When she said she had to go, or I had to go, I kissed her
goodbye and she said: "It was great seeing you again." I said:
"Yeah, same thing with me." As Jill and I got in the car with
her best friend Megan, Jill said: "You never told me she was
that beautiful." I said: "I didn't know." She said: "Well, why
on earth did you marry Andy? Because this person is such a nice
person!" And Jill never got on with Andrea very much. So I said:
"I don't know. I don't know about anything really . . ."'

Show-business encounters in hospitality rooms often reflect
warmth and bonhomie between old flames. But this one was
to be more dramatic than any. Lavinia had been in Phil's mind
intermittently; and the meeting, sparked by his first wife, was
set against the background of his declining marriage to Jill. As
Phil says of what was to unfold: 'If there's a crack in the door,
that's why something like this happens . . .'

He continues his story about Lavinia: 'So we went back and
that was the end of it. I had her phone number and she was
in the back of my mind. Next day I left to go to San Francisco
and before I left I called her just to say goodbye. Jill was still
on the road with me. I was on my own in the hotel. I phoned
to say, "I'm leaving, I don't know when I'm coming back, but
I'm calling to say it was great seeing you." She later told me
she rushed to the phone because she knew it was me.

'I said: "I guess I'll see you." And as I put the phone down I said: "I love you." And she said the same thing and it was like: Phew! So when I got to San Francisco I wrote to her. By this point, I was thinking: This is strange. I shouldn't be feeling this kind of thing. I'm happily married and I've got blinkers on. I shouldn't be feeling this. So I wrote to her saying: I'm feeling like this and I really shouldn't be, but then I *like* the way I'm feeling so I don't want not to have it.

'I came home from the tour. Somewhere out of the blue one day, when I got back, she called me at home in Sussex. She said: "I just got your letter." In fact, when she called, Jill was within ten feet of me at home. I never dreamed she would call. And I said: "I'll have to call you back." Then we went to have a meeting with one of the builders working at the house. Half-way through the meeting, I said: "I've got to go and make a phone call." I came back in and called her. She said: "I just got your letter and I feel exactly the same. We have to do something about this."

'So I said: "Yes, but what"? She said: "Well, I'm coming to England end of June, beginning of July for six weeks." I said I was on the road but I'll be here for a little while. So she said: "Well, please call me when I get there." So I did when she arrived. I was at home for a week or two, then we went to do the Genesis tour.

'Well, I called her every night. I spent hours on the phone. And then I had actually manipulated situations where I would fly back to England and we would see each other. And it was the most extraordinary period. And in Gothenburg we went through this period where we saw each other three or four times and literally we just stayed awake for the whole time, just talking. It was great.'

While the trysts were happening in Europe, Andrea sat in Canada with no knowledge of what had developed between the two old mates she had reunited. She expected an enthusiastic phone call from Lavinia straight after the concert. 'She didn't call. And, you know, a woman's intuition . . . I felt something had happened. But I kinda went: NO! But it was in the back of my mind. It was very strange that she didn't phone me to say she'd had a great time, or that it was great to see Phil again. There was just nothing. And I thought: Well, that's weird. We'd spent hours on the phone racking up phone bills and then she doesn't even phone to say the concert was great. No gossip about anything or anybody! We'd reconnected totally and had good conversations. It was lovely. I was really sick at the time with chronic fatigue syndrome and she sent me some catalogues of great Chinese herbal remedies. We were friends again.

'I'm kind of ticked off about it because it has kind of destroyed our friendship. I could phone her up and say: Listen, it doesn't matter about what's happened. But I feel a little betrayed in a way. I heard about Phil and Lavinia from Simon, who Phil had told. Simon knew before Jill, they were on tour and Phil and Jill were looking after them [the children] and taking them on the road and back to Sussex. Lily was there as well. Joely didn't know. But he told my son. When he had a couple of days off he would take off, saying, "I have to go to business meetings" and he was actually seeing Lavinia.'

Phil continues: 'Then it was coming to the time when she was going to go back to LA. Her husband [TV producer Brett Hudson] had been ringing her, saying she sounded very strange. He knew there was something going on somewhere along the line. So she actually went back to LA. And before she went back, I said: "I want to tell Jill, you have to tell Brett."

'Jill was actually wonderful throughout the whole thing. I remember her sitting by the lake at our house in Sussex and I said: "Listen, I don't know what's happening because Lavinia has gone back and they're talking, and I'm not able to reach her." And Jill said: "Well, you go and call her and find out if you're leaving or not." I went and called and I said: "She can't do it." So the Lavinia business didn't go anywhere. And Jill and I, to varying degrees of success, tried to pick up the pieces. But she never forgave me – she did, because she took me back, but at different times she never forgave me because it would rear its head. And we had some terrible shouting matches. And I could do nothing to change it. It had happened.'

His affair with Lavinia lasted only two or three months, says Phil, but the scene was set for the formal end of his ten-year marriage to Jill. 'Eventually, I knew that I wasn't *there* any more,' he says.

Phil had always buried his emotions deeply. Sometimes they would emerge in his songwriting, but often they lay dormant. Once, when he was in Jill's company, his old school friend Peter Newton, who stayed in touch with all the old school gang, casually mentioned the name of Lavinia Lang to Phil. Rather reprovingly, Phil said: 'Give me a break, Peter, I haven't thought about her since school.' Years later, when he asked Phil why he had shut him up at the mention of Lavinia's name, the reply was: 'I had to hide it somewhere.'

It was in Miami while on tour that Phil and Jill had had what he describes as a 'face to face'. 'I told her: we can't possibly try again because there is someone else.' That night, he says, Jill came to the gig and stood right at the front of the audience of between 12,000 and 15,000 people and just looked at him as he sang 'Separate Lives', which had been performed so prophetically, it now turned out, at their wedding.

What followed next has passed into rock folklore, and caused some of those who had thought of Phil as Mr Nice Guy to reconsider and dub him a 'bounder'. Jill, who normally kept her private life private, began to talk to the newspapers. 'I don't blame her,' says Andrea. 'She was trying to save her marriage. She wanted to try and get him back, give him a second chance or at least confront him with the situation publicly.'

Jill talked to the *Daily Mail*'s Baz Bamigboye and explained that the reason the couple were now leading separate lives was because family commitments clashed with the punishing schedule of touring. 'Lily is five years old now, and although I could take her on the road, it's just not the place for her,' said Jill. 'All I know is that he's there and I'm here. Two adults who love each other can be apart while one does one thing and the other does another thing. He's doing his music and I'm doing my thing with Lily. It doesn't mean it's the end of the world.' In the same interview Jill brought up the delicate subject of Lavinia. 'He [Phil] started talking to audiences about how he bumped into an old girlfriend who he first went out with before his first marriage. She's got children now but, when you see someone like that after twenty years, it hangs in your mind. It's a guy's thing and it means nothing at all but Phil probably made a bigger deal out of it than he perhaps should have done in public.'

An uncanny flashback to the storyline of an old song had caused some embarrassment to audiences during his tour. In 1989, he had written 'I Wish It Would Rain Down', for the . . . *But Seriously* album. 'The song,' Phil told the author, 'is actually about turning a corner, bumping into someone in the street that you haven't seen for years, and suddenly the memories of why you love that person come flooding back to you.'

> You know I never meant to see you again
> And I only passed by as a friend,
> All this time I stayed out of sight,

I started wondering why?
Now I, I wish it would rain down, down on me,
Yes, I wish it would rain down on me now.

You said you didn't need me in your life,
I guess you were right.
Well, I never meant to cause you no pain
But it looks like I did it again

Though your hurt is gone
Mine's hanging on, inside
And I know, it's eating me through every night and day,
I'm just waiting on your sign,

'Cos I know, I know I never meant to cause you no pain
And I realize I let you down
But I know in my heart of hearts
I know I'm never gonna hold you again.

The lyrics bore a real affinity to Phil's reconnection with Lavinia, and their subsequent split, although they were clearly written metaphorically because, as he pointed out, it was years earlier than his meetings with her. 'I would have this dream; sometimes our dreams are very jumbled and you wake up thinking you have thought about someone that you've not seen for years. But suddenly they enter your dream, and for the whole day you are trying to shake it off because it's trying to bring back what it was like, or could have been like.'

When Phil was introducing that song on stage, he lit a fuse under the story by creating some dialogue. Supposing, he told the audience by way of introducing 'I Wish It Would Rain Down', you go to a party with your loved one, your partner, 'and there you bump into someone of the opposite sex you haven't seen for a long time.' Phil then went into a monologue in the style of a favourite comedian, the late Sam Kinnerson: he wondered why this person never called him back. 'And it is the can of worms that gets opened . . . you had this conversation in the car on the way home with the person you came with [here he named his wife as that person] who noticed that you spent a lot of time with someone from your past. That was one of the stories I used to tell to summarize what the song was about. Then, of course, all this thing hit the press about Lavinia, and the audience was shuffling uneasily in embarrassment about the story. The song was still about the same thing, but suddenly people were actually thinking I was telling them what had happened. And it wasn't actually like that at all. It was meant to be a joke, a "what if" situation.'

He dropped the sketch from the tour.

'I Wish It Would Rain Down' is the kind of song which has made Phil Collins a fiercely individualistic artist. He has secured an international audience of millions, who empathize and identify with the crises he articulates . . . for himself and for them. And amid the turbulence of his personal life, which he has taken on to the stage, he strives to retain a sensitivity for his audience. He realizes now that the way he had been introducing the song was 'too close to the bone'. Having dropped the sketch now, he simply prefaces his performances of the song with the words: 'This is a song about relationships. I know a lot about relationships.' 'Phil doesn't need a therapist,' his wife, Jill, told the *Daily Mail* in July 1994. 'He can tell the whole world in his songs how he feels.'

Phil's album, *Both Sides*, released in September 1993 and compiled against the backdrop of his turbulent private life, was described by *Billboard* as 'The most reflective, personal album Collins has recorded since *Face Value*.' For the first time, Phil wrote explanatory sleeve notes – 'Songs are all things to all people but sometimes the wrong path is taken and the misinterpretation stays with you forever' – and introduced the lyrics to each song with a few thought-provoking words. 'I'm always whinging on about being misunderstood . . . I thought I'd try my best to try and explain to people what the songs were about, how they were recorded,' he reasoned.

Introducing the haunting ballad, 'Can't Turn Back the Years', in which he sings:

So we have to be strong, and I'm finding that hard,
We have to move on, but no matter how hard I try
If your heart's in pieces you look for the truth
And when I look deep inside I know, it's too bad I
   love you,

he wrote, 'No matter how much you think or want or need it, the past has to remain just that, the past . . .' And when asked to expand in a promotional interview, he added: 'There are things in your past that you believe you had laid to rest or have had laid to rest, have been laid to rest for you. And suddenly, they rear their heads. And maybe that, coupled with the fact that . . . turning forty maybe that has something to do with it . . . there were some things in my life that went on that are reflected in these songs. And I can't really get specific. People will jump to conclusions and add two and two and make five and say, "Oh, his marriage has broken up." Or, "Hasn't he got over his first wife yet?" Well, neither of those is true. I've got a very solid, great marriage and I'm well and truly over my first wife. That's history, it's dead and buried. We get on great and we have our children. But that's not in the ballpark any more. But there was an added element from way back that came and walked over my grave.'

Acknowledgements on the sleeve notes of *Both Sides* concluded: 'Jill, Lily, Simon and Joely, I love you.'

Both Sides had been recorded upstairs at Phil and Jill's home in his twelve-track demo room. 'The songs were becoming so personal, so private, I didn't want anyone else's input,' he said to *Billboard* in October 1993, explaining why he had recorded every instrument and lead vocal himself, using a set-up he could manage without an engineer. 'I only know two ways to write songs really,' he added. 'One way is being able to put into words my feelings, hopefully in a sort of conversational way, and therefore hit exactly those nerves in other people. Or you write songs from an observation point of view, about social issues that bother you and say, "Is anyone else bothered by this because it bothers me you know."'

Like 'Another Day in Paradise', the title track, 'Both Sides of the Story', was inspired by something that had pricked Phil Collins's social conscience. 'I saw a film called *Grand Canyon* and in the opening five minutes there is a scene where a white guy takes a short cut off a freeway in LA and suddenly finds himself in a war zone, a part of town he didn't think he was going to be in, all because he took a short cut. In my mind he suddenly saw what the other side of life was like. He breaks down in his car and these black kids start circling him. He's called a breakdown truck with his portable phone. Meanwhile the guys are starting to get a bit nastier. The breakdown truck arrives and the black driver persuades the black kids to leave the guy alone. As they walk away one of the teenagers who has pulled a gun says to the breakdown driver: "Let me just ask you one thing ... would you have been so nice to me if I didn't have this gun? Would you have kicked my arse if I didn't have it?" And the guy says, "Yes, I probably would have done," and the teenager says, "Well, that's why I carry it, see, because I'm fed up with people kicking my arse." That hit me like a ton of bricks. I thought, if you take away people's decency, and the rights and opportunity that everyone else gets, then it's the survival of the fittest. If you leave people in squalor you are going to have problems and tensions.'

Both Sides touched a lot of nerves. Released as a single, it reached number 7 in the British charts, and the album, which had entered the UK charts at number 1, sold about 6 million. 'It was not a commercial success in the same league as . . . *But Seriously* (which notched up sales of 16 million in the first eighteen months) but a lot of people would love to have commercial failures that sell 6 million records,' comments Tony Smith wryly.

Interviewers, Phil complained, especially in America, asked him time and again, 'You mean to say if these people were treated with more respect they would be more decent?' His response was, 'Yes, but obviously it's going to take time.' The third verse of 'Both Sides of the Story', he explained, 'is about the line that's drawn in the street and the wall that suddenly goes up, people suddenly can't relate to each other.' The tensions between black and white and the respect the ghetto kid feels his gun gives him only occur in the final verse.

After he'd written the song, Phil was watching a programme about the Enniskillen tragedy on TV and saw the father of one of those killed being interviewed. 'He started to cry and said: "Why can't people realize that we just think differently, that we have our beliefs and there are two sides to every story?" I sat there rigid. I had written the song and it was out and I'd faced criticism: "What does Phil Collins know about this?" and suddenly there is a real person who knows exactly how it feels, who said exactly the same thing as I said in the verse. I felt so good afterwards.' His daughter Joely remembers her father telling her that the songs on *Both Sides* were those he wanted to write rather than ones he knew people wanted to hear.

Respect is a word Phil uses a lot. Speaking personally, he says that in the early days of his musical career all he really ever wanted was to be respected by other musicians in the way that he respected the work of other drummers like Keith Moon and Ginger Baker.

Both Sides marked the final album under the three-company deals with WEA, Atlantic and Virgin. After that album, Phil's albums went to Warner round the world.

When the cracks in Phil's marriage to Jill became obvious, Andrea wondered if her ex-husband was going through a midlife crisis. Since Phil had dated Lavinia before he dated her, Andrea explained, it was fair to say that she was his first love. She empathized with Jill's position. 'His affair with Lavinia was a symptom of his already failing marriage,' she said. Interviewed in Hello magazine, she looked back on her own days with Phil: 'I didn't marry Phil so that I could live the life of a rock star's wife. I married the man but, by the time our marriage broke up, I realized I was married to the rock star, and I'd lost the man.'

Jill told the Sun: 'Phil is a perfectionist, he is obsessed with his career and his need to succeed . . . We [she and Lily] want Phil Collins, the husband, the father, back in our lives, not the rock star.' Even Lavinia's stepfather, Fred Lang, joined in the very public debate, giving his version of the story to the Sun a few days later: 'I think to be honest there were problems with Phil's marriage even before he met Lavinia again. But seeing her must have brought things to a head. I'm sure Lavinia still has fond feelings for Phil. But at the end of the day, she is a married woman and I don't think she would be prepared to risk her marriage and family for him.' An unnamed friend claimed that Lavinia felt the affair had been a huge mistake and was upset that it had been made public.

Lavinia herself kept a low profile throughout the media furore and as far as is known she has never publicly admitted to the affair.

Jill's friend Megan remembers the post-Lavinia period as one of considerable tension in the Collins household. 'The last time we were all under the same roof in England Phil swore that he wasn't going to leave Jill. He said to me: "I promise I won't leave," and I said, "Well, I'm afraid you're going to leave," and he said: "No, no, I love Jill, I won't leave."' Ruminating on what led to the ultimate break-up, Megan says: 'It was so awful. They were so in love it was ridiculous, he was just so sweet, we used to have so much fun. They were just so happy. It was impossible to see what went wrong. The idea of Phil being unfaithful was so *unheard* of. I have never seen a guy have so many women chase him and be so totally, genuinely, not interested,' says Megan. 'Not because they weren't attractive women – but he was a married man, period. He took it seriously. It was not possible to imagine Phil with another woman.'

All of a sudden, however, according to Megan, Phil didn't want Jill with him on tour. Nevertheless, Jill took Lily to join Phil in Germany. 'He spent minimum time with them,' says Megan. Jill, she says, got a suspicion that something was going on, that there was a girl in the picture, and returned home after only a few days with him. 'She rang me and said: "Megan, I can't handle it. What should I do?"

'Phil is such a romantic,' says Megan. 'I think he's one who always aspires to do better. He's one of the few people I can think of who has some fantasy ideal of how one should feel or behave. For Phil, things need to be perfect and by that time they weren't perfect, so it was going to be over. This was second time round to be dragged through the gutter.'

Greg Phillinganes, a fellow musician, was also among those who were shocked at the break-up of Phil's marriage to Jill. 'I thought they were joined at the hip. When I talked to friends about celebrity marriages, Phil's was always at the top of the list. Musicians are passionate people but we just cannot seem to get it right with women. We are in love with the idea of being in love, but we continue to make mistakes. I've made mistakes. It's sad really, because on one hand you have this massive talent that is responsible for some of the world's best music, and on the other side you have a guy who just can't seem to have a good relationship with a woman. There we have the paradox.'

For several months the Collinses' matrimonial problems were splashed in some detail over the pages of the tabloid press. One day the couple would be said to be trying to reconcile their differences, the next 'friends' would be quoted as saying 'It's over.' Even the more serious *Sunday Times* joined in the tabloids' public scrutiny of private foibles. A profile of Phil concluded: 'Collins made many pleas after all his charity work, his Live Aid double performance on both sides of the Atlantic, his hobnobbing with the royals, for decanonization. "I'm not as nice as everyone thinks I am," he urged. Now we believe him.'

Throughout July 1994 it seemed that very few days passed without screaming headlines in the tabloids about Phil Collins's private life. The *Daily Mirror* even went as far as getting a psychologist to analyse the meaning of the lyrics of some of the singer's songs. Dr Glenn Wilson's verdict on 'I've Forgotten Everything' from the *Both Sides* album was: "A lot of people have important relationships that are never formalized by marriage – that doesn't mean they weren't special. It sounds like this one left a vacuum in Phil's life.'

Looking back two years later, Phil poured scorn on the psychologist's interpretations of his lyrics. He told me: 'They included a song which I specifically wrote for the film *The War of the Roses*, for De Vito, which had nothing to do with my life at all. In 'Something Happened on the Way to Heaven' the lyrics say:

> We had a life, we had a love
> But you don't know what you've got
> 'Til you lose it . . .

This guy had obviously looked at the lyric and said: "This is about his marriage, blah, blah, blah." '

Instead of starving the controversy, Phil fed it, and finally in mid July 1994 he took matters into his own hands and issued the following statement, by fax, to newspapers:

> I feel the time has come for me to step in and offer my side of a sad story which has been unfolding in the press during the last few days. I can confirm that I have asked my wife, Jill, for a divorce.
>
> She is reluctant to give me this but we are however living separate lives at this time. The reason for my request is that because over the last year I have gradually come to realise that my emotional commitment to my marriage is not what it was or should be.
>
> Two years ago I met a person I had not seen for twenty years. She had been the pivotal woman in my teenage years. I spent ten years in and out of love with her. At our meeting two years ago we were both unable to resist the temptation to rekindle our relationship. It was our intention to carry on where we left off all those years ago. Of course this didn't happen for a variety of reasons too complicated to go into.
>
> I was very frank and honest with Jill who, though obviously hurt, said she understood how I had felt. After this 'affair' we tried to make our marriage work again but quite understandably Jill found it hard to forgive or forget and our relationship became more and more strained as time went on. Contrary to what has been

reported I am not going through a 40-something thing. In simple human terms I am not in love with my partner anymore. I love my daughter very much and will always be her proud father.

I will always try to be there for her. But I cannot stay in a relationship where the flame at least from my standpoint has burnt out. It is my intention to treat this parting in as dignified a manner as possible.

Under the circumstances I would therefore request that the spotlight be turned off my family at least so they can try to continue to function as normally as possible.

Thank you

Phil Collins

Phil Collins has always been an inveterate faxer. Rather than write letters or phone friends and family he sends faxes, even to Lily, but there was one fax he sent to his wife Jill, definitely not intended for publication, which found its way into the tabloids at the height of their marital difficulties and did much to dent his public image. It left no doubt in Jill's mind that Phil now wanted a divorce. (Coincidentally around this time his friend Prince Charles's liaison with Camilla Parker-Bowles was also hitting the headlines.)

'The Fax', as it became known, was in highly emotive language and led to Phil being labelled 'the first transcontinental celebrity to drop the axe by fax' (something he has consistently denied). The fax began: 'I am so sick and tired of your attitude Jill . . .' and concluded: 'I'm so fucking angry with you.' As he did when he broke up with his first wife, Andrea, Phil gave the impression that he felt he was the injured party. 'I'm astounded, yes astounded, by the things you say,' he wrote in the fax. Jill's suspicions about there being 'another woman' in Phil's life were confirmed.

With his marriage to Jill heading to its inevitable conclusion, at least in his mind, Phil had set off on a European tour on 1 April that year. On 24 April 1994, in Lausanne, a twenty-two-year-old interpreter, half Thai and half Swiss, was assigned to his party. Her name was Orianne Cevey and she and Phil had fallen instantly in love.

'I don't want to hear songs about this on your next record'

Once the identity of the new woman in Phil Collins's life was known, the tabloids renewed their interest in his personal life with a vengeance. Not surprisingly, it was Orianne's age (at twenty-two she was almost the same age as his daughter Joely) that provoked most comment. Phil, who can be petulant about press criticism of his music, frequently erupted about the continued intrusion into his private life. Admitting that the publication of The Fax had made a big dent in his image as Mr Nice Guy, Mr Perfect, he complained that certain newspapers now appeared to 'have it in' for him, publishing photographs that showed him in a bad light and writing articles that suggested he was having a midlife crisis. 'It angered me more than upset me,' he says, 'because I felt completely powerless.'

Journalists from the tabloid press followed him round the world, waiting for days in hotel lobbies while Phil and Orianne went in and out through back entrances. Reporters even searched through rubbish bins in their desperate hunt for information. Phil protests that he'd never sought his Mr Nice Guy image, it had been given to him by the media, and conjectures that if it had been Mick Jagger or Rod Stewart in the same situation, the press would have dismissed the story of a rock star leaving his wife simply as him being a rebel. Being cast as Mr Nice Guy wasn't a role that he had ever wanted, Phil told the author.

Orianne, he complained, had been dismissed as a bimbo. 'That's the last thing she is,' he asserted. 'She's a very, very intelligent young woman with a job as a communications and marketing consultant. At first the press described her as a millionairess, which of course she's not.' He described their meeting in Lausanne: 'The promoter arranged for her to meet us at the airport and take care of us at the hotel. On the way there I started to fall in love with her. It happened very quickly. It wasn't rock 'n' roll, it was actually very, very romantic and very sweet.'

News of Phil's liaison with Orianne came as a shock to his daughter Joely, who was born in the same year and is a few months older. Interviewed by the author in Los Angeles in March 1996, Joely said: 'I didn't even know that he had met somebody until I saw a picture in a newspaper that someone gave to me, and asked if that was me in the photograph. I looked at it and it was definitely not me. I've been told I look a little bit like her. I'm not one to judge in terms of relationships and age because I've dated people of various ages, and if you're happy with someone and you love that person for who they are, it doesn't matter how old they are. I find it odd, though. I think I'm actually a few months older than her. I'm not sure. I just know we were born in the same year.

'Obviously she is a very different person from me. I've talked to her on the phone and she was very, very sweet and sincere to me and I'm not one to judge who my dad is happy with. If that's who he's chosen to be happy with, all the power to him. And that's great. I can't say if it's going to last. It's not my business what he does but I don't recommend he gets married again. And I've told him that. Who knows what the outcome of that relationship will be? I mean, when she's in her prime he will be old and grey. He won't be grey, he'll be bald! Or even balder!'

On stage at the height of his very public break with Jill, Phil told his audience not to believe everything they read in the papers about him. Reviewing his performance at the NEC in Birmingham, the first of sixteen dates on a British tour, in October 1994, Paul Sexton reported in the *Daily Telegraph* that Phil had walked on stage 'in his usual shirtsleeves and studied insouciance' to open the show with 'I Don't Care Anymore', a choice, the reviewer opined, that was 'deliberate and defiant'.

As public curiosity intensified, Jill complained that she couldn't take Lily to school in Sussex without being followed by photographers, and in Switzerland, Orianne's family was also being plagued. Orianne's grandfather was dying of cancer and her father was also ill, says Phil, at the time the press were on her doorstep pestering her for photographs. He made a deal with Richard Young, a well-known London music business photographer whom he trusted. Richard was to fly out to Geneva to meet Phil and Orianne and take half a dozen pictures of the couple together which would be circulated to all the newspapers and, hopefully, stem the harassment.

But the ploy didn't work. 'It didn't stop anything. The pictures [that Richard Young took] were on the front page of every newspaper – but they were still interested,' says Phil. The pictures of Orianne and Phil together also added to Jill's distress. 'That was another nail in the coffin of her trying to think that this might not be true.'

This time Jill did not fuel the media furore. Whereas in July she had spiritedly defended her marriage, by September she was keeping a low profile. Questioned by the *Daily Mail*, she said that what she wanted most now was to protect Lily from the glare of publicity. 'All I can say is that Phil has gone and he will do what he has to do . . . I can make no further comment.' In Switzerland, Orianne's friends were interviewed by the press. They described her as 'intelligent and funny', said that she had been educated at an exclusive school which charged fees of £20,000 a year, and confirmed that she spoke fluent English, French and German.

Once again a psychologist (a female this time) was asked to look into the inner psyche of Phil Collins. Dr Dorothy Rowe, writing in the *Daily Mail*, concluded that, despite his protestations, he *was* going through a midlife crisis and that for many men having a young girlfriend proved that their sexual prowess was as great as ever. Phil's big problem, the psychologist thought, was other people's reaction to his new love. 'He needs to be liked. It's not enough for him that one or two people might continue to like him. He needs everybody to like him.' She cited his issuing of a statement about the state of his marriage as 'a desperate attempt to get everybody on his side', adding: 'Phil, if you want my admiration you'll have to show me that you've learned two of the hard facts of life. The first is that, if you don't die young, you get old. The second is that you can't have your cake and eat it too. Follow your heart and some people won't like you.'

Phil Collins complains about the tabloids but he reads them himself, especially on tour when his request is usually for 'something with pictures', and there can be no dispute that his life, away from his work, has been remarkable for the number of ingredients on which tabloids thrive; he is a multimillionaire celebrity who has had two divorces, a very public affair and been responsible for writing some headline-gripping faxes.

A firebrand in his relationship with the media, Phil does not hesitate to react; he is well known for firing off faxes to journalists whose articles he does not like and will phone editors direct if he thinks he can influence what newspapers plan to publish about him. Criticism of his music, he says, used to affect him more than it does now. He has now come to the conclusion, he told the author in 1996, that 'I've made the music I've made and those in the audience [at concerts] are those who do like me and what I do. They are very loyal . . . I've come to terms with the fact that the real man who matters is the man in the street who puts his hand in his pocket and buys a ticket and an album, who has no preconceptions because he is too busy getting on with his life . . . but I still get very frustrated at the sort of article that criticizes my life.' He cited a particular article written by a journalist he'd never met based on things written by other people who didn't know him. 'The circle gets wider all the time and the relationship to the truth becomes less and less . . . I get frustrated with that sort of criticism because they [the writers] have the last word. Criticism in that respect bothers me.' He'd written letters to the person who wrote the recent offending piece, he admitted, but torn them up. 'I thought better of it.'

It has always annoyed him when people get the story wrong. Not even the music press escapes criticism. In the old days he says people read the music papers to decide what records they would buy, based on the reviews. They trusted the opinion of the reviewer. 'It's not like that any more.'

Phil's bizarre obsession with newspaper reviews marks him out as different from other musicians. Most players regard adverse comments on their work by newspapers as uninformed and to be discarded. Phil pores over every review, and becomes particularly angry if facts are wrong. He will phone or write to the reviewer. 'That always struck me as very strange,' remarks Bill Bruford. 'His work was way beyond people's comments. That was the tetchy side of his personality.' Conversely, too much loyalty from writers was not wanted by Phil, either. He told me that the uncritical enthusiasm from the *Melody Maker*'s Chris Welch, one of Genesis's most rabid fans in the press corps, he sometimes found to be 'a bit too much'.

Although he is known as an affable man, Phil tries hard to grapple with the self-imposed difficulties of his relationships. In the words of one observer, he is totally self-sufficient, does not need friends, and needs to focus on one woman in his life. He prefers to cocoon himself with his partner, while outwardly keeping friendships with literally hundreds of people alive on a superficial plane. 'He has a lot of cordial relationships, but they are at a very show-business level,' says Martin Lewis. 'I don't think that situation comes from his being in show business, but from his personality. If he was a window cleaner, it would be the same for him. To lots of people, it's "Hi, how are you?" but he doesn't let anybody in closely.'

Phil appears to concur with that assessment, responding in the spring of 1995 to the author's question about his relationships: 'I'm not very good at staying in touch. That's something that really angers me about myself. Trouble is that when you have to do, workwise, what I do, it's like the guys at the circus with the plates on the end of a stick. I've got two older kids, Joely and Simon, and they still need me; it's not like they're old enough to fly off and do their own thing. So I have to stay juggling, keeping in contact with everybody, especially as they [Simon and Joely] live in Canada.'

He said he did not have time to sit down and say: 'Hello, Eric [Clapton], how are you? I never do that. And he doesn't do it either but when we meet we always pick up where we left off. He's probably my best friend. I am very close to the road crew and I have friends down the pub but I would consider Eric to be one of my best friends, if not my best friend. I don't actually call up anybody for chats. I'm closer now to my family than I have been. I've always been close but I communicate with them more, my brother, sister and mother probably more in the past nine or ten months. I don't know if I'm good at relationships or not, really. The other day I was thinking that in 1975 I got married and then that stopped, then I was married again [in 1984] and that stopped. And now I'm with Orianne . . .'

'I don't want to hear songs about this on your next record,' Jill told Phil when they split, but Phil Collins has always written about how he feels. 'The angst, the personal experiences really fuel the fire of my writing,' he says. He ponders on whether or not he could write without these life experiences. 'I'd hate to think that I subconsciously put myself through the angst just because of the artistic results.' He admits, however, that he finds writing the sadder, more love lost songs easier than the happier more up-beat ones.

Suffering acutely at the time of his separation from his children and amid the dying embers of his marriage to Andrea, Phil marshalled a hitherto untapped ability to touch people. His anguish became his inspiration. Unwittingly he was to draw from deep within himself to create a new artist. His emotions raw, he felt both sadness and anger when he returned alone from Vancouver, having failed to patch up his marriage, and found other members of Genesis immersed in creating their solo albums. Retreating alone to his Surrey home, he began making music on the unsophisticated equipment in his small studio. The passion and despair in the songwriting and in his pained vocals reflected Phil's despondency at his doomed marriage. The songs formed his open-heart diary and messages to a wife who at the time, he says, would not even speak to him by telephone; and in those songs out tumbled the starkness and angst which would begin his new career as a trenchant, autobiographical songwriter. Titles Like 'If Leaving Me Is Easy' (featuring Eric Clapton on guitar), 'In the Air Tonight', 'I Missed Again', 'Thunder and Lightning' and 'You Know What I Mean' were powerfully cathartic. Alone at home he remembers 'crying his eyes out' and then drifting to the synthesizer to divert his energy into making music.

He explains in his own words: 'The first album happened because of the falling apart of my first marriage . . . and I'd been to school with my wife so I couldn't quite deal with that . . . she went to Canada to be with her mother and her sister who also lived over there . . . I had nothing else to do other than to start to try to work on this eight-track recording equipment I had bought, and the other guys had also bought. So I started to write. I was enjoying wallowing in it a bit. I had my aunt's grand piano, a Prophet synthesizer, a Fender Rhodes piano and a couple of drum machines and I just started mucking about, recording at the same time, adding a bit of this and that . . .' He found those early autobiographical songs therapeutic to write. 'I could only write about things that I knew about. I was resisting the Genesis way of doing it which was "what if?" songs. I could do that and had done it with Genesis, but I didn't find it that satisfying. In the early days when I wrote lyrics for Genesis they were in line with what Genesis did, that is, escapism, surrealistic story songs, but the more recent stuff with Genesis, like "No Son of Mine" which is actually about the real problem of abused kids, about fathers and mothers who abuse their children . . . that's more my kind of lyric. And yet on the same album there's "Driving the Last Spike", which is a pictorial history of the building of the railways.'

With Genesis Phil found himself fitting into what Genesis did, whereas what he preferred and found more fulfilling and satisfying, he says, was being able to write about anything he wished, as he could on his solo albums. When that first solo album, *Face Value*, was such a success both artistically and commercially, he was surprised when asked if he was embarrassed that people knew so much about him from his own songs. His response was always: 'No, not at all. This is to me what songwriting should be about.' But the reason Jill had said she didn't want to hear all about the break-up of her marriage to Phil on his next record was, he admits, 'because she had to hear all about what happened before on *Face Value*, and so did my first wife'. He stresses that some of the lyrics are ambiguous. ''But if you're looking for it, you're going to say: "That's about you, that's about us, that's about her."'

But he is not thinking about what other people's reactions might be when he is writing, other than 'Will they like this?' he maintains. Simplicity is always his aim when writing lyrics. 'If you're talking about love you only have a certain number of scenarios: boy meets girl, boy loses girl or boy finds girl; what's important is the way the story is told. One of my favourite songs is "If Leaving Me Is Easy", from my first album. I love that song because it is direct, simple, and there can be no argument about what it's about. To me the song arcs, it jumps over the difficult areas; it's not stodgy, not over-romantic, it is just direct and the direct aspect of the lyrics are what people go for.' The lyrics to most of his songs, he says, most of the ideas, verses or choruses or even whole songs, come while he is writing. 'I start playing and as I'm playing I may start singing and that will start the ball rolling. When I've got a two-minute or four-minute verse, chorus or whatever, I take the microphone and sing, and because I've been doing it like this for such a long time, instead of singing la-da-da I'll sing words and lines and whole verses. It's an open-thought process: whatever the music is making me actually feel if you like will be the kind of the direction I will go in.

'Now in the song "Can't Turn Back the Years" the words wrote themselves. I routed the microphone to the track and started singing what you hear on the album. There were holes: the third line or the sixth line might not have been there but what you hear was spontaneous and improvised. "I've Forgotten Everything", also on the *Both Sides* album, which is another of my favourite songs, was written and recorded in two hours and I never even wrote down the words. All that was improvised. "In the Air Tonight" was all improvised. I re-sang it, but my way of writing lyrics is not that of writing down on a piece of paper, it's actually singing spontaneously on three or four tracks of a multi-track and then listening to what I've sung and writing down anything that sounds like a word. If at the end of a line I sing something that sounds like a word, even though it isn't, I will try to find a word that sounds the same. So all the songs are based on gut feelings, gut reactions to what I felt at the time or what the music I've written has made me feel. Sometimes they both come together, sometimes the lyrics come in ten minutes, sometimes three furlongs past the music.

'The criticism I've always read about Genesis and my music, my albums, is that it always sounds clean, perfect, professional, and really most of the things you hear on my records are first or second takes; there's no slaving over a tape machine trying to get it right. I play with very good musicians who actually get it right first time or second time, and on *Both Sides*, when I was doing everything, I kept lots of things that weren't technically perfect by any means. I was playing bass with one hand and dropping in the machine with the other and sometimes if you isolated the bass track you could hear clicks all the time. I'm not a perfectionist from that point of view because I am only interested in the feel, whether the thing feels right or not. Until *Both Sides* I'd always worked with a co-producer, Hugh Padgham, and with Genesis there was always a period where the recording hat came off and suddenly someone put on a mixing hat and said: "Right, I know this has sounded great for the last three months, but now we're going to make it sound really great," and the whole thing was strained and strained and strained.' The simple way, Phil reminds us, is how recording used to be in the days of his idols, the Beatles, and the great bands he grew up with.

He puts songwriting on a different level from his other talents, 'because everything else is reproducing what you've done. The only time you actually do anything really new is when you're writing. To me, the writing and recording is pretty much the same stage because of the way I write. I'll get an idea and put it down on a multi-track so I can then sing and maybe the thing that will make that interesting will be a guitar part. I need the facility to be able to overlay things, to see if the idea is going to work.'

Being on stage he sees as 'presenting to people the best of your work, i.e. the work that has been popular and therefore people want to hear, mixed with a few of the things you think they should have heard.'

He is often asked whether he sees himself as a singer, drummer, actor or songwriter. 'On a different day, you'll get a different answer,' he says. 'I used to say that I was a drummer who sang. And I still think like a drummer when I'm writing. My writing has to be from there [drumming] upwards; and finding a drummer for the band . . . if I was having problems with that part of the band I'd be in big trouble. So I think of myself as a drummer, but I spend more time writing songs and singing them than I do anything else.'

He considers himself an entertainer, 'but there's a stigma in the word: Des O'Connor! Entertainer is what I am, I suppose, though I hate to say it. Then, when I'm acting I don't think about anything else other than what I'm doing then. The last two or three years have been pretty much non-stop music, so I'm much more of a singer than an actor.'*

He views his audience relationship as one of trust, mostly. 'Even if they didn't buy the album they'd come and see the show. If they had a choice of three or four people to see, they'd say: "Well, we know Phil's going to put on a good show." That kind of trust. I am aware of it; I do get the feedback of affection and I think it is because of a vulnerability, that I seem to be fallible. That has something to do with it. They know that I fucked up or I am capable of doing this, getting it wrong, having the same problems as them, and telling everybody and not trying to cover it up. And I think that's something that goes towards what people want.'

Did he want his audiences to leave a concert entertained by the show, or stimulated by the lyrics? 'I think most of them go away saying: "Good show." Because a lot of people don't think of it beyond that. The way the show finished is so up, and so light. The second half is deliberately like a steamroller party, so anything you told them in the first half, like in 'Another Day in Paradise', has an introduction that is usually slightly humorous. Because people will remember something they laughed at, rather than something they were told deeply and earnestly. I've always used the psychology that if an audience laughs, it relaxes. And it if relaxes, it listens and absorbs.

'In the early days of Genesis people used to sit there with notebooks making notes of tempo changes. Campus rock 'n'

* On a recent promotional tour Phil chatted happily about his life and work on the Des O'Connor show on TV.

roll! If you're telling stories, make 'em laugh. People relax and enjoy it more. Obviously it works both ways and to have a good speech on something, a serious speech, is just as effective. I've found it best to make them laugh first, then go in and say something that maybe they'll remember.'

In the first half of his show for the last tour, he said, 'Any feelings they've had, like during "Can't Turn Back the Years" . . . if a couple of people have had tears in their eye during that, or during 'Another Day in Paradise' or 'We Wait and We Wonder', which are actually songs about important things, I think by the time we come out at the end with 'Sussidio' or 'Take Me Home', they've forgotten.' Maybe in the car on the way home, people might be thinking about his serious stuff; maybe they would play the album to remind themselves, 'in the way that you see a movie and you watch the whole film and later you think about different scenes. And that's what the show is: a movie with different scenes in it.'

Apart from music, films are Phil Collins's great passion and he confesses to being moved to tears often by what he sees on screen, and by soundtrack albums. Dimitri Tiomkin's music for The Alamo, his favourite film, which he describes as 'a very sad, patriotic movie', makes him cry every time he hears it. He wept, too, watching Zeffirelli's film of Romeo and Juliet and when he heard Nino Rota's inspirational music. Rota's soundtrack album reached number four in the charts and so impressed the movie music maestro Henry Mancini that he did his own arrangement of the theme; Mancini's intrumental recording of 'The Love Theme' from Romeo and Juliet went to the top of the Billboard list in 1969. 'Like a lot of guys my age I was in love with Olivia Hussey [who played Juliet],' says Phil, remembering that he had auditioned for the part of Romeo himself when at stage school.

*   *   *

On stage, Phil Collins The Entertainer combines a laddish, matey accessibility with some extrovert running around that stems directly from his youth as an actor. 'I feel totally at home on stage,' he says. 'That came from doing the Dodger; I've never felt scared. Nervous yes, but scared, no. I'm not comfortable being an exhibitionist.' At a Johannesburg press conference, he disarmed the journalists and particularly the photographers by entering the room and telling them: 'All I do is sit down and stand up; I can sit down and smile or not smile; or I can stand up and do the same thing. You have four variations!' He has a good intuitive feeling about what the media wants, but feels reticent about preening. 'I always feel they want something more,' he reflected on the journalists, 'and that picture is going to make a difference.' In most places in the world, people knew what he did and didn't do, but in a new territory like South Africa, 'I feel there should be more coming from me. Why isn't there more? Whereas someone like Jagger and the late Freddie Mercury, they go out there and deliver more. But maybe that in itself makes what I do different, and therefore has a charm about it. I'm not forcing anything unnatural from myself.'

Despite all his professionalism and hard work Phil Collins can be engagingly discomfited by the resulting adulation. 'Sometimes it's almost embarrassing, actually,' he says. 'On stage there may be moments when I feel awkward, that I'm not worth the money people have paid in terms of what they are seeing.' Occasionally he has what he calls a 'grey day', when everything he does feels contrived or awkward or not enough to deserve the applause he receives. Then, he says, panic sets in as he wonders whether the audience is applauding because they are enjoying the show or because they are too embarrassed not to applaud.

Because of his familiarity with appearing on stage since his earliest years, large audiences hold no fears. 'I've always found walking on stage in front of a crowd of 10,000 or 20,000 much easier than walking into a room, like at a press conference, of twenty people applauding. I don't feel very comfortable in those situations.' He is uneasy with the 'star' label too. 'I feel a bit inadequate,' he says, 'and I get embarrassed by all the kerfuffle arriving at an airport.'

On his *Far Side of the World* tour in 1995, tour manager Deborah Sandvik found Phil less demanding than many of his contemporaries. 'Some artists want certain kinds of flowers or certain foods brought in and have very strict requirements about the size of bed they want and location of hotel rooms. Some are adamant that they want a suite.' Phil, she found, didn't care whether he had a suite or not, as long as he had space to set up his musical equipment, though he appreciated the availability of a steam room, as he takes a steam treatment every day on tour to keep his vocal chords in good working order. 'Some artists feel the need to be pampered and spoiled. Phil really isn't like that,' she says. He has only one 'special requirement', and that is for the herb tea that Brad Marsh, his drum technician, prepares for him before every show to soothe his throat. When travelling by train Deborah found Phil ambivalent about being put in first or second class. On the tour, which included 158 shows seen by 2 million fans in thirty-two countries, occasionally Phil would put on his baseball cap and walk around the streets unnoticed. 'I remember in Dublin I was walking back to the hotel and I saw this lonely figure wearing a baseball cap and glasses with a book under his arm and he seemed familiar. When he waved I realized it was Phil going out for a meal. Of course I was a little concerned about him walking down the street by himself.'

Since John Lennon's murder on 8 December 1980, many rock icons have cultivated an aura of inaccessibility, but Phil

Collins's appeal has always been based on what his fans perceive as a lack of remoteness. 'I'm the same person off stage as on,' he insists. 'I think one of the things people like about me is that I'm like one of them.' Film-maker Taylor Hackford elaborates on Phil's Everyman quality: 'He's reached incredible heights as a performer but every time I see him he's a down to earth guy, he has a deep well of talent that makes him secure; I love to watch him perform. He's unlike any other rock 'n' roll star because he's up there and he's kinda saying: "Hey, look at me, if I can do this, you can."'

Daryl Stuermer thinks Phil almost resisted stardom: 'I think he wanted success but not the hassle that goes with being a star. Because Phil looks like the average guy (he's good-looking but he's not like a TV hunk, doesn't dress like a movie star or a rock star), I think he wants to keep that certain level of the average guy but at the same time have the success of a pop star. He wants the credibility and to be very well known, he puts his face on the covers of his records so you know who he is, but at the same time he does not want everybody to be into his personal life.'

Many of his friends testify to how little success has changed Phil Collins over the years. Jack Gee, who knew him as a schoolboy queuing to get into the Marquee, went to see one of Phil's shows at Wembley over twenty years later. 'He was by now a superstar and Dennis Waterman and Rula Lenska were with him backstage but he rushed forward to see me. I couldn't believe it. He hadn't changed at all, he was not at all big time; we reminisced about his visits to the club.' Nathan East, who has known Phil since they worked together on Phil Bailey's *Chinese Wall* project, says: 'Success has not changed him one bit. He is always very humble and kind. I have a Christmas card from him every year.'

Phil works hard at creating a good impression and insists on good public relations from those who work for him. 'If Tony [Smith, his manager] or Carol [Willis Impey, his assistant at the management company Hit and Run Music] are a bit hard on people I say: "Listen, don't be, because they will think that is the way I am." It matters to me that people are impressed with the crowd I have around me; every time we do a show people say they've never worked with such a nice bunch of guys.'

His attention to detail is legendary. He refuses to have photographs for fans with his signature imprinted and signs every one personally. As well as being actively involved in the minutiae of the look of album and CD covers and handwriting the labels, he still wants to know how they are going to be advertised and what the posters will look like. Until four years ago he even answered his own letters. Now he has a secretary based in Guildford. He still has no press agent.

For a man who hates racism, loves black music and has always worked with black musicians, the accusations that followed a chance remark Phil made at the *Billboard* Music Awards ceremony in December 1993 were particularly distressing. He was hosting the show at the Universal Amphitheatre in Universal City, California, which was broadcast on television, and among the winners was Dr Dre. 'I'd listened to Dr Dre because I felt I had to check out why this album had sold between 6 and 8 million copies and I couldn't believe it. What they say is so negative. Fortunately rap is changing now, you get bands like Boyz II Men, Warren G, rappers who have melody. But after Dr Dre came up on stage to collect their awards the atmosphere changed completely; it had been a very light evening and I said: "It's suddenly got dark in here," meaning the atmosphere.' The backlash at the time, and afterwards, was considerable. The following night Phil appeared on the *Arsenio Hall Show* and defended himself against the racist charges: 'I said: "As a musician I am trying to build bridges across some of this racial trouble with songs like 'Both Sides of the Story' and these rappers are digging ditches to make the problem bigger by singing 'get a gun and kill the white mother fucker'. Surely this is wrong?" There is still racism in music with rap.'

For Phil, who has always admired and worked with black musicians, this was not his first personal encounter with racism in music. Recalling the time he produced Philip Bailey, he recounts: 'Philip met a black American DJ who was very powerful at the time, who asked him, "What are you going to England for?" Philip said, "To do an album with Phil Collins." The DJ's reply was: "Don't make no soft white album, boy, because we ain't gonna play it."' Phil and Phil made the record, and one of the tracks, 'Easy Lover', which they co-wrote, was a hit in the black music charts, as was Collins's 'Sussudio' a few months later.

Phil's friend from stage school, Peter Newton, confirms that Phil came from a family where racism was anathema. 'Phil's dad, a traditional Englishman who addressed people as "old bean" and "old boy", welcomed me with open arms; a black boy in East Acton was unusual at that time.'

'He does nothing spontaneously, he has his life mapped out'

'**I** go out there and do the best I possibly can every night, forget about whatever is in the back of my mind before I go on and try to play and sing as well as possible. And I fully expect everybody else to be doing the same.' Phil Collins is tough on himself and tough on those who work for him. He does not suffer fools gladly and will not accept second best. Sometimes you get the feeling that he is concealing a volcanic temper, that his fuse could blow at any moment and that he is only too well aware of that fact.

Greg Phillinganes, who first worked with Phil on Eric Clapton's album *August*, finds him 'demanding and bossy – but appreciative' and Nathan East, who was seventeen when he first joined Phil's band, describes him as 'Driven, just driven . . . To work with Phil you've got to get up really early and have your stuff together. Because otherwise you won't make the bill. He's challenging.' Daryl Stuermer, who has played alongside Phil for many years, too, says: 'The only time he flies off is

when he thinks someone is incompetent. You know you're
doing all right if you're not told you've done wrong. It's not
Phil's style to say: "You're fantastic" – occasionally he will
say: "That's great, I like that," but it's never over the top. Phil
knows me probably better than anyone else in the band and
I know him better than probably anyone else. I don't have to
tell him he's fantastic and visa versa.'

Chester Thompson remarks that Phil has always been a tough
taskmaster who works himself, as well as his musicians, very
hard, and Nathan East, who considers Phil to be one of the
hardest-working musicians he knows, remembers that on . . .
But *Seriously* Phil was always the first to arrive at the recording
studio. 'Our schedule was midday to midnight and at twelve
midday Phil was ready to go. Dinner was at 7 p.m. and if at
6.45 p.m. we'd finished with a song he'd put up another,
work for fifteen minutes, go to eat and at 7.45 p.m., while
he was still chewing, he was on his way back to the studio. I
have never seen anything like it. So much output, productivity,
energy and life.'

Nathan sees Phil as 'a true leader' who pushes for perfection.
'You can make a mistake, but he wants you to know that you
made a mistake and that he knows. He's really demanding,
but he's careful about the way he puts things. He has radar,
there's not one note that you can slip past him. Not one
light bulb can be out without him noticing it. There may
be ten people on stage besides himself and I've played one
note out of place and got a turn of the head that showed
that he knew. I've worked with some really great people:
George Benson, Anita Baker, Eric Clapton, Randy Newman,
all perfectionists who work very hard, and like Phil none of
them would ever let anything get out to the public that was
not of the highest quality. What I learned from working with
Phil is his attitude that you can demand more from yourself

than anyone else would ever demand from you; and that rubs off.'

Setting up a drummer's kit is like dealing with his heartbeat. Brad Marsh, Phil's drum technician, found working for Phil, whom he refers to by the nickname Elvis, 'like working for an angel compared with Prince', one of his previous employers. 'Everybody says Phil is meticulous and demands perfection and if he doesn't get it, once in a while he gets testy, but if he does it's deservedly so,' says Brad. Since Phil is left-handed and Brad right-handed, at first he found it odd setting up Phil's equipment. 'If you're right-handed you play your hi-hat and cymbals with your right hand and your snare drum with your left for the most part and your bass drum with your right foot and your hi-hat with your left. If you are left-handed you play the opposite. I made a mistake and got reprimanded and I deserved it. It didn't happen again. If ever Phil comes down on you, you don't make the same mistake again.'

But although he is respected by his fellow musicians primarily for his professionalism, Phil's sense of humour is also renowned. Nathan East remembers many occasions on stage when Phil has had the band in hysterics and recalls Phil often diffusing potentially difficult situations with a joke.

Phil soundchecks punctiliously, says Nathan. 'If you play the same things five days in a row he will soundcheck five days in a row.' His obsession for checking that things are OK spills over into his personal life too. He admits to returning home time after time after he's locked the door to make sure the oven is turned off. 'And on my way to the airport the other day I turned around and came back to check I'd locked the door . . . I had.'

When Phil was producing Eric Clapton's album in Montserrat he confesses that he drove Eric's band 'a lot harder than they are normally driven . . . I tend to work twelve till twelve and Eric works twelve till four, two till six or something. I work long hours because I enjoy it . . . after the first week or so Eric said, "I think we should back off a little bit, give the boys some rest." '

He readily admits he can be tough with his own band. 'I'm by no means a dictator but I have got hold of the wheel,' he says. If he spots a mistake, a wrong note or thinks a musician might have played something slightly differently with better effect he will tell them immediately after the show. 'Even when I come off stage at the interval I will get my roadie to remind me of something I want to bring up later. If I have something to say I have to say it before I forget, or it might happen again. It's probably not psychologically the best thing to do, to go in after a show and say what's wrong because then I find myself digging a hole and saying, "The rest of it was great." ' He is not aiming for perfection, he insists, but 'completeness'.

Greg Phillinganes, who has also worked with Eric Clapton and Stevie Wonder, admires Phil and has great respect for him as 'a total musician who does his homework' and is meticulous. 'It's scary,' he says. 'He has a set-up on stage for when things go wrong. He can go in the corner and talk into a mike . . . he is literally taking notes during the performance. I think it's great. You have to respect the guy.' He marvels, too, at Phil's singing: 'I just don't understand how he sings night after night, his vocal chords must be made out of plutonium or something. I've worked with some artists who, if they sneeze they don't do a show, but this guy, man, could have one leg, one arm, be bleeding out of the side and have a strep throat and be brought out on a stretcher and it would still be: "Boom . . . let's go." That's why he has the audience he has and why he makes big bucks.'

Just quite how many bucks Phil Collins makes is uncertain, but in the *Sunday Times*'s 1996 survey of the 500 richest people in Britain he was listed at number 140, along with landowners the Duke of Beaufort and the Marquess of Salisbury. All three were estimated to have fortunes conservatively put at £115 million. Phil's entry, based on the 1994 accounts of Philip Collins Limited, pointed out that he had taken a £17 million pay cut, the largest ever in Britain. Some of his business ventures, including a salmon farm and an estate company, according to the *Sunday Times* survey, proved to be much less successful than his music, however. Phil's divorce from Jill, the *Sunday Times* noted, was reputed to have cost him 'at least £17 million.' Among the 'music millionaires' Phil was listed number six, after Andrew Lloyd Webber, Paul McCartney, Cameron Mackintosh, Robert Stigwood and Elton John. Eric Clapton came in at number thirteen. In February 1996 the *Observer* (using 1993 figures) had put Phil at the top of the list of the UK's highest-earning rock stars, with annual earnings of £24.286 million. The point was made that 'UK artists are responsible for 24 per cent of the global market'.

Another survey, published in *Labour Research* magazine in 1995, put Phil as the second highest-paid director in the UK, earning £22.28 million in the previous financial year, an increase of 110.1 per cent on the year before. The top spot went to Bernie Ecclestone of Formula One Promotions. Elton John was listed at number four and Eric Clapton at number seven.

'The music business is earning more overseas income for Britain than the armaments, china and brewing industries,' reported *The Times* the same year, adding: 'Recording artists such as Elton John, Eric Clapton and Phil Collins earned £1.158 billion gross overseas in 1993, compared with £307 million earned by armaments, excluding aircraft; china and ceramics, £392 million, and brewing, £216 million.' The news story was based on a report by British Invisibles, the trade association which promotes Britain's invisible exports.

But Phil Collins is not a natural multimillionaire. 'He doesn't know how to enjoy his money,' says his first wife, Andrea. 'He doesn't have houses all around the world or live the lifestyle of the rich and famous. He tries to live like an ordinary person with all this money.' And Phil says himself that money has never been his motivation. As a teenager he expected to play in a band 'until the bubble burst' and then end up in a pit orchestra.

His mother remembers Phil having a number of lean years when he first became a musician. 'It used to worry me because he would ask me for money and I'd say, "But you've been playing every night for two weeks, doesn't that get you any money?" And he'd say: "Oh, no they [his employers] haven't got any money so I can't have any." I couldn't understand that and it went on for years, him playing for free. He'd say, "But I love playing, it doesn't matter about the money." As a businesswoman I thought, "This isn't right."' Even now, it seems, Phil can scarcely believe his good fortune. He saves for a rainy day like his mother and father taught him, he says.

Phil's manager, Tony Smith, confirms that he has always been ill at ease with the trappings of fame. And Jill's friend Megan Taylor is convinced that Phil doesn't actually know or care how much money he has. 'I'm sure the divorce settlement was the first time he ever reviewed the figures,' she says.

Success and a big house with a swimming pool and tennis court would not be allowed to cloud Phil's frugality. Showing his friend Ronnie Caryl round his new home in Sussex for the first time, they walked into the biggest room to take a look at the piano, and Phil flicked a switch to light up an avenue of trees outside. Ronnie remarked on its beauty, and then Phil switched the light off. 'Why have you turned it off?' asked a puzzled Ronnie. 'I got the first electricity bill,' Phil replied, 'and it was £800. I'm not having that.' He had been checking the oil levels to get the most economical temperature for the central heating system. 'And he was marking it with a pencil,' Ronnie recalls. 'I asked how much he was earning. I can do that with him. And he told me. And I thought: "You're really worried about electricity bills and oil levels?"

'But he explained to me that he puts himself on a wage, or tries to, and tries to live within it. So that when the bills come in, he can feel that they are somewhere near reality. I don't think he has the ability to spend money. I think it's absolutely wonderful what he does for charity, but he doesn't really seem to know how to have fun.' Ronnie remembers Phil admiring a pair of Armani trousers and a jacket that Eric Clapton was wearing and asking how much they cost, and Eric replying: 'Phil, you could buy one hundred pairs of these trousers and a hundred of these jackets every day. You don't have to worry about it any more.' Phil would find it difficult to justify that kind of expenditure says Ronnie.

Phil's attitude to his phenomenal wealth has always been 'Why not give some back?' and he has gained a reputation for being a tireless worker for charity. He abhors waste. Looking round his sumptuous hotel accommodation on tour he said to the author: 'I could have done with a room a quarter this size and the rest of the cost could have gone somewhere more useful.' The free champagne and other generous gifts heaped on him make him uncomfortable. 'And when I think of the money that Eric [Clapton] and I used to spend on a Versace suit ... well, instead of buying another suit why not give the money to somebody else?'

He is, he admits 'riddled with guilt ... I don't know why.' Collections for the homeless are a familiar part of his concerts and he makes personal donations to a variety of good causes, including children's charities and an organization called Promat, which specializes in funding the teaching of black teachers, to which he has given nearly 3 million rand. 'Everything Phil earns in relation to record royalties in South Africa goes straight to Promat,' says Tony Smith.

From time to time he gives to needy people on an individual basis. 'Ever since Live Aid and the story came out that I loaned eight grand to a guy who came to my front door [he paid me back] I get loads of letters asking me for money. My secretary Annie is very good at weeding out the ones that are really really needy, like the person who needs a new wheelchair and the kid who needs a guide dog or whatever. I feel great about that, about helping people individually, as well as supporting things like the Prince's Trust. I like to get involved, to meet the people involved with the charities we collect for at the gigs.'

In 1994 Phil was made a Lieutenant of the Victorian Order for his charity work, and at the time of writing he had just been nominated Person of the Year by MusiCares, the musicians' charity, set up by the recording artists' organization, NARAS.

Phil's philanthropic streak was in evidence early in his life. When he and Phil were both in *Oliver!* as teenagers, Jack Wild recalls that one Christmas the youngsters in the show went carol singing to raise money for Doctor Barnardo's. 'We had a placard that announced us, "all the boys from the show, *Oliver!*" . . . the management was not pleased. We sang our hearts out and got sore throats for the show.'

A sign of Phil's meticulously tidy mind, as well as his watchful eye over the minutiae of his finances, came in the Brand X years. He was leaving a recording session at the Trident Studios in Soho; it was Christmas-time, and in heavy traffic he had parked his car at Hyde Park Corner and got a taxi into the centre of London. Tony Smith recalls: 'We came out of the studio and he said: "I'll have to get a cab back to the car park.

I haven't got any money. Can you lend me some money?" So I gave him a fiver. Standing there in Wardour Street, he wrote a cheque out for this £5 and gave it to me, which was funny in itself.'

Smith stuck the cheque in his pocket and forgot he had it. About three weeks later he was sitting at home on a Sunday, preparing to have lunch. 'The phone rang. It was Phil. "You know that cheque I gave you?" "Yeah?" "You haven't cashed it yet." Phil explained that he could not get his bank statement to balance. Smith tells the story as highly indicative of the man, then and now. 'That could take place tomorrow. He is not into money, but he is interested in making sure that everything is in its right place.'

Phil is also concerned to see fair play. When one of his American concerts was recorded and put out on CD in Germany without his consent, he brought injunction proceedings in 1992 to stop further distribution by the record company; as a result of his challenge in the Munich State Court the scope of Article 6 of the EC Treaty was judged to extend the protection of copyright and performers' rights under German law equally to members of other EEA countries as well as German nationals. The case set an important precedent.

It was in June 1993 that Phil first realized he was on the way to leaving Genesis. The catalyst was the making of his album *Both Sides* which was released in November of that year. Even though he had done several solo albums, 'That was the first time I was being totally me, really baring my soul, playing everything. And it was in my home studio so it was really do-it-yourself, warts and all.'

While he was mixing the album, Mike Rutherford, because of his involvement with polo and with charities, had asked Genesis to play for a charity show at Cowdray Park. He assembled a rock conglomerate of musicians interchanging in a band including Eric Clapton, Pink Floyd, and members of Queen. Mike Rutherford was the musical director.

Phil felt that he was creating, with *Both Sides*, his most powerfully personal album. When he came to appear on stage with Genesis, 'I really felt that I didn't belong there [at Cowdray Park]. I felt like I was an actor. Because I had come from doing something that was totally me . . . and then suddenly I was in this group in another place. We sang four or five songs, and three or four of them I'd written the lyrics to which is even stranger. But I couldn't convince myself. And that was the final thing.' He felt privately of Genesis that 'It was fun and it was great and there was some work to be proud of, but I don't know if I want to do it any more.'

It was three years later, on 29 March 1996, that Phil Collins announced he was quitting Genesis to concentrate on his solo career. Many wondered what took him so long. News of the break came in an official statement from Hit and Run Music, curiously headed: 'Genesis end 20 year experiment, decide to replace Peter Gabriel as vocalist.' Phil's twenty-year stint with the band as singer was described as 'temping', and the announcement explained that Phil had 'decided to move on in order to concentrate on his solo projects'. Mike Rutherford was sympathetic. 'I quite understand Phil's reasons for leaving – being in two highly successful outfits is very hard work.' And Tony Banks added: 'Of course we'll miss him. We have had some fantastic times together.' Phil, underlining that the parting was amicable, spoke of the last album the group had done together, *We Can't Dance*, as 'the best album, the most fun to write'.

After leaving Genesis, Phil declared that as well as pursuing his solo career as a writer and performer he planned to do more music for movies; and he hoped other acting roles in films would be forthcoming. A comic version of *The Three Bears* with Bob Hoskins and Danny De Vito was mentioned, a project which he has talked about for some time but which has not yet taken off.

After *Buster*, the director David Green expected Phil to go on to a 'Brilliant film career ... certainly as good as Frank Sinatra's thirty or forty years before. Sinatra was a very good actor and kept his music career running as well. I think Phil Collins could have done that. I hope it's not too late. My guess is that he hasn't missed the boat. He is still in his forties and Hollywood is still there.' Hollywood's verdict on Phil's performance in *Buster*, according to David Green, was that he had talent and ability. Later, he remembers: 'He had a little part in a film called *Hook* which came to nothing and a couple of other flirtations – he was in a gay rights movie, *And the Band Played On*, and he did *Frauds*, which was a disaster – I'm sad that he's not done more; I would certainly like to work with him again.'

Tony Smith, Phil's manager, says that Phil has had two or three offers of roles in fairly major movies in the past twelve months but has not been available to do them. 'Two years ago it was all movies; he spent a lot of time in Los Angeles meeting people and putting his face around,' says Smith. 'He's still interested in doing the right roles but there is not quite the same impetus as when he was still with Jill and they had a house in LA.'

Phil says himself that he 'really loves' making films. 'It's a great challenge because I don't do it very often; I get a great buzz when I put on my acting hat.' He would like to do more, he says, but that would mean spending time away from Switzerland, where he now lives with Orianne. 'I've found a little nest here and I really am the happiest I've been for years, and filming probably means having to leave. When Orianne's business is up and running we want to work it so with technology the way it is she can work out of hotels so she could be away as long as I need to be. I am serious about doing more acting in the long term but I'm still recoiling from what's happened in my personal life. I've found peace now and I want to enjoy that.'

It is a peace that has been a long time coming, due in no small part to the public's seemingly insatiable appetite for information about Phil's private life. The very public wrangling over his divorces has led to some unkind digs at the man who had hitherto been dubbed the Housewives' Choice. In January 1995, when *Cosmopolitan* named Prince Charles the most hated man in Britain, Phil, along with David Mellor and James Hewitt, appeared in the list of 'love rats'. His attempts to redress the balance by giving numerous personal interviews to journalists continue even though he now lives permanently in Switzerland.

For the first time he can remember, Phil had the experience of spending several months doing nothing and enjoying it when he and Orianne first moved to Hermance, near Geneva. His friends comment on his new-found personal contentment. 'As soon as I saw Orianne,' says Peter Newton, 'I thought she was the absolute composite of the great loves of Phil's life all in one.' 'With Orianne he seems to be genuinely happy,' says Ronnie Caryl. 'I met them both at a backstage party in Paris and Phil's new family was there and there was a wonderful spread of seafood, oysters and champagne and suddenly Phil said: "This is great, I'm actually enjoying myself." Maybe for the first time, he actually admitted he was having fun.' It is left to producer Hugh Padgham to question, reluctantly, the effect Phil's new relaxed life could have on his music. 'I love the guy dearly and I am very happy that he's happy. The only thing that worries me is that happiness does not bring out the best in musicians.'

Despite the fact that Phil is one of rock's royalty, delivering immaculate concerts and beautifully refined records, he faces criticism from many who were initially his admirers. The theory is that he took the soft option in his music, that he no longer walks the artistic highway of *Face Value*, but has settled for something more conservative. This criticism is only one step behind the cynical view that 'Mr Nice Guy' is too wimpish, and somehow not dangerous enough, to be a valid artist. This is transparent nonsense, overlooking a central fact about Phil Collins and his music. In my view he has never been a hardcore rock artist; he is much more of a Frank Sinatra than a Robert Plant; more of a Ray Charles than a Randy Newman.

Phil dispenses high-quality, wide-ranging popular music. He does not need to be aligned with the rock fraternity in particular, because his interest and talent is infinitely wider than most of the artists who populate it. Fundamentally, he's a musician from whom a splash of cabaret, also, has become expected.

Nevertheless, there is a core of attack which brands him too soft. 'Phil is like one of those really nice, smooth pebbles that you pick up off the beach and skim. He skims across things,' says his old friend and admirer Martin Lewis. 'He's a little bit of everything; there's no *there* with Phil. Listen to *Face Value*. Here's a man who needs to be permanently in pain, starving in a garret, in emotional torture, to give his best work.'

Asserting the time-honoured theory that the more domesticated Phil gets, the more bland the songs become, Martin Lewis states: 'He's well-meaning, but there isn't a substance to Phil. I don't think he's very deep intellectually; he's bright but not that bright. Either that or he is intimidated by brightness because there is a something about him, a veneer quality about his perceptions of the world. I don't think he has a world view, but a blinkered view on life. He seems unadventurous, lacking a sense of curiousity.

'He must have been immensely proud of what he achieved on *Face Value* and on some of the songs on *Hello, I Must Be Going*. But to have continued on in that vein would have necessitated him being in touch with his feelings. I think Phil, the minute he was through that intense pain, was so glad to get it behind him again, and he doesn't have anything further to say personally. Woody Allen said that if there is a God, the very least you'd have to say is that he's a bit of an under-achiever. Phil Collins has achieved a state in his career which holds up well. He's on the radio all the time; we're not getting sick of him. But I think he touched greatness. He could return to it if he wanted to. But he's gone for the soft option, the easy way out. He is not driven, and has not pushed or stretched himself. He has a good heart. He's not malicious or evil. Quite the reverse. But he's undercut by an artistic laziness. Is he a nice guy? Yes, he is. But there is a lack of depth to the niceness. He was never ruthless with me. He was at worst distracted and nonchalant.'

Phil's sensibility had shifted from rock around the time of his fourth album, says Hugh Padgham. 'And he had so much influence at that time, he could have asked anybody to take part in his work. I thought: OK, Phil writes great pop songs, but pop songs can be shallow and he has the ability to write with a bit more depth.' Agreeing with the theory that Collins took the middle-ground option, becoming an entertainer rather than an artist, Padgham declared in 1995: 'I think he needs to get his credibility back together as a musician and a drummer. He was regarded in the hierarchy of musicians as being one of the best drummers in the world, and also a fantastic singer ... To me, the person singing 'Groovy Kind of Love' is a

consummate pop star, but that isn't the same Phil. I see him
as a much more serious musician and I wish that was able to
come out more on his records.' He is in such a strong position
with his record company now, says Padgham, that 'as long as
he's got a couple of good pop songs on an album, he can do
what the hell he likes on the rest of the record. Obviously
record companies get confused if you have two pop songs
and a lot of Miles Davis-type jazz. You can't be as diverse
as that. But in a way he can put one finger up to the record
company.'

Summarizing his trenchant views on Phil, Martin Lewis adds:
'If he'd never done *Face Value*, it wouldn't matter. But he *has*
done that album, and he has touched real life. He slid away
from it. He could have been a John Lennon, but opted to
be a Paul McCartney.' Even though it contains a germ of
validity, such waspishness implies that there is some shame
in being McCartney, whose body of work, in and out of the
Beatles, lifts him well beyond the confines of rock. Paul is
also the world's most successful songwriter. If Phil Collins
has sinned by somehow following a similar route, he can
hardly be accused of veering off-course from his eclectic tastes
in music.

An incurable romantic, even in his teenage years, Phil is
remembered by his peers at stage school for not being afraid
to show his emotions. Peter Newton recalls one occasion
when he and Phil were practising harmonies with the rest
of their school pop group, The Real Thing, and Phil broke off
and suddenly began serenading Lavinia. 'He sang "I've Been
Trying", right through, while we all watched, squirming —
Lavinia, of course, was loving it. Even at fifteen Phil was very
mature. When he loves someone, a woman, a man or a child,
he has no qualms about showing it,' says Newton.

At a charity concert in Los Angeles with Plácido Domingo, Diana Ross, Neil Diamond and Natalie Cole, Phil surprised many there by singing the evergreen Jerome Kern love song, 'The Way You Look Tonight'. Quincy Jones, who was in the audience, went backstage after the show to see Phil. 'He admired the way I'd sung that song, saying, "I forget you sing, I think of you as a drummer,"' recalls Phil. The meeting led to a new musical direction for Phil and a big boost to his confidence. 'It was wonderful having had a battering from the English press, because of the divorce, for someone to say, "Man, this sounds great, I'd love to do an album with you."' In a studio in Zürich, with Quincy Jones producing in Los Angeles, Phil recorded Duke Ellington's 'Do Nothing Till You Hear from Me' on Q's Jook Joint. 'Gloria Estefan and I are the only white people on the record,' says Phil. 'Other tracks include Ray Charles.'

Quincy Jones, who remembered watching Duke Ellington leading Al Hibbler (both dressed in white) to the spotlight to sing the tune on stage, commented on Phil's rendition: 'I know in my heart that if Duke were here he wouldn't be able to resist the urge to say, "I love you madly."'

Working with Quincy Jones made Phil ponder on whether he should return to working with a producer again on his own albums, rather than doing so much himself. 'Sometimes I'm better off when I don't hold the reins . . . one side of me thinks only I know really how I want my stuff to sound but maybe I should let it go.' Future plans at the time of writing include a big band album, probably with Quincy, featuring another of Phil's musical idols, Tony Bennett. He remembers asking Bennett for his autograph in an Italian restaurant in St Louis. 'It was on my first solo tour. I said: "Excuse me, Mr Bennett, could I have your autograph?" He said: "Sure." I said: "I'm a singer too," and he replied: "Well, good luck."' A few years later Bennett interrupted his show to announce: 'We have in the audience one of the finest contemporary songwriters . . . Phil Collins.' Phil is still star-struck as he discusses his plan to work with Bennett. 'Tony Bennett and the Phil Collins Orchestra . . . wow.' He wants to tour with Bennett with a big band, 'about twenty-two people on a bus doing the jazz festivals at Montreux, Nice and Antibes and various small concert halls around Europe'.* He is also working on the music for Walt Disney's *Tarzan*, due out in 1998.

Phil the Romantic enjoys listening to ballads as much as he enjoys the sharper R & B music. On tour in the early days of his romance with Orianne, he recalls returning to his hotel room and, after phoning her, putting on Tony Bennett's tribute album to Frank Sinatra, *Perfectly Frank*, every night. Another favourite was Charlie Watts's *Warm and Tender*. 'You'd never dream it was by the Rolling Stones' drummer,' he remarks. Phil, who is still in awe of his idols despite having got to know many of them personally, was surprised and delighted when Watts, who was rehearsing in Toronto when Phil was playing there, came to visit and see his show. 'He said he'd bought my latest record. The thought of Charlie Watts going to a record shop and buying one of my records completely threw me.' It was many years after they became friends before Phil, who kept scrapbooks of newspaper and magazine cuttings of all his favourite bands in his teens, confessed to Eric Clapton: 'I have a scrapbook of your past.'

Phil is not religious, but after being introduced by Eric to the pre-concert 'huddle' he adopted the practice of a few quiet moments with fellow musicians before going on stage. 'We put our arms round each other in a big circle and take it in

* Since writing, Bennett and Collins have toured together, with Quincy Jones conducting.

turns to say a prayer. It's a very spiritual moment. We pray for the crew and hope the audience go away with a smile on their face; it's a nice thing to do.'

To his mother, every son is wonderful, and June Collins's view of Phil is no exception. 'He's so caring,' she says. 'As a child he was marvellous to my mother when she was old and ill. When she had to go into a home he'd go along and entertain her and the other residents; she loved that.' She describes the happy holiday she spent recently with Phil and Orianne in Switzerland: 'He went out of this way to give me a lovely time.' He has always phoned home regularly, but these days his calls are more spontaneous and she was thrilled when he recently called her on impulse from his boat in the middle of Lake Geneva simply to say he was feeling great. June Collins hesitates to comment, but admits she worries that Phil often wonders if people are being nice to him because of who he is. 'It does rankle; it's a question he's always asking. Plenty of girls would like to go out with him. They say to me: "Introduce me to him, I'll be a good wife." I feel sorry for him really. He gives pleasure to so many people and what has he got apart from money? Not a lot really. Orianne is lovely, a lovely girl, but I've seen it all before – twice. We all want the best for our kids but I don't know. I had dinner with Bert Weedon and he asked me how I felt about Phil and Orianne. I said: "She's a lovely girl but the only thing I worry about is the difference in age, it's like talking to my granddaughter." Bert replied: "Well, if it's any consolation to you there's twenty years difference between my wife and me and we're as happy as anything." And when I talked about it to Paul Daniels and his wife Debbie, Paul said: "Think nothing of it, we're as happy as anything and there's twenty-two years difference in our ages." Orianne is what I'd call an old twenty-four-year-old. I just hope she doesn't change, and if she does, I hope I'm not around to pick up the pieces.'

Phil, sitting in his local restaurant in Hermance, a few minutes along the lakeside from his home, wearing his customary baseball cap as he tucks into the local speciality, perch and frites, washed down with fizzy water, exudes the impression of a man utterly content with his lot. After a year's stand-off he is now back in frequent contact with his older children, Joely and Simon, and Lily comes to see him and Orianne on regular visits. His divorces, from one woman who stayed behind when he toured and another who accompanied him round the world, and an intense romance with an old flame, now confined to the past, he has even started to walk more slowly alongside whoever he is with. He has noticed recently an astonishing new development: his hair has started to grow! 'Maybe it's because I am happy.'

As he drives around Geneva in his immaculately kept sleek black jeep or potters along in his motorboat or lies out in the sun reading biographies, he is, as his great friend Eric Clapton has done many times before, in the process of 're-inventing' himself, he says. 'Dad does nothing spontaneously, he has his life mapped out,' comments his daughter Joely.

People expect all rock stars to come with a chippy attitude. Phil Collins, articulate and street sharp, came with *none* – just flawless musicianship, strong songs and a fine voice. He is not a rock singer with attitude, but a singer of popular music more in common with Sinatra and Tony Bennett than with Robert Plant or Michael Jackson. His solo albums have sold 70 million copies and with Genesis he has sold 100 million. His total worldwide record sales (including singles) are put at 200 million. The figures speak for themselves.

His fans and his friends wish him well for the future. After a turbulent life lived, particularly in recent years, in the full glare of the media, they think he deserves a period of peace and calm in his middle years. He is, after all, still a nice guy. It falls to Joely to strike a resonant if heartfelt postscript. In a letter to her father soon after she learned of his new romance she pleaded: 'Please don't have any more kids.'

Discography

SOLO

Face Value
   (16029–2/Atlantic, 1981) (Virgin V 2185, 1981)
'In the Air Tonight', 'This Must Be Love', 'Behind the Lines',
'The Roof Is Leaking', 'Droned', 'Hand in Hand', 'I Missed
Again', 'You Know What I Mean', 'Thunder and Lightning',
'I'm Not Moving', 'If Leaving Me Is Easy', 'Tomorrow Never
Knows'.

Hello, I Must Be Going!
   (80035–2/Atlantic, 1982) (Virgin V 2252, 1982)
'I Don't Care Anymore', 'I Cannot Believe It's True', 'Like
China', 'Do You Know, Do You Care?', 'You Can't Hurry
Love', 'It Don't Matter to Me', 'Thru These Walls', 'Don't Let
Him Steal Your Heart Away', 'The West Side', 'Why Can't It
Wait til Morning'.

No Jacket Required
   (81240–2/Atlantic, 1985) (Virgin V 2345, 1985)
'Sussudio', 'Only You Know and I Know', 'Long Long Way to
Go', 'I Don't Wanna Know', 'One More Night', 'Don't Lose

My Number', 'Who Said I Would', 'Doesn't Anybody Stay Together Anymore', 'Inside Out', 'Take Me Home', 'We Said Hello Goodbye'.

12″ ERS
   (81847–2/Atlantic, 1988)
'Take Me Home', 'Sussudio', 'Who Said I Would', 'Only You Know and I Know', 'Don't Lose My Number', 'One More Night'.

... But Seriously (82050–2/Atlantic, 1989)
   (Virgin V 2620, 1989)
'Hang In Long Enough', 'That's Just the Way It Is', 'Do You Remember?', 'Something Happened on the Way to Heaven', 'Colours', 'I Wish It Would Rain Down', 'Another Day in Paradise', 'Heat on the Street', 'All of My Life', 'Saturday Night and Sunday Morning', 'Father to Son', 'Find a Way to My Heart'.

Serious Hits ... Live!
   (7 82157–2/Atlantic, 1990) (Virgin PCLP 1, 1990)
'Something Happened on the Way to Heaven', 'Against All Odds (Take a Look at Me Now)', 'Who Said I Would', 'One More Night', 'Don't Lose My Number', 'Do You Remember?', 'Another Day in Paradise', 'Separate Lives', 'In the Air Tonight', 'You Can't Hurry Love', 'Two Hearts', 'Sussudio', 'A Groovy Kind of Love', 'Easy Lover', 'Take Me Home'.

Both Sides
   (82550–2/Atlantic, 1993) (Virgin CDV 2800, 1993)
'Both Sides of the Story', 'Can't Turn Back the Years', 'Everyday', 'I've Forgotten Everything', 'We're Sons of Our Fathers', 'Can't Find My Way', 'Survivors', 'We Fly So Close', 'There's a Place for Us', 'We Wait and We Wonder', 'Please Come Out Tonight'.

Dance into the Light
  (Face Value/Warner 0630–1600–2, 1996)
'Dance into the Light', 'That's What You Said', 'Lorenzo', 'Just Another Story', 'Love Police', 'Wear My Hat', 'It's in Your Eyes', 'Oughta Know by Now', 'Take Me Down', 'The Same Moon', 'River So Wide', 'No Matter Who', 'The Times They are A-Changin''.

Music for Films

'Against All Odds (Take a Look at Me Now)'
(Atlantic single, 1984)

'Separate Lives' (Love Theme from 'White Nights')
(Atlantic single, 1985)

Buster (Original Motion Picture Soundtrack)
(Atlantic, 1988)
'A Groovy Kind of Love', 'Two Hearts', 'Big Noise'.

SOLO HOME VIDEOS

Video 45
  (Sony – 1983 – 17 minutes)
'In the Air Tonight', 'I Missed Again', 'Thru These Walls', 'You Can't Hurry Love'.

Live at Perkins Palace

(Thorn EMI Video TVF 2454 – 1983 – 60 minutes)
'I Don't Care Anymore', 'I Cannot Believe It's True', 'Thru
These Walls', 'I Missed Again', 'Behind the Lines', 'The Roof
Is Leaking', 'The West Side', 'In the Air Tonight', 'You Can't
Hurry Love', 'It Don't Matter to Me', 'People Get Ready'.

No Jacket Required EP

(Atlantic Video 50104–3 – T – 1985 – 27 minutes, 51
seconds)
'Sussudio', 'One More Night', 'Who Said I Would', 'Don't Lose
My Number', 'Take Me Home'.

No Ticket Required

(A *Vision 50313–3 – 1986 – 89 minutes, 16 seconds)
'Only You Know and I Know', 'Against All Odds', 'Who Said I
Would', 'Sussudio', 'Behind the Lines', 'Westside', 'One More
Night', 'In the Air Tonight', 'Like China', 'You Can't Hurry
Love', 'It Don't Matter to Me', 'Hand in Hand', 'Take Me
Home', 'It's Alright', 'Droned'.

The Singles Collection

(Atlantic Video 50145–3 – 1989 – 65 minutes)
'Don't Lose My Number', 'I Missed Again', 'A Groovy Kind of
Love', 'Who Said I Would' (Live), 'You Can't Hurry Love',
'Thru These Walls', 'Sussudio', 'One More Night', 'Two Hearts',
'In the Air Tonight', 'Easy Lover', 'Against All Odds (Take a Look
at Me Now)' (Live), 'Take Me Home'.

. . . But Seriously, The Videos

(A *Vision Entertainment 50322–3 – 1992 – 77 minutes)
'Hang In Long Enough', 'Another Day in Paradise', 'Do You
Remember?', 'Colours', 'Something Happened on the Way to
Heaven', 'All of My Life', 'I Wish It Would Rain Down', 'Heat
on the Street', 'That's Just the Way It Is', 'Saturday Night and

Sunday Morning', 'Father to Son', 'Find a Way to My Heart', 'Around the World in 80 Presets' (under titles – audio only).

Seriously Live

(A *Vision Entertainment 50170–3 – 2 hours, 40 minutes) 'Hand in Hand', 'Hang In Long Enough', 'Against All Odds (Take a Look at Me Now)', 'Don't Lose My Number', 'Inside Out', 'Do You Remember?', 'Who Said I Would', 'Another Day in Paradise', 'Separate Lives', 'Saturday Night and Sunday Morning', 'The West Side', 'That's Just the Way It Is', 'Something Happened on the Way to Heaven', 'Doesn't Anybody Stay Together Anymore', 'One More Night', 'Colours', 'In the Air Tonight', 'You Can't Hurry Love', 'Two Hearts', 'Sussudio', 'A Groovy Kind of Love', 'Easy Lover', 'Always', 'Take Me Home'.

A Closer Look: Both Sides Tour '94

(1994, 55 minutes)
Home video of the tour rehearsals.

With Flaming Youth

ARK 2

(Phonogram, 1969) (Fontana STL 5533, 1969)
'Guide Me Orion', 'Earthglow', 'Weightless', 'The Planets (Mars – Bringer of War, Venus – Bringer of Peace, Mercury – The Winged Messenger, Jupiter – Bringer of Jollity, Saturn – Bringer of Old Age, Uranus – The Magician, Neptune – The Mystic)', 'Changes', 'Pulsar', 'Space Child', 'In the Light of Love', 'From Now On (Immortal Invisible)'.

With Genesis

Nursery Cryme
(82673–2/Atlantic, 1971) (Charisma CAS 1052, 1971)
'The Musical Box', 'For Absent Friends', 'The Return of the Giant Hogweed', 'Seven Stones', 'Harold the Barrel', 'Harlequin', 'The Fountain of Salmacis'.

Foxtrot
(82674–2/Atlantic, 1972) (Charisma CAS 1058, 1972)
'Watcher of the Skies', 'Time Table', 'Get 'Em Out by Friday', 'Can-Utility and the Coastliners Horizons', 'Supper's Ready': 'Lover's Leap', 'The Guaranteed Eternal Sanctuary Man', 'Ikhnaton and Itsacon and Their Band of Merry Men', 'How Dare I Be So Beautiful?', 'Willow Farm', 'Apocalypse in 9/8 (co-starring the delicious talents of Gabble Ratchet)', 'As Sure as Eggs Is Eggs (Aching Men's Feet)'.

Genesis Live
(82676–2/Atlantic, 1973) (Charisma CLASS 1, 1973)
'Watcher of the Skies', 'Get 'Em Out by Friday', 'The Return of the Giant Hogweed', 'Musical Box', 'The Knife'.

Selling England by the Pound
(82675–2/Atlantic, 1973) (Charisma CAS 1074, 1973)
'Dancing with the Moonlit Knight', 'I Know What I Like (In Your Wardrobe)', 'Firth of Fifth', 'More Fool Me/The Battle of Epping Forest', 'After the Ordeal', 'The Cinema Show', 'Aisle of Plenty'.

The Lamb Lies Down on Broadway
(82677–2/Atco, 1974) (Charisma CGS 101, 1974)

'The Lamb Lies Down on Broadway', 'Fly on a Windshield',
'Broadway Melody of 1974', 'Cuckoo Cocoon', 'In the Cage',
'The Grand Parade of Lifeless Packaging', 'Back in NYC', 'Hairless
Heart', 'Counting out Time', 'Carpet Crawlers', 'The Chamber of
32 Doors', 'Lilywhite Lilith', 'The Waiting Room', 'Anyway',
'Here Comes the Supernatural Anaesthetist', 'The Lamia', 'Silent
Sorrow in Empty Boats', 'The Colony of Slippermen (The Arrival, A
Visit To The Doktor, The Raven)', 'Ravine', 'The Light Dies Down
on Broadway', 'Riding the Scree', 'In the Rapids', 'It'.

A Trick of the Tail
   (38101–2/Atco, 1976) (Charisma 4001, 1976)
'Dance on a Volcano', 'Entangled', 'Squonk', 'Mad Man Moon',
'Robbery, Assault & Battery', 'Ripples', 'A Trick of the Tail',
'Los Endos'.

Wind and Wuthering
   (82690–2/Atco, 1977) (Charisma CDS 4005, 1977)
'Eleventh Earl of Mar', 'One for the Vine', 'Your Own Special
Way', 'Wot Gorilla?', 'All in a Mouse's Night', 'Blood on the
Rooftops', 'Unquiet Slumbers For The Sleepers . . .', '. . . In
That Quiet Earth', 'Afterglow'.

Seconds Out
   (82689–2/Atlantic, 1977) (Charisma GE 2001, 1977)
'Squonk', 'The Carpet Crawl', 'Robbery, Assault & Battery',
'Afterglow', 'Firth of Fifth', 'I Know What I Like', 'The Lamb
Lies Down on Broadway', 'The Musical Box' (closing sec-
tion), 'Supper's Ready', 'Cinema Show', 'Dance on a Volcano',
'Los Endos'.

. . . And Then There Were Three
   (82691–2/Atlantic, 1978) (Charisma CDS 4010, 1978)
'Down and Out', 'Undertow', 'Ballad of Big', 'Snowbound',
'Burning Rope', 'Deep in the Motherlode', 'Many Too Many',

'Scenes from a Night's Dream', 'Say It's Alright Joe', 'The Lady Lies', 'Follow You, Follow Me'.

Duke

(16014–2/Atlantic, 1980) (Charisma CBR 101, 1980)
'Behind the Lines', 'Duchess', 'Guide Vocal', 'Man of Our Times', 'Misunderstanding', 'Heathaze', 'Turn It on Again', 'Alone Tonight', 'Cul-De-Sac', 'Please Don't Ask', 'Duke's Travels', 'Duke's End'.

Abacab

(19313–2/Atlantic, 1981) (Charisma CBR 102, 1981)
'Abacab', 'No Reply at All', 'Me and Sarah Jane', 'Keep It Dark', 'Dodo', 'Lurker, Who Dunnit?', 'Man on the Corner', 'Like It or Not', 'Another Record'.

Three Sides Live

(82694–2/Atlantic, 1982) (Charisma GE 2002, 1982)
'Turn It on Again', 'Dodo', 'Abacab', 'Behind the Lines', 'Duchess', 'Me and Sarah Jane', 'Follow You, Follow Me', 'Misunderstanding', 'In the Cage' (Medley: Cinema Show/Slippermen), 'Afterglow', 'Paperlate', 'You Might Recall', 'Me and Virgil', 'Evidence of Autumn', 'Open Door'.

Genesis

(7 80116–2/Atlantic, 1983) (Charisma GENLP 1, 1983)
'Mama', 'That's All', 'Home by the Sea', 'Second Home by the Sea', 'Illegal Alien', 'Taking It All Too Hard', 'Just a Job to Do', 'Silver Rainbow', 'It's Gonna Get Better'.

Invisible Touch

(7 81641–2/Atlantic, 1986) (Charisma GENLP 2, 1986)
'Invisible Touch', 'Tonight, Tonight, Tonight', 'Land of Confusion', 'In Too Deep', 'Anything She Does', 'Domino' (Part One – In the Glow of the Night, Part Two – The Last Domino), 'Throwing It All Away', 'The Brazilian'.

We Can't Dance
   (7 82344–2/Atlantic, 1991) (Virgin GENLP 3, 1991)
'No Son of Mine', 'Jesus He Knows Me', 'Driving the Last Spike',
'I Can't Dance', 'Never a Time', 'Dreaming While You Sleep',
'Tell Me Why', 'Living Forever', 'Hold on My Heart', 'Way of
the World', 'Since I Lost You', 'Fading Lights'.

Live/The Way We Walk – Volume One: The Shorts
   (82452–2/Atlantic, 1992) (Virgin GENCD 4, 1992)
'Land of Confusion', 'No Son of Mine', 'Jesus He Knows Me',
'Throwing It All Away', 'I Can't Dance', 'Mama', 'Hold on My
Heart', 'That's All', 'In Too Deep', 'Tonight, Tonight, Tonight',
'Invisible Touch'.

Live/The Way We Walk – Volume Two: The Longs
   (82461–2/Atlantic, 1993) (Virgin GENCD 5, 1993)
'Old Medley' ('Dance on a Volcano', 'The Lamb Lies Down on
Broadway', 'The Musical Box', 'Firth of Fifth', 'I Know What I
Like'), 'Driving the Last Spike', 'Domino' (Part I: In the Glow
of the Night, Part II: The Last Domino), 'Fading Lights', 'Home
by the Sea'/'Second Home by the Sea', 'Drum Duet'.

Genesis Home Videos

Three Sides Live
   (Thorne EMI Video TVF 1422 – 1982 – 90 minutes)
'Behind the Lines', 'Duchess', 'Misunderstanding', 'Dodo',
'Abacab', 'No Reply at All', 'Who Dunnit', 'In the Cage'
(Medley: Cinema Show/Slippermen), 'Afterglow', 'Me and
Sarah Jane', 'Man on the Corner', 'Turn It On Again'.

Genesis Live — The Mama Tour

   (Atlantic Video 50111–3 – B – 1983 – 102 minutes)
'Abacab', 'That's All', 'Mama', 'Illegal Alien', 'Home by the Sea',
'Second Home by the Sea', 'Keep It Dark', 'It's Gonna Get Better',
Medley: 'In The Cage'-'Cinema Show', 'Afterglow', 'Turn It on
Again', Final Medley: '(I Can't Get No) Satisfaction'.

Visible Touch

   (Atlantic Video 50117–3 – 1987 – 33 minutes)
'Anything She Does', 'Throwing It All Away', 'Tonight, Tonight,
Tonight', 'Land of Confusion', 'In Too Deep', 'Invisible Touch'.

Genesis Videos, Volume 1

   (Atlantic Video 50129–3 – 1988 – 55 minutes)
'Mama', 'No Reply at All', 'Land of Confusion', 'That's All',
'Tonight, Tonight, Tonight', 'Duchess', 'Anything She Does',
'Robbery, Assault & Battery', 'In Too Deep', 'Abacab', 'Follow
You, Follow Me'.

Genesis Videos, Volume 2

   (Atlantic Video 50130–3 – 1988 – 57 minutes)
'Illegal Alien', 'Throwing It All Away', 'Misunderstanding',
'Ripples', 'Keep It Dark', 'A Trick of the Tail', 'Home by the
Sea', 'Second Home by the Sea', 'Man on the Corner', 'Turn It
on Again', 'Many Too Many', 'Invisible Touch'.

Invisible Touch Tour

   (Virgin Music Video 3–50139 – 1988)
'Mama', 'Abacab', 'Domino (Pt. 1: In The Glow of The Night)',
'Domino (Pt. 2: The Last Domino)', 'That's All', 'Brazilian',
'Land of Confusion', 'Tonight, Tonight, Tonight', 'Throwing It
All Away', 'Home by the Sea', 'Invisible Touch', 'Drum Duet',
'Los Endos', 'Turn It on Again' (Medley), 'Do The Neurotic'.

Genesis: A History

(Polygram Home Video 082 769–3 – 1990 – 90 minutes)

Live: *The Way We Walk in Concert*
  (Polygram Video 440 086 497 – 3 – 155 minutes)
'Land of Confusion', 'No Son of Mine', 'Drawing the Last Spike', 'Old Medley', 'Fading Lights', 'Jesus He Knows Me', 'Dreaming While You Sleep', 'Home by the Sea', 'Hold on My Heart', 'Domino', 'I Can't Dance', 'Tonight, Tonight, Tonight', 'Invisible Touch', 'Turn It on Again'.

With Brand X

Unorthodox Behavior
  (Passport, 1975) (Charisma CAS 1117, 1976)
Phil: Drums, percussion.
Nuclear Burn', 'Euthanasia Waltz', 'Born Ugly'/'Smacks of Euphoric Behavior', 'Unorthodox Behavior', 'Running on Three', 'Touch Wood'.

Moroccan Roll
  (Passport, 1977) (Charisma CAS 1126, 1977)
Phil: Drums, lead vocals, accoustic piano
'Sun in the Night', 'Why Should I Lend You Mine (When You've Broken Yours Off Already)' . . . into 'Maybe I'll Lend You Mine After All', 'Hate Zone', 'Collapsar', 'Disco Suicide', 'Orbits', 'Malaga Virgen', 'Macrocosm'.

Livestock
  (Passport PB9824, 1977) (Charisma CLASS 5, 1977)
Phil: Drums

'Nightmare Patrol', 'ISH', 'Euthanasia Waltz', 'Isis Morning', 'Malaga Virgen'.

Masques
  (Passport, 1978) (Charisma CAS 1138, 1978)

Product
  (Passport PB9840, 1979) (Charisma CAS 1147, 1979)
'Don't Make Waves', 'Dance of the Illegal Aliens', 'Soho, . . . and so to F/Algon (Where An Ordinary Cup Of Drinking Chocolate Costs $8,000,000,000', 'Rhesus Perplexus', 'Wal to Wal', 'Not Good Enough – See Me!', 'April'.

Do They Hurt?
  (Passport 9845, 1980) (Charisma CAS 1151, 1980)
Phil: Drums on 'Voidarama' and 'Triumphant Limp'

Is There Anything About
  (Passport PBC6016, 1982) (CBS 85967, 1982)
Phil: Drums on 'Ipanaemia', 'A Longer April', 'Modern, Noisy and Effective'.

As Producer

John Martyn: *Glorious Fool*
  (Duke/Atlantic, 1982)

Frida: *Something's Going On*
  (Atlantic, 1982 – Includes 'You Know What I Mean' written by Phil and a Frida/Phil duet on 'Here We'll Stay')

Adam Ant: *Strip*

(Epic, 1984)

Philip Bailey: *Chinese Wall*
(Columbia, 1984 – Includes the Collins/Bailey duet co-written by Phil, 'Easy Lover')

Eric Clapton: *Behind the Sun*
(Duck/Warner Bros, 1985)

Howard Jones: *No One Is to Blame*
(Elektra single, 1986)

Eric Clapton: *August*
(Duck/Warner Bros, 1986)

Stephen Bishop: *Bowling in Paris*
(Atlantic, 1989)

David Crosby: *Thousand Roads*
(Atlantic, 1993 – Includes the Crosby/Collins duet, 'Hero')

As Sideman

Brian Eno: *Another Green World* (Editions EG, 1976)
Thin Lizzy: *Johnny the Fox* (Mercury, 1976)
Cafe Jacques: *Round the Back* (Columbia, 1977)
John Cale: *Guts* (Island, 1977)
Elliott Murphy: *Just a Story from America* (Columbia, 1977)
Brian Eno: *Before and After Science* (Editions EG, 1978)
Brian Eno: *Music for Films* (Editions EG, 1978)

Rod Argent: *Moving Home* (MCA, 1978)
Robert Fripp: *Exposure* (Polydor, 1979)
Peter Gabriel: *Peter Gabriel* (Mercury, 1980)
    (Played drums on 'Intruder' and 'No Self Control', snare on 'Family Snapshot', and surdo on 'Biko')
Robert Plant: *Pictures at Eleven* (Swan Song/Atlantic, 1982)
Robert Plant: *The Principle of Moments* (Es Paranza/Atlantic, 1983)
Eric Clapton: *Journeyman* (Duck/Reprise, 1989)
Tears For Fears: *The Seeds of Love* (Fontana/Polygram, 1989)
    (Played drums on 'Woman in Chains')
Tina Turner: *Break Every Rule* (Capitol, 1986)
    (Played drums on 'Girls' and 'Typical Male')
Fourplay: *Elixer* (Warner Bros, 1995)
    (On Phil's song, 'Why Can't It Wait Till Morning')
Quincy Jones: *Q's Juke Joint* (Quest, 1995)
    (Sings 'Do Nothing 'Til You Hear from Me')
Soundtrack: *Porky's Revenge*
    (Part of 'The Crawling King Snakes')

Various

The Secret Policeman's Other Ball
    (Island, 1983)
Sings 'In the Air Tonight' and 'The Roof Is Leaking'
Do They Know It's Christmas (Single – Columbia, 1984)

Music From The Television Series Miami Vice
    (MCA, 1985)
Includes 'In the Air Tonight'

Miami Vice II
   (MCA, 1986)
Includes 'Take Me Home'

The Prince's Trust All-Star Rock Concert
   (MGM-UA Home Video – 1986)
Sings 'In the Air Tonight'

Eric Clapton and Friends
   (Vestron Music Video – 1986)
Plays drums, sings 'In the Air Tonight'

Knebworth: The Album
   (Polydor, 1990)

Two Rooms: Celebrating the Songs of Elton John & Bernie Taupin
   (Polydor, 1991)
Sings 'Burn Down the Mission'

Two Rooms: Celebrating the Songs of Elton John & Bernie Taupin
   (Polygram Video 083 589–3)

The Prince's Trust Rock Gala
   (MGM-UA Home Video – 1992)
Sings 'In the Air Tonight'

Grammy's Greatest Moments Volume 1
   (82574–2/Atlantic, 1994)
Sings 'Another Day in Paradise' with David Crosby

A Tribute to Curtis Mayfield
   (9 45500–2/Warner Bros, 1994
Sings 'I've Been Trying'

The Songs of West Side Story
   (09026–62707–2/RCA Victor, 1996)
Sings 'Somewhere'

Films

Buster
   1988 – Dir. David Green – 102 minutes

Hook
   1991 – Dir. Steven Spielberg – 142 minutes

Frauds
   1993 – Dir. Stephan Elliot – 94 minutes

Balto
   1995 – Dir. Simon Wells – 77 minutes (Voice only – it was animated)

Phil also acted in a 1984 episode of NBC TV's *Miami Vice* and the made-for-cable movie *And the Band Played On* (1993 – Dir. Roger Spottiswoode – 140 minutes).

Index